LUCY MAUD MONTGOMERY: A PRELIMINARY BIBLIOGRAPHY

by

Ruth Weber Russell
D. W. Russell
Rea Wilmshurst

Waterloo, Ontario
University of Waterloo Library
© 1986

Canadian Cataloguing in Publication Data

Russell, Ruth Weber.
    Lucy Maud Montgomery : a preliminary bibliography

(University of Waterloo Library bibliography,
ISSN 0829-948X ; 13)
Includes index.
ISBN 0-920834-42-6

1. Montgomery, L. M. (Lucy Maud), 1874-1942 –
Bibliography.   2. Novelists, Canadian (English) –
20th century – Bibliography.*   I. Russell, Delbert
Wayne, 1944-   II. Wilmshurst, Rea.
III. University of Waterloo.   Library.   IV. Title.
V. Series.

Z8591.2.R88 1986   016.81352   C86-093506-X

The following titles have been published in the bibliography series at the University of Waterloo Library:

No. 1.   *Business: A Guide to Select Reference Sources,* 1978. $5.00.

No. 2.   *Comparative Provincial Politics of Canada: A Bibliography of Select Periodical Articles, 1970-1977,* 1978. $5.00.

No. 3.   *A Catalogue of the Dance Collection in the Doris Lewis Rare Book Room, University of Waterloo Library,* 1979. $5.00.

No. 4.   *Terrorism: 1970-1978,* 1979. $5.00.

No. 5.   *A Catalogue of the Library of George Santayana in the University of Waterloo Library,* 1980. $5.00.

No. 6.   *Aspects of Negotiations Between States,* 1981. $10.00.

No. 7.   *A Catalogue of the Lady Aberdeen Library on the History of Women in the University of Waterloo Library,* 1982. Reprinted 1984. $10.00.

No. 8.   *Ralph Nader Bibliography 1960-1982,* 1982. $10.00.

No. 9.   *A Guide to Research Collections in Microform in the Arts Library,* 1983. $10.00.

No. 10. *A Catalogue of the Dance Collection in the Doris Lewis Rare Book Room, University of Waterloo Library.* Second edition, revised and enlarged, 1983. $10.00.

No. 11. *A Guide to the John Herbert Papers in the University of Waterloo Library,* 1984. $15.00.

No. 12. *The Nature and Properties of Very Sensitive Clays: A Descriptive Bibliography,* 1985. $15.00.

Order from:
University of Waterloo
Publications Service
Dana Porter Library
Waterloo, Ontario, Canada
N2L 3G1

CONTENTS

PREFACE

Research on this bibliography was made possible by two grants from the Social Sciences and Humanities Research Council of Canada, one to Ruth Russell and D.W. Russell, one to Rea Wilmshurst. We wish to thank the SSHRC for their generous support of our work. We would also like to express our thanks to the French Department and the Dean of Arts of the University of Waterloo for their subventions in aid of publication, and to the Publications Committee of the University of Waterloo Library for sponsoring the publication of our research in their series of bibliographies.

INTRODUCTION

The purpose of this bibliography is to make available, for the first time, a listing of works by and on Lucy Maud Montgomery, who is one of the most widely-read authors that Canada has yet produced. The bibliography is a preliminary one. The works of LMM have appeared in so many editions, in both English and other languages, that it would take time well beyond that available to the present bibliographers to produce an absolutely complete listing. (Also, because LMM was a "popular" author, worn copies of her books have been systematically discarded by public libraries and certain editions have, as a result, disappeared from any library system where they would be identifiable, or accessible.) The preliminary nature of this bibliography was dictated by a different set of circumstances where it lists reviews of her work. Most of the reviews have not been listed in any indexes; the University of Guelph owns one 500-page scrapbook of reviews of LMM's work which the author compiled, but this compilation, the only such in existence, will not be available to researchers until 1992 or later.

The organization of the bibliography is, generally speaking, chronological. By far the largest group of listings is contained in Part 1: Novels by Lucy Maud Montgomery. (We have stretched the definition of a novel in this case to include *Chronicles of Avonlea*, 1912, and *Further Chronicles of Avonlea*, 1920.) Within this section are 22 subsections, one for each of LMM's novels, listed in chronological order of publication, beginning with *Anne of Green Gables* in 1908 and ending with *Anne of Ingleside* in 1939. Publication information for the first edition of each novel is given where it first appears. Editions of a given title are divided into "Editions in English" and "Translations." Under the first of these divisions, there are four geographical sections, arranged alphabetically (LMM has been published in English in Australia, Canada, Great Britain and the United States), with editions organized chronologically within each section. The translations have been organized first alphabetically by language, and then chronologically.

Part 2: Other Books by Lucy Maud Montgomery is the next section; it is organized by subject, and then chronologically. This section includes the subsections "Collected Poems," "Non-Fiction," "Autobiography," "Letters," "Published Journals," and "Posthumous Collected Stories." Any translations are listed after the English-language versions of a work, as in Part 1.

Part 3: Adaptations for Other Media lists adaptations of the novels and stories for the stage, movies and television. Only those adaptations whose existence is confirmed by a printed source are included here.

Part 4: Stories, Poems, Miscellaneous Pieces, Anthologized Works: A Selected Listing, is almost entirely the work of Rea Wilmshurst. (Our own search of all available indexes produced a few pieces of information which we were able to add to the body of her research.) Ms. Wilmshurst has made an extensive search of library holdings to verify bibliographical details on the large number of published stories and poems collected in scrapbooks by

LMM. Additional information was obtained from LMM's personal ledger list of stories and poems, which records payment received for each item. In each subsection of this part, items are listed chronologically, with separate listings at the end of "Stories" and "Poems" of undated items found in the scrapbooks, or reprinted in the collections of stories or poems, but not otherwise identified. A final list in each of these subsections gives titles from the ledger which have not been found. The subsection "Miscellaneous" includes LMM's student essays, her early journalism pieces, and her later articles.

In Part 5: Archival Holdings, the general structure is different. Archival holdings are listed alphabetically, by location, with brief descriptions where applicable.

Part 6: Works on Lucy Maud Montgomery is divided into eight types of works, ranging from "Books and Theses" to "Selected Newspaper Articles." It should be noted that the first three categories here -- "Books and Theses," "Articles, Chapters in Books and Theses," and "Audio-Visual Studies" -- are as comprehensive as we were able to make them. The following five categories, though, are all selected: "Selected Articles from Reference Works," "Selected Newspaper Articles," "Selected Reviews: Novels," "Selected Reviews: Other Books," and "Selected Reviews and Study Guides: Film and Stage Versions." In some cases the selection was done by the bibliographers; for example, there seemed little to be gained by citing every brief reference to LMM in an encyclopedia or a textbook; only those from what might be termed basic reference texts, or which were representative of a certain fashion in critical thinking, have been included. Similarly, we chose to list only a selection of the newspaper articles written on her. (And the number of which we became aware was only a small fraction of the total; there are four 100-page scrapbooks at Guelph -- inaccessible until 1992 -- which LMM compiled of newspaper clippings.)

Entries in some other categories, however, might be said to be preselected. For example, prior to the first listings of the *Canadian Periodical Index* in 1928, book reviews in Canadian newspapers and periodicals have not been indexed, so the only Canadian reviews prior to this which we have listed are, with a few exceptions, those preserved in the Canadian Literature Scrapbooks at the Toronto Reference Library. An index to 20 Canadian periodicals between the years of 1920 and 1928 has been prepared at York University, but this material is at present irretrievable due to technical difficulties. What a small fraction our listing represents of the total number of reviews can be judged from a statement by LMM in a letter to G. B. MacMillan; in this letter of August 31, 1908, she says she had received copies of 66 reviews since *Anne of Green Gables* was published on June 10 of that year.

The listing of adaptations of LMM's works for stage, film, television and radio does not reflect accurately the number of productions (both amateur and professional) or broadcasts based on LMM's work around the world. We have listed only the known published versions of plays, although we have heard of productions from Poland to Korea; similarly, the television and radio adaptations listed are only those for which we could find documented verification. Although one of the researchers remembers listening to a CBC radio version of *Anne of Green Gables* in the 1950s, and although Norman Campbell states that he first produced *Anne of Green Gables* as a live musical for CBC television in 1953, we were unable to obtain verification from the CBC for these productions, and consequently do not list them. We have not attempted to trace the production history of such well-known recent adaptations as the Campbell/Harron musical, but we should note here that it has been produced in such varied places as Sweden and Japan, and won the "1969 Musical of the Year Award" from London critics.

The final section of our bibliography, Part 7: Index of Names and Titles, gives a single alphabetical listing of the names of authors, translators, editors, directors and titles of works cited in Parts 1-5. Only some of the names and titles from Part 6 are indexed, as follows: for "Books and Theses" both the author's name and the title are indexed; for "Articles, Chapters in Books and Theses" only the author's name is indexed; for "Audio-Visual Studies" and "Selected Articles from Reference Works" only the titles of the studies and reference works are indexed; reviews are indexed only under the title of the work reviewed.

This bibliography contains a number of items which the bibliographers have not personally examined. It was decided to proceed in this way because to examine every item listed was a virtual impossibility; many early editions no longer exist, at least where it is possible to trace them, and most translated versions are not available in North America. We have attempted to examine, however, as many editions as possible, through visiting in person major libraries in the Toronto, Ottawa, Guelph, Hamilton and Kitchener areas, as well as all appropriate and available collections in Prince Edward Island; we have also received interlibrary loans from across North America.

In terms of the methodology for indicating what has been examined and what has not, an important change has been made mid-way in the listings. In Parts 1, 2 and 3 (Novels by LMM, Other Books by LMM, Adaptations for Other Media) those works which *have* been seen have been identified with an asterisk. In all the following sections, some form of annotation identifies works which have *not* been seen. (We should note that this system applies to Part 4: Stories, Poems and Journalism, because in this section most of the information was generated from materials *seen* (in scrapbooks) but not necessarily identified -- whereas the reverse is true for Parts 1, 2 and 3.)

The sources of information which we have used have been many and varied. It is an unfortunate fact that while some publishers keep a full record of every title they have printed -- title, date, number of copies -- many more publishers do not. (Harrap of London, for example, supplied us with a detailed history of their publishing of LMM's works.) In cases where direct information from a publisher was not available to check against other sources, information from those other sources -- from detailed searches of every available index, catalogue, bibliography, or other reference tools, as well as from personal searches of library holdings and letters from national libraries -- was checked against itself. In some cases it seemed probable that additional reprintings were made, besides those for which we found direct references and therefore cited, but we did not proceed to list any such assumed reprints; we have listed only those to which we found a direct reference of some kind.

We had hoped to obtain some information on editions and reprintings through Dr. Stuart Macdonald, LMM's last surviving son and literary executor, but he died suddenly in September of 1982, just as we were beginning our research.

Information on translations of LMM's works into other languages came in small part from isolated references to a variety of works; in larger part from the *Index Translationum*, and in largest part from librarians at national libraries around the world. (Some information on English-language editions was also generated through this last source; for example, the Urban Council Public Libraries of Hong Kong sent information on certain recent Angus and Robertson (Sydney) editions not listed by the Australian National Library, and it was from the librarian at Trinity College, Dublin, that we learned that the Pitman 1908 edition of *Anne of Green Gables* was, in fact, printed in the United States.) In virtually every case where a national library held copies of works by LMM, whether in English or another language (and 40 of the 63 national libraries who replied to our inquiries had holdings) we were given very full and precise information: photocopies from card-catalogue listings, carefully compiled lists, extra annotations from the librarian.

Listings in our bibliography distinguish between editions of a title, and reprints of an edition, in that all reprints of an edition are listed together in one entry, whereas a new edition is given a separate entry. It was not always easy to distinguish between the two, and some arbitrary decisions had to be made. A new edition (rather than a new reprint of a previous edition) was identified as occurring when one of the following conditions was met: significantly different pagination, implying a re-setting of the type; being part (or ceasing to be part) of a distinctive and easily identified series; a change from hard to soft cover; a significant difference in illustrations; bearing a different publisher's imprint. (This last point was not always as obvious as it sounds; for example, the first Australian editions of many of LMM's novels were published in the 1920s by the Cornstalk Publishing Company. Angus and Robertson later absorbed this company and reissued the titles under their own imprint; these we termed new editions.)

Sometimes there was isolated information about a certain series (for example, Ryerson's "Canada editions") which could not be fitted into any coherent sequence, so it was omitted. (A copy of *Anne of Green Gables* printed by Ryerson in 1958, for example, bore on its copyright page the dates of every printing by Ryerson of that title since 1942; we know that

"Canada editions" were published of this title during that time; but because it was impossible to state which dates in the list denoted these particular editions, the series title was not considered information sufficiently precise to be included.) Similarly, the otherwise comprehensive information sent by Harrap included the statement that they have no records of a "uniform edition" of LMM's works being published between 1925 and 1935. Therefore, even though we had a number of other references to this series, we were unable to tell where these "uniform editions" fit into the large general list, and we do not refer to it in our bibliography.

Anomalies abound; in the early years, the LMM titles were simultaneously published by the original publisher, L.C. Page of Boston, and by two other American publishers: A.L. Burt and Grosset and Dunlap. (The Burt company apparently specialized in reprints, and a note on one of the early Burt editions says that it was "printed by arrangement with the Page company." A note on the 1938 Grosset and Dunlap edition of *Anne of Windy Poplars* says this edition was printed from the original plates but sold at a lower price since the author had agreed to accept a reduced royalty.) Many books that we examined bore no date of printing, only the original copyright date for that title; among this group were most of McClelland and Stewart's Cavendish editions, published mostly in the 1940s, and recent Angus and Robertson editions. All such questionable dates have been noted. Square brackets are used around dates which we have supplied from evidence not found on the copyright page, and around our approximations of dates. Thus, in items 533 and 534 of our listing, [1930s or 1940s?] indicates that the date of the reprint is unknown, but presumed to be sometime between the original date of 1933 and the appearance of the Cavendish editions sometime in the 1940s; similarly, [1940s?] and [1950s?] indicate that we presume from external evidence that the Cavendish editions began in the 1940s, and that the reprint was in the 1950s. In some of the translations that we examined, there had been no indication in any reference to the book (in the *Index Translationum* listing, or in information from the relevant national library) that this particular title was anything but a translation of the complete original text. However, it was obvious on examining the book that this was in fact a condensation or abridged version.

As the varied listings of this bibliography gradually assumed a coherent shape, it became possible to see the outlines of a publishing history of some complexity, stemming from the day that the publishing firm of L. C. Page in Boston decided to publish the five-times-rejected first novel by the Maritimes writer. Because *Anne of Green Gables* was such an immediate success, LMM was commissioned to write a sequel, and *Anne of Avonlea* was published in the following year, 1909. LMM published five more books with Page in the next few years: *Kilmeny of the Orchard* in 1910, *The Story Girl* in 1911, *Chronicles of Avonlea* in 1912, *The Golden Road* in 1913, and *Anne of the Island* in 1915. During this time she was becoming increasingly dissatisfied with her relationship with Page, and decided to change publishers. Her next book, and only volume of poetry -- *The Watchman, and Other Poems* -- was published in 1916 by the Canadian firm of McClelland, Goodchild and Stewart. Her next two novels, *Anne's House of Dreams* in 1917 and *Rainbow Valley* in 1919, were released simultaneously by McClelland, Goodchild and Stewart in Toronto (changed to McClelland and Stewart by the time of publication of *Rainbow Valley*) and Stokes of New York, but the first several years of the Canadian editions of each title bore the Stokes copyright. Her next book, *Rilla of Ingleside*, was the first to appear in identical Stokes and McClelland and Stewart editions, each with its own copyright, although in this case there are McClelland and Stewart editions dated a year earlier than the American ones. All her remaining novels -- from *Emily of New Moon* in 1923 to *Anne of Ingleside* in 1939 -- were published simultaneously by McClelland and Stewart in Canada and Stokes in the U.S. The novels first published by Page, however -- from *Anne of Green Gables* in 1908 to *Anne of the Island* in 1915, and then *Further Chronicles of Avonlea* in 1920 -- first appeared in real Canadian editions only beginning in 1942, when they were published by Ryerson in Toronto.

The Page-McClelland and Stewart sequence had one exception. This was Page's publication in 1920 of *Further Chronicles of Avonlea*. This was a collection of stories published without the author's permission from manuscripts in the publisher's possession. To quote from LMM's handwritten note in the presentation copy of the first edition sent to her (with considerable bravura) by L. C. Page, "This book was published by the Page Co. from manuscripts which I had never given them permission to use. Hence it is full of sentences and passages which have already been published in my other books. Also, they interpolated in 'Tannis of the Flats' several paragraphs that injured it as an artistic unit. In 1920 I entered suit against the Page Co. for an injunction to restrain them from publishing this book. In 1928 after pending nearly nine years I won the suit."

The lengthy, expensive and acrimonious lawsuit was watched with considerable interest by the literary community in Canada. In spite of the legal victory LMM obtained, however, *Further Chronicles of Avonlea* is still in print in four English-language versions (published by Angus and Robertson in Australia, McGraw-Hill Ryerson in Canada, Harrap in Great Britain and Grosset and Dunlap in the U.S.) and in Japanese and Spanish translations.

From these North American publishers who first published her works, a network of other editions grew in spurts to eventually circle the globe. Her novels have indeed been widely translated, though not as widely as popular wisdom would have it. *Anne of Green Gables*, the most widely translated of her works, has been translated into 16 languages. Translations of this best-seller began to appear almost immediately after the English-language editions: the Swedish in 1909, the Dutch in 1910, the Polish in 1912. The greatest European popularity of LMM's work has been in the Scandinavian countries and in Poland, where *Anne of Green Gables* alone has been published continuously since 1912, in some 13 editions and reprintings. New translations of various titles continue to appear: Hebrew in the 1950s, Spanish in the 1950s and 1960s, Slovak in the 1960s, Portuguese in 1972, Turkish in 1979, Italian in 1980, French in 1983.

The most phenomenal sales of LMM's writings in recent years, though, have been in Japan. Since her work first began to be translated into Japanese in the 1950s, there have been hundreds of editions and reprints: hard and soft cover, illustrated and unillustrated, complete texts and abbreviated versions for young children, books printed by arrangement with the copyright owners and pirated editions as well. (The popularity of the novels has created spin-off works as well: *Anne's Cooking Notes*, and *Anne's Picture Book of Cakes*, two books consisting of recipes and quotations from the LMM books, and *Anne's Handicraft Picture Book*, an expensive 3-volume set often given as a wedding gift, with photos of such objects as "Rag dolls of Anne and Gilbert," "Sweaters for Anne and Gilbert," etc.)[1] Three of her books have been translated only into Japanese: *Pat of Silver Bush*, *Mistress Pat*, and *Anne of Ingleside*. Our Japanese colleague Dr. Okabe, a Visiting Professor of Physics at Waterloo who was kind enough to translate for us information received from the National Diet Library in Japan, assured us that it was an easy task as he had read most of the books himself, and also that a senior colleague of his in Japan had told him that he must visit Prince Edward Island and the Green Gables Museum (as he himself had done) while in Canada. The musical stage play of *Anne of Green Gables*, first produced in Japan at Osaka in 1970, has been translated into Japanese and staged in Japan in 1981.

The large number of recent translations into Korean imply a surge of popularity in that south-east Asian nation as well; a Korean colleague who helped us obtain information from Korean publishers of LMM's works told us that she herself had, as a student, seen several stage adaptations of LMM's works and that these productions are very popular in Korea. We were unable to obtain any precise information about these adaptations, though, and have not listed them.

If an excess of enthusiasm has led to exaggeration in the number of languages into which LMM's works have been translated, there has been no exaggeration of the immense popularity of her work -- popularity defined in the most concrete way, by the number of editions printed and books sold. To attempt a global sales figure for her books, individually or in total, is to leap from bibliography into never-never land. Instead, we will cite a few specific individual figures. *Anne of Green Gables* has been the single title with the largest sales (and the most frequent appearance on best-seller lists), followed by *Anne of Avonlea*. The Page edition of *Anne of Green Gables* went through 37 printings between June 1908 and May 1914, with the latter printing producing 150,000 copies. In October 1933 the 68th impression was printed, with a cumulative total (Page editions only) of 553,000 copies. A Page edition printed in September 1951 states on the copyright page that 1,250,000 copies have been printed. *Anne of Green Gables* still sells very well in the United States today; the Bantam paperback edition went through 11 printings between August of 1976 and January of 1981.

---

[1]   See our entry 1804, below.

No cumulative Canadian figures are available, but 19 of her 22 novels are still in print in Canadian editions. (The exceptions are *Kilmeny of the Orchard*, *The Story Girl*, and *Further Chronicles of Avonlea*.)

Some round totals are available for British sales. The size of early British sales of the Pitman editions of the Page titles is unknown, although the Pitman edition of *Anne of Green Gables* went through 9 printings by July 1909. Hodder and Stoughton sold over 100,000 copies of the later novels (from *Rilla of Ingleside* on) between 1921 and 1933. Harrap began publishing LMM's work in 1925 and does so to the present day. (They have published all her novels except *A Tangled Web*, released in the 1930s by Hodder and Stoughton as *Aunt Becky Began It*.) Between 1925 and the present they have printed 1,725,000 copies of LMM's works, with *Anne of Green Gables* alone accounting for almost half a million books of this total.

The Australian publisher Angus and Robertson now has all 22 of LMM's novels in print, in addition to *The Road to Yesterday*. In their letter to us outlining dates of printings, they were unable to give definitive quantities, as this was considered confidential information, but they did say that they currently reprint at the rate of five or six thousand copies per print run. Using the lower of these figures to calculate a total reveals that since 1972 some 325,000 copies have been printed of her works.

Slovak translations of LMM's work are relatively recent, and only the first three titles in what is usually considered the "Anne series" have been published: *Anne of Green Gables*, *Anne of Avonlea*, and *Anne of the Island*. Nonetheless, since 1969 some 200,000 copies of these titles have been printed in Slovak. Polish printings (continuous since 1912 for *Anne of Green Gables*), have been not only frequent but large. Some recent representative figures follow. Fifty thousand copies of the combined *Anne of Green Gables*; *Anne of Avonlea* were printed in 1967, with a reprint in 1973; 50,000 copies of the combined *Anne of the Island*; *Anne's House of Dreams* were printed in 1968, with reprints in 1971 and 1974; 50,000 copies of *Anne's House of Dreams* in 1977, with a reprint in 1982; 50,000 copies of the combined *Rainbow Valley*; *Rilla of Ingleside* in 1970, with reprints in 1972 and 1974; 50,000 copies of *Anne of Windy Poplars* in 1977, with a reprint in 1981.

The overwhelming and abiding popularity of the works of LMM is one factor contributing to the obvious imbalance in this bibliography -- the remarkable disparity between the *works by* and the *works on* sections. The other contributing factor to this imbalance, of course, is the shortage of critical attention paid to LMM. Historically, the reasons for this are several. LMM was a "popular writer," a writer of best-sellers and then pot-boilers and many variations on a tried-and-true theme to reach an eager, ready-made audience. She was also Canadian and primarily a writer of children's books, both factors working to some extent against making her work a focus of serious critical attention.

The big names in the Canadian literary establishment have had no diffi-
culty in casting her work aside (though her novels usually received favoura-
ble reviews when they were published, even by such reviewers as Arthur
Deacon). Archibald MacMechan, under whose direction LMM studied for a
year at Dalhousie College, in 1924 wrote that *Anne of Green Gables* "just
misses the kind of success which convinces the critics while it captivates
the unreflecting general reader." What is lacking is what "makes the difference between a clever book and a masterpiece."[2] Arthur Phelps was
much more harsh in his assessment of her writings. In his discussion of
LMM in *Canadian Writers*, published in 1951,[3] he classed LMM as one of a
number of "romantic and sentimental writers" (this number included Ralph
Connor, Robert Service, and Mazo de la Roche) whom "no critic would
think of . . . as having made any serious contribution to art" and yet who
have been very popular abroad. Yet, he conceded, "There may still be a
place for the stories of LMM." Desmond Pacey set the firm stamp of critical disapproval on LMM in his *Creative Writing in Canada*, published in
1961. Her writings were representative, he said, of the "age of brass" in
Canadian literature, from 1900 to 1920. Typical of a "new fashion in esca-
pism . . . to write idylls of the more secluded areas," the works produced by
LMM and other contemporary successful novelists were not even of the
second rank. *Anne of Green Gables* was such a popular success because "it
had all the features of . . . escape literature which a materialistic and vul-
gar generation craved."[4]

The tide of disfavour has to some extent begun to ebb; several theses
have given serious study to LMM's novels, and some recent critical articles
have found merit in her work. But there is still a massive reversal that
must take place before this writer receives the attention she is due -- due
not because she is Canadian, or a woman, or has been neglected, but
because her books have spoken so directly to so many millions of young
adolescent girls (and boys) and continue to do so today, seventy-five years
later and in the disparate cultures of Japan, Korea, Poland, Czechoslovakia, Argentina. There are qualities in her books that touch the deepest
places in the heart of childhood. Among the purposes which we hope this
bibliography will serve, will be to direct some serious attention to examining these qualities.

                                                            RWR
                                                            DWR

---

[2] Archibald MacMechan, *Head-Waters of Canadian Literature*, Toronto:
McClelland and Stewart, 1924, pp. 209-213.

[3] Toronto: McClelland and Stewart, pp. 85-93.

[4] Toronto: McGraw-Hill Ryerson, 1961, pp. 89-92, 102-06.

ACKNOWLEDGEMENTS

In the course of our research we have received help from a great many sources. We wish to thank the many librarians from national libraries who responded to our requests for information on their holdings of the works of LMM: from Argentina, Julio Zolezzi, of the Biblioteca Nacional, Buenos Aires; from Australia, Glenys McIver, Senior Reference Librarian, National Library of Australia, Canberra; from Austria, the reference service, Austrian National Library; from Brazil, Zeneida C. Queiroz Barros, Chief, Reference Division, National Library, Rio de Janeiro; from Belgium, N. Tassoul, Sub-keeper, Bibliothèque Royale Albert Ier, Brussels; from Britain, C.B. Smith, Bibliographic Information Service, British Library, London; from Bulgaria, Yordanka Parvanova, Deputy Director, Cyril and Methodius National Library, Sofia; from Chile, Maria Teresa Sanz, Coordinadora de la Biblioteca Nacional, Santiago; from China (Taiwan), Hsiu-wei Ho Kang, National Central Library, Taipei; from Czechoslovakia, Dr. M. Bielik, Director, Slovak National Library, Martin; from Cuba, Xonia Jiménez López, Biblioteca Nacional José Martí, Havana; from Denmark, Birgitte Hvidt, Rigsbibliotekarembedet, Copenhagen; from Finland, Torbjörn Söderholm, Director, Åbo Akademis Bibliotek, Åbo, and Esko Rahikainen, Helsinki University Library, Helsinki; from France, Andrée Lheritier, Conservateur, Catalogues et Bibliographies, Bibliothèque Nationale, Paris; from Germany, Heinz Wegehaupt, Director, Children's Department, Deutsche Staatsbibliothek, Berlin; Director Schroeter, Deutsche Bücherei, Leipzig; Dr. Rumpf, Berliner Gesamtkatalog, Berlin; Gisela Kitrowski, Stadt- und Universitäts-Bibliothek, Frankfurt; Dietmar Buschey, Niedersächsische Staats- und Universitätsbibliothek, Göttingen; Christiane Kraft, Deutsche Bibliothek, Frankfurt; the Director, Norddeutscher Zentralkatalog, Hamburg; Dr. Schneiders, Head, Reference Division, Bayerische Staatsbibliothek, Munich; and Dr. Gunther, Director, Zentralkatalog Baden-Württemberg, Stuttgart; from Ghana, Christina D.T. Kwei, Assistant Director, Ghana Library Board, Accra; from Greece, Dr. P.G. Nicolopoulos, Director, National Library of Greece, Athens; from Hungary, Dr. Lidia Ferenczy, Head, Reference Service, National Széchényi Library, Budapest; from Hong Kong, Lai-bing Kan, University Librarian, Chinese University of Hong Kong, and Barbara Luk, Chief Librarian, Urban Council Libraries, Hong Kong; from Iceland, Nanna Bjarnadóttir, Icelandic National Library, Reykjavík; from India, H.C. Cupta, Deputy Librarian, the National Library, Belvedere, Calcutta; from Ireland, M. Hewson, Director, National Library of Ireland, Dublin, and M. Pollard, Keeper of Early Printed Books and Special Collections, Trinity College, Dublin; from Israel, Libby Kahane, Reference Service, Jewish National and University Library, Jerusalem; from Italy, Dr. Stefania Guardati, Director, Biblioteca Nazionale, Bari; the Director, Biblioteca Nazionale Centrale, Florence; the Director, Biblioteca Nazionale Braidense, Milan; Dr. Maria Cecaro, Director, Biblioteca Nazionale Vittorio Emanuele III, Naples; the Director, Biblioteca Nazionale Centrale Vittorio Emanuele II, Rome; from Jamaica, Anita Johnson, National Library of Jamaica, Kingston; from Japan, the Director, Reference Division, National Diet Library, Tokyo; from Jordan, Dr. Kamel Asali, Director, The Library, University of Jordan, Amman; from Korea, Kwak

No-Hee, Director, International Exchanges, the Central Library, Seoul; from Luxembourg, the Reference Division, Bibliothèque Nationale, Luxembourg; from Mexico, Luz Maria Mendoza Hernandez, Head, Public Services, Instituto de Investigaciones Bibliograficas, University of Mexico, Mexico City; from the Netherlands, Marieke T.G.E. van Delft, Koninklijke Bibliotheek, The Hague; from New Zealand, Aileen Claridge, Director, User Services, National Library of New Zealand, Wellington; and Nicola Woodhouse, Reference Librarian, School Library Service, National Library of New Zealand, Tawa; from Nigeria, J.A. Orebiyi, National Library of Nigeria, Lagos; from the Philippines, Beatriz R. Diaz, Chief, Reference Division, National Library, Manila; from Poland, Mirosława Kocięcka, Head, Reference Service Dept., Biblioteka Narodowa, Warsaw; from Portugal, Pedro Mendonça da Silveira, Biblioteca Nacional, Lisbon; from Roumania, the Director, Biblioteca centrala de stat, Bucharest; from Scotland, June Cormack, National Library of Scotland, Edinburgh; from Sierra Leone, G.E. Dillsworth, Chief Librarian, Sierra Leone Library Board, Freetown; from Singapore, Fiona Mill, National Library, Singapore; from Spain, Hipólito Escolar Sobrino, Director, Biblioteca Nacional, Madrid; from Sweden, Lars Olsson, The Royal Library-National Library, Stockholm; from Switzerland, Dr. F.G. Maier, Director, Bibliothèque Nationale Suisse, Bern; from Thailand, Kullasap Gesmankit, Director, National Library of Thailand, Bangkok; from Turkey, Dr. Müjgân Cunbur, Directress, National Library, Ankara; from the USSR, I.F. Grigorieva, Chief, Foreign Acquisitions and International Exchange, M.E.Saltykov-Shchedrin State Public Library, Leningrad; and I.V. Pereslegina, Director, The All-Union State Order of the Red Banner of Labour Library of Foreign Literature, Moscow; from Vietnam, Trinh Ngoc Hanh, Assistant Director, Bibliothèque des Sciences Générales, HoChiMinh City; from Wales, Menna Phillips, The National Library of Wales, Aberystwyth; from Yugoslavia, Dragan Chirovich, Director, Narodna Biblioteka, Belgrade; from Zimbabwe, N. Johnson, National Free Library of Zimbabwe, Bulawayo.

Special thanks are also due to the many people who have responded to our requests for information on a myriad of points, ranging from translations of material in languages unknown to us, to details about particular archival holdings: these people include Dr.Yutaka Okabe; Mrs. J.J. Kim; Mrs. Kyunghae Lee; Mr. Deok-Kyo Choi of Changjosa Publishing; Mr. Michio Kondo of Shinozaki Shorin Press; Judy MacDonald, Registrar, Confederation Centre; Elinor Vass, Confederation Centre Library; Irene Aubrey, National Library of Canada; Frank Piggot and Francis W.P.Bolger, University of PEI; Ruth Campbell, Park Corner; Charlotte Stewart, Mills Memorial Library, McMaster University; Margaret Beckman, John Moldenhauer and Nancy Sadek, University of Guelph Library.

Our gratitude, also, goes to our many colleagues at the University of Waterloo who supplied countless services, among whom are the Interlibrary Loan librarians, and the Arts Computing Group. Particular thanks go to Vic Neglia and Susan Bellingham for their expertise and encouragement, to Lois Claxton and Stuart MacKinnon for their support, and to Debbie Geddes and Shelley Martin for their typing help. We are indebted, as well, to Esther

Millar, of the University of Waterloo Library, for her meticulous proofreading. We would also like to thank our collaborator, Rea Wilmshurst, for allowing us to incorporate many of the results of her separate research on the periodical publications of LMM in Part 4 of our bibliography.

Part 1

NOVELS BY LUCY MAUD MONTGOMERY

Items in Parts 1, 2 and 3 marked with an asterisk have been personally examined.

ANNE OF GREEN GABLES

First edition. Boston: Page, 1908.

Editions in English

Australia:

1.   *Anne of Green Gables.* Platypus series. Sydney: Cornstalk Publishing Co., 1924. 431 pp. Frontispiece.

2.   -----. Bellbird series. Sydney: Cornstalk Publishing Co., 1925.

3.   -----. Sydney: Angus and Robertson, 1934. vii, 283 pp. Reprinted 1948, 1949.

4.   -----. Sydney: Angus and Robertson, 1953. iv, 274 pp. Illustrated with line drawings. Reprinted *1955.

5.   -----. Sydney: Angus and Robertson, 1966. 256 pp. Reprinted 1974, 1976, 1977, 1979 (ISBN 0207123233), 1981, 1982.

Canada:

6.   *Anne of Green Gables.* Toronto: Ryerson, *1942. viii, 396 pp. Reprinted 1943, 1944, *1945, 1946, 1948, 1950, 1952, *1954, *1955, 1956, *1958, *1960, *1962.

7.   -----. Toronto: Ryerson, *1964. vi, 329 pp. Illus. Hilton Hassell. Reprinted *1965, 1967.

8.   -----. Toronto: Ryerson, *1968. vi, 329 pp. Illus. Hilton Hassell. Paperback. Reprinted *1972 (ISBN 0770000061), *1975.

9.   -----. Toronto: McGraw-Hill Ryerson, *[1970s]. 329 pp. Paperback. ISBN 0770000088.

10.   -----. Large print ed. London, Ont.: Gatefold Books, *1980. 329
         pp. Paperback. ISBN 0919155006.

11.   -----. Toronto: Seal Books, McClelland and Stewart-Bantam,
         *1981. 309 pp. Paperback. ISBN 0770416934. Frequently reprint-
         ed with new ISBN but no change in date; current (1985) ISBN
         077042001X.

Great Britain:

12.   *Anne of Green Gables*. London: Pitman, 1908. viii, 429 pp. With
         seven full-page illustrations, frontispiece and cover by M.A. and
         W.A.J. Claus. This edition, printed in the U.S., is probably identi-
         cal to the original Page edition, except that the publisher's imprint
         has been changed from Page to Pitman. It bears the Page copy-
         right.

13.   -----. London: Harrap, 1925. 351 pp. Reprinted 1926, 1927
         (twice), 1928, 1929, 1930, 1931, 1933, 1934 (twice), *1935 (twice),
         1936, 1937, 1941 (twice).

14.   -----. London: Harrap, 1933. 351 pp. Larger reprint of 1925 edi-
         tion, with 8 colour illustrations by Sybil Tawse. Reprinted 1936
         (twice), 1937 (twice), 1938, 1939, 1940, 1941, 1959, 1967.

15.   -----. London: Harrap, 1943. 256 pp. No illustrations. Reset.
         Reprinted 1944, 1945, 1946 (twice), 1949, 1950 (twice), 1952
         (twice), 1953, 1954, 1956, 1958, 1959, 1961, 1962, 1964, 1965, 1968,
         *1971 (ISBN 0245551263 for this and the following reprints), *1972,
         1974, 1975, 1976, 1978, 1980.

16.   -----. Harmondsworth: Penguin, Peacock Books, *1964. 253 pp.
         Paperback. Reprinted 1966, *1968, 1970 (ISBN 140470301), 1972,
         1974, 1975.

17.   -----. Harmondsworth: Penguin, Puffin Books, 1977. Paperback.
         Reprinted 1981. ISBN 140309454.

United States:

18.   *Anne of Green Gables*. Boston: Page, *1908. viii, 429 pp. With
         seven full-page illustrations, frontispiece and cover by M.A. and
         W.A.J. Claus. Reprinted *1908 (seven times--have examined 4th
         and 5th impressions), *1909 (nine times--have examined 12th and
         15th impressions), 1910 (nine times), 1911 (six times), 1912 (twice),
         1913 (three times), 1914, *1916 (Personal copy of LMM, signed,
         examined at Guelph), 48th reprint 1920, 50th reprint June *1920,
         52nd reprint Aug. *1921, 1923. 68 printings through 1942.

19.   -----. New York: Grosset and Dunlap, *1908. viii, 429 pp. With seven full-page illustrations, frontispiece and cover by M.A. and W.A.J. Claus. This edition is identical to the original Page edition, except that the publisher's imprint has been changed from Page to Grosset and Dunlap. It bears the Page copyright. Reprinted *1914.

20.   -----. Mary Miles Minter ed. Boston: Page, 1920. Illustrated with 24 reproductions of scenes from the motion picture starring Mary Miles Minter.

21.   -----. Boston: Page, 1931. 396 pp. Illustrated and with frontispiece by Elizabeth R. Withington. Reprinted 1940, 1943, 1947.

22.   -----. Silver anniversary ed. Boston: Page, 1933. 396 pp. With eight colour illustrations by Sybil Tawse. Reprinted 1953.

23.   -----. New York: Grosset and Dunlap, *1935. viii, 299 pp.

24.   -----. Thrushwood Books. New York: Grosset and Dunlap, 1948. viii, 299 pp. Reprinted 1949.

25.   -----. Boston: Page, *1951. viii, 299 pp. With six full-page black-and-white illustrations by Elizabeth R. Withington. Cameo illustration of Anne by M.A. and W.A.J. Claus from original Page edition pasted on front cover.

26.   -----. Condensed and abridged by Mary W. Cushing and D.C. Williams. New York: Grosset and Dunlap, *1961. 105 pp. Illus. Robert Patterson.

27.   -----. Tempo Books. New York: Grosset and Dunlap, 1964. 317 pp. Paperback. Reprinted *1965, *1969.

28.   -----. An Anne of Green Gables Book. New York: Grosset and Dunlap, *1970. viii, 299 pp. Reprinted 1972, *1980 (ISBN 0448025442).

29.   -----. Literary Guild ed. n.p., 1972.

30.   -----. New York: Bantam, *1976. 309 pp. Paperback. ISBN 0553028170. Published in Canada as a Seal Book. 11 printings through 1981.

31.   -----. Cutchogue, N.Y.: Buccaneer Books, 1977. 429 pp. ISBN 0899662625. Reprinted, without illustrations, from original 1908 edition.

32.   -----. Skylark Books. New York: Bantam, *1981. 310 pp. Paperback. ISBN 0553151541. Illustrations. Larger type than Bantam-Seal edition; for younger readers. Reprinted *1982.

33.   -----. Illustrated Junior Library. New York: Putnam Publishing
        Group (Grosset and Dunlap), 1983. 382 pp. ISBN 0448060302.
        Illustrated with eleven colour and thirty-eight black and white
        illustrations by Jody Lee. Reprinted 1984. Published by arrange-
        ment with Farrar, Straus and Giroux.

34.   -----. Condensed and retold by Deirdre Kessler. Charlottetown:
        Ragweed Press, 1983. 43 pp. Illus. Floyd Trainor. Paperback.
        ISBN 0920304117.

35.   -----. Bridgeport, Conn.: Airmont Publishers. This edition was
        published in violation of copyright and withdrawn from the market.

Translations

Danish:

36.   *Anna fra Grønnebrink*. Tr. Anna Erslev and Dagmar Gade. Copen-
        hagen: H. Aschehoug, 1918. 199 pp.

Dutch:

37.   *In Veilige Haven*. Tr. Betsy de Vries. Haarlem: Tjeenk Willink,
        *1910. 360 pp. Colour illustration on hard cover. Personal copy of
        LMM, signed, examined at Guelph.

38.   *Anne van het Groene Huis*. Tr. Betsy de Vries. Haarlem: Tjeenk
        Willink, 1920. 355 pp. Reprinted 1924, 1927.

39.   *Anne van het Groene Huis*. Kramers pocket reeks series, no. 21.
        Tr. Clara de Groot. The Hague: Kramers, 1960. 222 pp.

40.   *Anne van het Groene Huis*. Tr. E.R. Kuitenbrouwer-Dickson and H.
        Vermeulen-Smit. 2 vols. Baarn: De Fontein, *1979. Illus. B. Bou-
        man. Vol. 1 (ISBN 9026112254), 121 pp. Vol. 2 (ISBN 9026112262),
        127 pp.

Finnish:

41.   *Annan nuoruusvuodet*. Tr. Hilja Vesala. Porvoo: Werner Söder-
        ström, 1920. 390 pp. Reprinted 1930, 1943, 1944, 1947, 1950,
        1955.

42.   *Annan nuoruusvuodet*. Rev. ed. Tr. Hilja Vesala. Porvoo and Hel-
        sinki: Werner Söderström, 1961. 284 pp. Reprinted 1964, *1968,
        1973, 1981 (ISBN 9510043788).

French:

43.   *Anne ou les illusions heureuses.* Tr. S. Maerky-Richard. Geneva:
        Jeheber, *1925. 382 pp. Illus. W.F. Burger, 8 line drawings. Per-
        sonal copy of LMM, signed, examined at Guelph. Paperback.

44.   *Anne et le bonheur.* Tr. and abridged by Suzanne Pairault. Paris:
        Hachette, *1964. 254 pp. Illus. Jacques Fromont, colour plates
        and line drawings. Reprinted *1971.

Hebrew:

45.   *Ha-asufit.* Tr. Israel Fishman. Tel-Aviv: M. Newman, 1951. 468
        pp. Illustrated. Reprinted 1969.

Icelandic:

46.   *Anna í Grænuhlíð.* Anna í Grænuhlíð series. Tr. Axel Guðmundsson.
        Reykjavík: Ólafur Erlingsson, 1933. 208 pp. Condensation of the
        novel. Reprinted, Reykjavík: Draupnisútgáfan, 1951; Reykjavík:
        Iðunn, *1964. Four condensed novels published in this series; see
        also *Anne of Avonlea; Anne of the Island; Anne's House of Dreams.*

Italian:

47.   *Anna di Green Gables.* Tr. Luisa Maffi. Milan: Mondadori, 1980.
        322 pp. Illus. Giovanni Mulazzani.

Japanese:

48.   *Akage no Anne.* Tr. Hanako Muraoka. Tokyo: Mikasa Shobo, 1952.
        268 pp. Paperback. Illustrated. Reprinted 1954, 1955.

49.   *Akage no Anne no monogatari.* Tr. Hanako Muraoka. Tokyo:
        Kōdan Sha, 1954. 315 pp.

50.   *Akage no Anne.* Tr. Hanako Muraoka. Tokyo: Shincho Sha, 1954.
        407 pp.

51.   *Akage no Anne.* Tr. Hanako Muraoka. Tokyo: Mikasa Shobo, 1956.
        247 pp. Paperback. Illustrated with colour plates and photo of
        P.E.I. Reprinted *1966.

52.   *Akage no Anne.* Tr. Sakiko Nakamura. Tokyo: Kadokawa Shoten,
        1957. 373 pp. Paperback.

53.   *Akage no Anne.* Tr. Hanako Muraoka. Tokyo: Mikasa Shobo, 1959.
        460 pp.

54.   *Akage no Anne.* Tr. Hanako Muraoka. Tokyo: Kaisei Sha, 1960.
       314 pp.

55.   *Akage no Anne.* Tr. Hanako Muraoka. Tokyo: Kōdan Sha, 1960.
       422 pp.

56.   *Akage no Anne.* Tr. Hanako Muraoka. Tokyo: Kōdan Sha, 1962.
       294 pp.

57.   *Akage no Anne.* Tr. Hanako Muraoka. Tokyo: Iwasaki Shoten,
       1963. 205 pp. Illustrated.

58.   *Akage no Anne.* Tr. Hanako Muraoka. Tokyo: Shōgakkan, 1963.
       317 pp. Reprinted 1967.

59.   *Akage no Anne.* Tr. Hanako Muraoka. Tokyo: Kōdan Sha, *1964.
       334 pp. Illustrated with one colour and several black and white
       illustrations. Reprinted *1971, *1973.

60.   *Akage no Anne.* Tr. Junkichi Kōbe. Tokyo: Popura Sha, 1964. 158
       pp.

61.   *Akage no Anne.* Tr. Taeko Nakamura. Tokyo: Kōdan Sha, 1965.
       414 pp.

62.   *Akage no Anne.* Tr. Ayako Sono. Tokyo: Kawade Shobō, 1966. 358
       pp.

63.   *Akage no Anne.* Tr. Hanako Muraoka. Tokyo: Kōdan Sha, 1966.
       270 pp.

64.   *Akage no Anne.* Tr. Hanako Muraoka. Tokyo: Popura Sha, 1966.
       294 pp. Illustrated with colour plate, sketches, photos of LMM and
       Green Gables. Reprinted *1967, *1971.

65.   *Akage no Anne.* Tr. Hanako Muraoka. Tokyo: Shōgakkan, 1966.
       497 pp.

66.   *Akage no Anne.* Tr. Hanako Muraoka. Tokyo: Kaisei Sha, 1967.
       270 pp. Illustrated with one colour plate, many sketches, photo of
       LMM. Reprinted *1971.

67.   *Akage no Anne.* Tr. Hanako Muraoka. Tokyo: Ōbun Sha, *1967.
       284 pp. Illustrated with many coloured drawings, photos of Green
       Gables and LMM, map of P.E.I. Reprinted *1973.

68.   *Akage no Anne.* Tr. Hanako Muraoka. Tokyo: Popura Sha, 1967.
       325 pp. Illustrated.

69.   *Akage no Anne*. Tr. Hanako Muraoka. Tokyo: Shūei Sha, 1967. 161 pp.

70.   *Akage no Anne*. Tr. Saiko Hida. Tokyo: Shūei Sha, 1968. 155 pp.

71.   *Akage no Anne*. Tr. Hanako Muraoka. Tokyo: Bunken Shuppan, 1970. 270 pp.

72.   *Kojika monogatari; Indian minwa; Akage no Anne*. Tokyo: Shōgaku Kan, 1970. 423 pp. Illustrated. Combined translation of Marjorie Kinnon Rawlings' *The Yearling*, an American Indian folk tale, and *Anne of Green Gables* (probably condensed).

73.   *Akage no Anne*. Tr. Hanako Muraoka and Shinsuke Tani. Tokyo: Kaisei Sha, 1972. 206 pp.

74.   *Akage no Anne*. Tr. Hanako Muraoka. Tokyo: Kōdan Sha, 1973. 284 pp.

75.   *Akage no Anne*. Tr. Taeko Kamiyama. Tokyo: Ōbun Sha, 1973. 444 pp. Paperback.

76.   *Akage no Anne*. Tr. Mieko Maeda. Tokyo: Gakushū Kenkyū Sha, 1974. 414 pp.

77.   *Akage no Anne*. Tr. Toshiko Yamanushi. Tokyo: Shūei Sha, 1974. 180 pp.

78.   *Akage no Anne*. Tr. Yoko Inokuma. Tokyo: Kōdan Sha, 1975. 426 pp. Paperback.

79.   *Akage no Anne*. Tr. Mieko Maeda. Tokyo: Kokudo Sha, 1977. 277 pp.

80.   *Akage no Anne*. Tr. Toshiko Yamanushi. Tokyo: Shunyodo, 1977. 291 pp.

81.   *Akage no Anne*. Illustrated children's ed. Tr. Yoshihiko Shiroyanagi. Tokyo: Popura Sha, 1978. 206 pp.

Korean:

82.   *Bbalganmeori Aen; Aeneui Cheongchun*. Tr. Ji-Shik Shin. Seoul: Yugminsa, 1963. 158 pp. Translation of *Anne of Green Gables* and *Anne of Avonlea*.

83.   *Bbalganmeori Aen; Aeneui Cheongchun*. Tr. Ji-Shik Shin. Seoul: Changjosa, 1964. Translation of *Anne of Green Gables* and *Anne of Avonlea*.

84.   *Bbalganmeori Aen; Aeneui Cheongchun.* Seoul: Daehan Publishing
        Company, 1966. 149 pp. Translation of both *Anne of Green Gables*
        and *Anne of Avonlea.*

85.   *Palkan mori Anne.* Tr. Pak Hwa-mok. Seoul: Yukyoungsa, *1974.
        320 pp.

86.   *Palkan mori Anne.* Tr. Sok Yong-won. Seoul: Kwang'um Sa, *1975.
        245 pp.

87.   *Bbalganmeori Aen; Aeneui Cheongchun.* Tr. So-Hee Shon. Seoul:
        Dongseo Publishing, 1977. 447 pp. Translation of *Anne of Green
        Gables* and *Anne of Avonlea.*

88.   *Bbalganmeori Aen; Aeneui Cheongchun.* Tr. Sin-Hang Lee. Seoul:
        Sinmoon Publishing, 1977. 356 pp. Translation of *Anne of Green
        Gables* and *Anne of Avonlea.*

89.   *Green Gables Anne* (Phonetic transcription in Korean). Tr. Shun-
        Yen Park. Seoul: Dong Seo Publishing, 1981. This volume is the
        first of 12 volumes in the Anne series; we are not able at present
        to establish the correspondence between the Korean and English
        titles, so we list here all twelve volumes, with our guess at the
        original title: *Chaneu shijeul* (almost certainly *Anne of Avonlea*);
        Chutsalang (almost certainly *Anne of the Island*); *Yaksok* (perhaps
        the last part of *Anne of the Island*); *"Wedding Dress"* (Phonetic
        transcription in Korean) (perhaps part of *Anne of Windy Poplars*);
        Nowanaeui djip (perhaps part of *Anne's House of Dreams*); *Ghumeui
        "dessert" (Phonetic transcription in Korean)* (perhaps part of *Anne's
        House of Dreams*); *Dja mudjigai* (probably *Rainbow Valley*); *Adule
        gua daldule* (perhaps last part of *Rainbow Valley*); *Dali kago haega
        kago* (perhaps part of *Anne of Ingleside*); *Haengbok han nanal* (per-
        haps part of *Anne of Ingleside* or of *Rilla of Ingleside*); *Oendjaek
        ajina* (probably part or all of *Rilla of Ingleside*).

90.   *Bbalganmeori Aen.* Anne Story series, vol. 1. Tr. Ji-Shik Shin.
        Seoul: Changjosa, *1984. 256 pp. Paperback. Illustrated, black
        line drawings.

Norwegian:

91.   *Anne fra Birkely.* Tr. Elise Horn. Kristiania: H. Aschehoug, 1918.
        208 pp.

92.   *Anne fra Bjorkely.* 4th ed. Tr. Mimi Sverdrup Lunden. Oslo:
        Aschehoug, 1954. 159 pp. Reprinted 1974.

Polish:

93.   *Ania z Zielonego Wzgórza.* Tr. Rozalia Bernsteinowa. Warsaw: M. Arct, 1912. 232 pp.

94.   *Ania z Zielonego Wzgórza.* Tr. Rozalia Bernsteinowa. Warsaw: M. Arct, 1919. 361 pp.

95.   *Ania z Zielonego Wzgórza.* Tr. Rozalia Bernsteinowa. Warsaw: M. Arct, 1921. 355 pp.

96.   *Ania z Zielonego Wzgórza.* Tr. Rozalia Bernsteinowa. Warsaw: M. Arct, 1925. 351 pp.

97.   *Ania z Zielonego Wzgórza.* Tr. Rozalia Bernsteinowa. Warsaw: M. Arct, 1928. 279 pp.

98.   *Ania z Zielonego Wzgórza.* Tr. Rozalia Bernsteinowa. Warsaw: M. Arct, 1935. 292 pp. Reprinted 1937.

99.   *Ania z Zielonego Wzgórza.* Tr. Rozalia Bernsteinowa. Warsaw: M. Arcti Dom Książki Polskiej, 1947. 296 pp.

100.   *Ania z Zielonego Wzgórza.* Tr. Rozalia Bernsteinowa. Warsaw: Nasza Księgarnia, 1956. 345 pp. Illus. Bogdan Zieleniec.

101.   *Ania z Zielonego Wzgórza. Ania z Avonlea.* Tr. Rozalia Bernsteinowa. Warsaw: Nasza Księgarnia, *1967. 562 pp. Illus. Bogdan Zieleniec. Reprinted 1973. Translation of both *Anne of Green Gables* and *Anne of Avonlea.*

102.   *Ania z Zielonego Wzgórza.* Tr. Rozalia Bernsteinowa. Warsaw: Nasza Księgarnia, 1976. 412 pp. Illus. Bogdan Zieleniec. Reprinted 1980.

Portuguese:

103.   *Anne e a sua aldeia.* Série Juvenil Civilização series. Tr. Olinda Gomes Fernandes. Porto: Livraria Civilização Editora, 1972. 368 pp.

Slovak (Czechoslovakia):

104.   *Anna zo Zeleného domu.* Tr. Jozef Šimo. Bratislava: Mladé léta, 1959. 332 pp. Illus. Otakar Fuchs.

105.   *Anna zo Zeleného domu.* 2nd ed. Tr. Jozef Šimo. Bratislava: Mladé léta, 1964. 309 pp. Illus. Jozef Trepáč. Reprinted *1969.

106.   *Anna zo Zeleného domu.* Tr. Jozef Šimo. Bratislava: Mladé léta,
        1972. 321 pp. Illus. Jozef Trepáč. Reprinted 1975.

Spanish:

107.   *Anne, la de tejados verdes.* 3rd ed. Tr. José García Díaz. Buenos
        Aires: Emecé Editores, 1962.

Swedish:

108.   *Anne på Grönkulla.* Tr. Karin Lidforss Jensen. Lund: Gleerup,
        *1909 (personal copy of LMM, signed, examined at Guelph). 332
        pp. Reprinted 1914, 1917, 1920, 1923, 1929, 1935, 1943, 1946,
        1949.

109.   *Anne på Gröntorpa.* Tr. Aslög Davidson. Stockholm: Wahlström,
        1941. 251 pp. Reprinted 1944, 1946.

110.   *Anne på Grönkulla.* Tr. Karin Lidforss Jensen. Lund: Gleerup,
        1951. 328 pp. Illus. Britt G. Hallqvist. Reprinted 1952, 1954,
        1955.

111.   *Anne på Grönkulla.* Tr. Karin Lidforss Jensen. Lund: Gleerup,
        1961. 330 pp. Illus. Britt G. Hallqvist. Reprinted *1967, *1971.
        First volume of eight in a series: *Anne på Grönkulla; Vår vän
        Anne; Drömmens uppfyllelse; Anne på egen hand; Drömslottet;
        Regnbågens dal; Lilla Marilla; Grönkullagrannar.*

112.   *Anne på Grönkulla.* Abridged ed. Tr. and illus. Margareta Sjögren-
        Olsson. Stockholm: Lindblad, *1962. 158 pp.

113.   *Anne på Grönkulla.* Abridged ed. Tr. Karin Lidforss Jensen. Lund:
        Liber Läromedel, 1976. 142 pp. Illus. Christina Birgander and Bir-
        gitta Hvidberg. ISBN 9140038904.

114.   *Anne på Grönkulla.* Tr. Karin Lidforss Jensen. Lund: Liber Läro-
        medel, 1980. 328 pp. Illus. Britt Hallqvist. ISBN 9140022110.

Turkish:

115.   *Yuvasiz çocuk.* Tr. Ipek Ongun. Istanbul: Altin Kitaplar Basimevi,
        1979. 215 pp.

ANNE OF AVONLEA

First edition. Boston: Page, 1909.

Editions in English

Australia:

116.   *Anne of Avonlea.* Sydney: Cornstalk Publishing Co., 1925. vi, 364
        pp.

117.   -----. Platypus series. Sydney: Angus and Robertson, 1927. 364
        pp.

118.   -----. Sydney: Angus and Robertson, 1953. viii, 268 pp. Illustrated.
        Reprinted *1955.

119.   -----. Sydney: Angus and Robertson, 1965. 252 pp. No illustra-
        tions. Reprinted 1972, 1973, 1974, 1977, 1980, 1981, 1982.

Canada:

120.   *Anne of Avonlea.* Toronto: Ryerson, *1942. viii, 367 pp. Reprint-
        ed 1944, *1946, 1947, 1949, 1952, *1956, 1960, *1963, *1966,
        *1969.

121.   -----. Toronto: Ryerson, *1968. viii, 367 pp. Paperback.

122.   -----. Toronto: Seal Books, McClelland and Stewart-Bantam,
        *1981. 277 pp. ISBN 0770416969. Frequently reprinted with new
        ISBN but no change in date; current (1985) ISBN 0770420206.

123.   -----. Large print ed. London, Ont.: Gatefold Books, *1982. 430
        pp. ISBN 0919155049.

Great Britain:

124.   *Anne of Avonlea.* London: Pitman, 1909. viii, 367 pp. With fron-
        tispiece and cover in colour by George Gibbs. This edition, printed
        in the U.S., is probably identical to the original Page edition,
        except that the publisher's imprint has been changed from Page to
        Pitman. It bears the Page copyright. Reprinted 1913.

125.   -----. London: Harrap, 1925. 320 pp. Reprinted 1926, 1927, 1928,
        1929, 1930, 1931, *1933, 1934 (twice), 1935, 1936, 1937, 1938,
        1939, 1940, 1941.

126.   -----. London: Harrap, 1943. 252 pp. Reset from the 1926 edition.
        Reprinted 1945, 1946, 1947, 1949, 1950, 1952, 1953, 1954, 1956,

1957, 1960, 1961, 1963, 1965, 1967, 1969, 1971, 1972 (ISBN 0245551271), *1974 (twice), *1975, *1976, 1978.

127.   -----. Harmondsworth: Penguin, Peacock Books, 1974. viii, 240 pp. Paperback. ISBN 0140470808. Reprinted *1975.

128.   -----. Harmondsworth: Penguin, Puffin Books, 1979. 240 pp. Paperback. ISBN 0140312501.

United States:

129.   *Anne of Avonlea*. Boston: Page, *1909. viii, 367 pp. With frontispiece and cover in colour by George Gibbs. Reprinted *1909 (twice in September; all first three impressions have been examined; four subsequent impressions in 1909 have not been examined), 1910 (five times), 1911 (three times), 1912, 1913 (three times), 1914, 1915 (three times), *1916 (personal copy of LMM, signed, examined at Guelph, is 24th impression); other reprints include the 30th (1919), the 40th (*1928), the 44th (1943 -- the last known reprint of this edition).

130.   -----. New York: Grosset and Dunlap, 1909. viii, 367 pp. With frontispiece and cover in colour by George Gibbs. This edition seems to be identical to the original Page edition, except that the publisher's imprint has been changed from Page to Grosset and Dunlap. It bears the Page copyright. Reprinted *1917, *1919, 1920.

131.   -----. New York: Grosset and Dunlap, *1909. vii, 367 pp. This edition is not a Thrushwood Book, nor does it have illustrations.

132.   -----. n.p.: Michigan Young People's Reading Group, 1923.

133.   -----. Thrushwood Books. New York: Grosset and Dunlap, 1936. vii, 366 pp. Reprinted 1949, 1961.

134.   -----. An Anne of Green Gables Book. New York: Grosset and Dunlap, *1970. vii, 366 pp. Reprinted *1973 (ISBN 0448025442), 1975.

135.   -----. New York: Bantam, *1976. 277 pp. Paperback. ISBN 055302816. Published in Canada as a Seal Book. Reprinted 9 times through 1983.

136.   -----. New York: Bantam Skylark, *1983. viii, 274 pp. ISBN 0553151142.

137.   -----. Bridgeport, Conn.: Airmont Publishers. This edition was published in violation of copyright and withdrawn from the market.

Translations

Danish:

138.   *Anne som voksen.* Tr. Jenny Erslev and Dagmar Gade. Copenhagen: H. Aschehoug, 1919. 192 pp.

Dutch:

139.   *Anne van Avonlea.* Tr. Betsy de Vries. Haarlem: Tjeenk Willink, 1912. viii, 298 pp. Reprinted 1920, 1924.

140.   *De nieuwe juf van Avonlea.* Anne van het Groene Huis series, vol. 3. Tr. Martha Heesen. Baarn: De Fontein, *1980. 112 pp. Illus. B. Bouman. Translation of Part One of *Anne of Avonlea.* ISBN 9026112327.

141.   *Een bruiloft in Avonlea.* Anne van het Groene Huis series, vol. 4. Tr. Martha Heesen. Baarn: De Fontein, *1980. 122 pp. Illus. B. Bouman. Translation of Part Two of *Anne of Avonlea.* ISBN 9026112335.

Finnish:

142.   *Anna ystävämme.* Tr. Hilja Vesala. Porvoo: Werner Söderström, *1921 (personal copy of LMM, signed, examined at Guelph). 344 pp. Reprinted 1944, 1945, 1947, 1950, 1955.

143.   *Anna ystävämme.* Tr. Hilja Vesala. Porvoo: Werner Söderström, 1961. 260 pp. Reprinted *1964, *1973 (ISBN 951004377X).

Hebrew:

144.   *An mi'avonli.* Tr. Israel Fishman. Tel-Aviv: M. Newman, 1957. 364 pp.

Icelandic:

145.   *Davið kemur til sögunnar.* Anna í Grænuhlíð series, vol. 2. Tr. Axel Guðmundsson. Reykjavík: Ólafur Erlingsson, 1934. 192 pp. Reprinted by another publisher, Reykjavik: Iðunn, 1951-66, *1964. 183 pp. Condensed version.

Japanese:

146.   *Anne no seishun.* Tr. Hanako Muraoka. Tokyo: Mikasa Shobo, 1954. 259 pp. Illustrated. Paperback. Reprinted 1955.

147.   *Anne no seishun.* Tr. Hanako Muraoka. Tokyo: Shincho Sha, 1955. 386 pp. Paperback.

148.   *Anne no seishun*. Tr. Hanako Muraoka. Tokyo: Mikasa Shobo, 1956.
        226 pp. Paperback.

149.   *Anne no seishun*. Tr. Sakiko Nakamura. Tokyo: Kadokawa Shoten,
        1958. 330 pp. Paperback.

150.   *Anne no seishun*. Tr. Hanako Muraoka. Tokyo: Kōdan Sha, *1964.
        302 pp. Illustrated with photos of Green Gables and LMM.
        Reprinted 1966, 1971, 1973.

151.   *Anne no seishun*. Tr. Hanako Muraoka. Tokyo: Mikasa Shobo,
        *1966. 221 pp. Illustrated with photos of Green Gables and other
        P.E.I. scenes.

152.   *Anne no seishun*. Tr. Hanako Muraoka. Tokyo: Kaisei Sha, 1967.
        276 pp. Illustrated. Reprinted *1970.

153.   *Anne no seishun*. Tr. Hanako Muraoka. Tokyo: Popura Sha, *1967.
        274 pp. Illustrated with one photo of P.E.I. and one drawing.
        Reprinted *1978.

154.   *Anne no seishun*. Tr. Taeko Kamiyama. Tokyo: Ōbun Sha, 1976.
        388 pp. Paperback.

Korean:

155.   *Aeneui Cheongchun*. Tr. Ji-Shik Shin. Seoul: Daedongdang, 1960.
        209 pp.

156.   *Bbalganmeori Aen; Aeneui Cheongchun*. Tr. Ji-Shik Shin. Seoul:
        Yugminsa, 1963. 324 pp. Translation of both *Anne of Green
        Gables* and *Anne of Avonlea*.

157.   *Bbalganmeori Aen; Aeneui Cheongchun*. Tr. Ji-Shik Shin. Seoul:
        Changjosa, 1964. Translation of *Anne of Green Gables* and *Anne of
        Avonlea*.

158.   *Bbalganmeori Aen; Aeneui Cheongchun*. Seoul: Daehan Publishing
        Company, 1966. 149 pp. Translation by Uryang Eorynie Publishing
        Company of *Anne of Green Gables* and *Anne of Avonlea*.

159.   *Bbalganmeori Aen; Aeneui Cheongchun*. Tr. So-Hee Shon. Seoul:
        Dong Seo Publishing, 1977. 447 pp. Translation of *Anne of Green
        Gables* and *Anne of Avonlea*.

160.   *Bbalganmeori Aen; Aeneui Cheongchun*. Tr. Sin-Hang Lee. Seoul:
        Sinmoon Publishing, 1977. 356 pp. Translation of *Anne of Green
        Gables* and *Anne of Avonlea*.

161. *Aeneui Cheongchun.* Anne Story series, vol. 2. Tr. Ji-Shik Shin.
      Seoul: Changjosa, *1984. 256 pp. Paperback. Illustrated with
      black line drawings.

Norwegian:

162. *Anne som frøken.* Tr. Elise Horn. Kristiania: H. Aschehoug, 1920.
      176 pp.

163. *Anne som frøken.* 3rd ed. Tr. Mimi Sverdrup Lunden. Oslo:
      Aschehoug, 1955. 160 pp. Reprinted 1974.

Polish:

164. *Ania z Avonlea.* Tr. Rozalia Bernsteinowa. Warsaw: B. Rudzki,
      1924. 284 pp.

165. *Ania z Avonlea.* Tr. Rozalia Bernsteinowa. Warsaw: M. Arct,
      1927. 262 pp.

166. *Ania z Avonlea.* Tr. Rozalia Bernsteinowa. Warsaw: M. Arct,
      1935. 251 pp.

167. *Ania z Avonlea.* Tr. Rozalia Bernsteinowa. Wrocław: M. Arcti
      Dom Książki Polskiej, 1948. 232 pp.

168. *Ania z Avonlea.* Tr. Rozalia Bernsteinowa. Warsaw: Nasza Księ-
      garnia, 1957. 268 pp. Illus. Bogdan Zieleniec.

169. *Ania z Avonlea.* Tr. Rozalia Bernsteinowa. Warsaw: Nasza Księ-
      garnia, 1976. 318 pp. Illus. Bogdan Zieleniec. Reprinted 1980.

170. *Ania z Zielonego Wzgórza; Ania z Avonlea.* Tr. Rozalia Bernstei-
      nowa. Warsaw: Nasza Księgarnia, *1967. 562 pp. Illus. Bogdan
      Zieleniec. Translation of both *Anne of Green Gables* and *Anne of
      Avonlea.* Reprinted 1973.

Slovak (Czechoslovakia):

171. *Anna z Avonlea.* Tr. Jozef Šimo. Bratislava: Mladé letá, *1969.
      286 pp. Illus. Jozef Trepáč. Reprinted 1972, 1975.

Spanish:

172. *Anne, la de Avonlea.* Tr. José García Díaz. Buenos Aires: Emecé
      Editores, 1951, 1968. 290 pp.

Swedish:

173.   *Vår vän Anne.* Tr. Karin Jensen. Lund: Gleerup, 1910. 301 pp.
        Reprinted 1917, 1920, 1926, 1935, 1943, 1946, 1950, 1952, 1954,
        1955, 1962.

174.   *Anne växer upp.* Tr. Aslög Davidson. Stockholm: B. Wahlström,
        1946. 251 pp.

175.   *Vår vän Anne.* Tr. Karin Jensen. Hfors: H. Schildt, Lund: Berling,
        1946. 302 pp. (Co-publication with Gleerup?)

176.   *Anne växer upp.* Abridged ed. Tr. and illus. Margareta Sjögren-
        Olsson. Stockholm: Lindblad, *1963. 154 pp.

177.   *Vår vän Anne.* Tr. Karin Lidforss Jensen. Lund: Gleerup, *1966.
        279 pp. Reprinted *1972.

178.   *Vår vän Anne.* Tr. Karin Lidforss Jensen. Stockholm and Lund:
        Liber Läromedel and Br. Ekstrand, *1977. 279 pp. Illus. Vibeke
        Wennerberg. ISBN 9140022145. Reprinted *1980.

KILMENY OF THE ORCHARD

First edition. Boston: Page, 1910.

Editions in English

Australia:

179.   *Kilmeny of the Orchard.* Bellbird series. Sydney: Cornstalk Pub-
        lishing Co., 1925. 238 pp. Frontispiece.

180.   -----. Sydney: [Angus and Robertson?], 1934.

181.   -----. Sydney: Angus and Robertson, 1982. 218 pp.

Canada:

182.   *Kilmeny of the Orchard.* Toronto: Ryerson, *1944. viii, 256 pp.
        Reprinted 1945, *1947, *1956, *1965, *1968, *1972 (ISBN
        0770001033).

Great Britain:

183.   *Kilmeny of the Orchard.* London: Pitman, *1910. xii, 256 pp. With
        illustrations, frontispiece and cover in colour by George Gibbs.

This edition, printed in the U.S., is identical to the original Page edition, except that the publisher's imprint has been changed from Page to Pitman. It bears the Page copyright. Reprinted 1910.

184.   -----. London: Harrap, 1925. 221 pp. Reprinted 1926, 1929, 1931, 1932, 1934, *1935, 1936, 1937, 1940.

United States:

185.   *Kilmeny of the Orchard.* Boston: Page, *1910. xii, 256 pp. With illustrations, cover and frontispiece in colour by George Gibbs. Reprinted 1910 (five times), *1911, 1912.

186.   -----. New York: A.L. Burt, 1910. Reprinted 1924. 256 pp. (Copy bearing only 1910 date, presumed to be 1924 reprint was examined.)

187.   -----. Juveniles of Distinction series. New York: Grosset and Dunlap, 1943. 256 pp.

Translations

Japanese:

188.   *Kajuen no serenade.* Tr. Hanako Muraoka. Tokyo: Shincho Sha, 1957. 171 pp.

189.   *Kajuen no serenade.* Tr. Hanako Muraoka. Tokyo: Shincho Sha, *1961. 215 pp. Paperback.

190.   *Kajuen no serenade.* Tr. Hanako Muraoka. Tokyo: Kōdan Sha, 1966. 204 pp.

191.   *Kajuen no serenade.* Tr. Hanako Muraoka. Tokyo: Kaisei Sha, 1967. 268 pp. Illustrated with one colour plate, many drawings, photos of LMM and P.E.I. Reprinted *1970.

192.   *Kajuen monogatari.* Tr. Hanako Muraoka. Tokyo: Iwasaki Shoten, 1973. 207 pp.

Polish:

193.   *Dziewczę z sadu.* Tr. Władsyława Wielińska. Warsaw: J. Przeworski, 1936. 147 pp. Illus. Jan Szancer.

Spanish:

194.   *El Bosque encantado.* Tr. Juan J. Llobet. Buenos Aires: Acme. 3rd printing *1967. 192 pp. Illus. E. Cuschie.

Swedish:

195.   *Kilmeny.* Tr. E.M.R. Lund: Gleerup, 1932. 151 pp.

THE STORY GIRL

First edition. Boston: Page, 1911.

Editions in English

Australia:

196.   *The Story Girl.* Bellbird series. Sydney: Cornstalk Publishing Co., 1925. 352 pp. Frontispiece.

197.   -----. Sydney: Angus and Robertson, 1976. 286 pp. ISBN 0207133786. Reprinted 1980.

Canada:

198.   *The Story Girl.* Toronto: Ryerson, *1944. viii, 365 pp. Reprinted 1946, *1953, *1961, 1966, *[1970s] (ISBN 0770001963 under the McGraw-Hill Ryerson imprint).

Great Britain:

199.   *The Story Girl.* London: Pitman, 1911. vi, 365 pp. With frontispiece and cover in colour by George Gibbs. This edition, printed in the U.S., is probably identical to the original Page edition, except that the publisher's imprint has been changed from Page to Pitman.

200.   -----. London: Harrap, 1925. 291 pp. Reprinted 1926, 1929, 1930, 1932, *1934, *1935, 1936, 1937, 1939, 1941.

201.   -----. London: Harrap, 1943. Reset from previous edition, reprinted 1945, 1948, 1950.

United States:

202.   *The Story Girl.* Boston: Page, 1911. vi, 365 pp. With frontispiece and cover in colour by George Gibbs. Reprinted *1911 (five times, of which the 2nd and 5th reprintings have been examined).

203.   -----. New York: A.L. Burt, *1911. vi, 365 pp. With frontispiece and cover in colour by George Gibbs. This edition is identical to the original Page edition, except that the publisher's imprint has been changed from Page to Burt. It bears the Page copyright.

Copy signed by LMM, examined at National Library, Ottawa. Reprinted 1926.

204.   -----. New York: Grosset and Dunlap, *n.d. viii, 365 pp. With frontispiece in colour by George Gibbs.

205.   -----. Juveniles of Distinction series. New York: Grosset and Dunlap, 1943. vi, 365 pp.

Translations

Japanese:

206.   *Sutōrī-Gāru.* Vol. 1. Tr. Yuriko Kimura. Tokyo: Shinozaki Shorin, *1980. 196 pp. Illustrated.

207.   *Sutōrī-Gāru.* Vol. 2. Tr. Yuriko Kimura. Tokyo: Shinozaki Shorin, *1980. 202 pp. Illustrated.

Polish:

208.   *Historynka.* Tr. Janina Zawisza-Krasucka. Warsaw: J. Przeworski, 1936. 363 pp. Illus. Stefan Haykowskiego.

Spanish:

209.   *La Niña de los cuentos.* Tr. J.J. Llobet. Buenos Aires: Acme, 1956. 270 pp.

210.   *La Niña de los cuentos.* Robin Hood series. Tr. J.J. Llobet. Buenos Aires: Acme, *1966. 218 pp. Illus. Ely Cushie. Third reprinting.

CHRONICLES OF AVONLEA

First edition. Boston: Page, 1912.

Editions in English

Australia:

211.   *Chronicles of Avonlea.* Bellbird series. Sydney: Cornstalk Publishing Co., 1925. 275 pp.

212.   -----. Sydney: Angus and Robertson, 1932. 275 pp.

213.   -----. Sydney: Angus and Robertson, 1938. 234 pp.

214.   -----. Sydney: Angus and Robertson, 1954. vi, 217 pp.

215.   -----. Sydney: Angus and Robertson, 1972. 236 pp. ISBN
        0207123535. Reprinted 1974, 1976, 1980, 1983.

Canada:

216.   *Chronicles of Avonlea.* Toronto: Ryerson, *1943. viii, 306 pp.
        Reprinted *1945, *1947, *1949, 1953, *1961, 1967, *1970 (ISBN
        0770000436).

217.   -----. Toronto: McGraw-Hill Ryerson, *1980. 306 pp. Paperback.
        ISBN 007092368.

Great Britain:

218.   *Chronicles of Avonlea.* London: Sampson Low, Marston & Co.,
        1912. 314 pp. With frontispiece in colour by George Gibbs.

219.   -----. London: Simpkin, 1914. 314 pp.

220.   -----. New ed. London: Simpkin, 1915. 315 pp.

221.   -----. London: Harrap, 1925. 236 pp. Reprinted 1925, 1928, 1929,
        *1930, 1931, 1933, 1935, 1936 (twice), *1937, 1939, 1940, 1941
        (twice), 1942, 1945, 1946, 1951, 1955, 1957, 1961, 1964, 1966, 1969,
        1971, 1972, *1974 (ISBN 0245555617), 1976, 1977, 1979, 1982.

United States:

222.   *Chronicles of Avonlea.* Boston: Page, *1912. viii, 306 pp. With
        frontispiece and cover in colour by George Gibbs. Reprinted fre-
        quently: *1912 (4th impression, LMM's personal copy, signed, exam-
        ined at Guelph), 1916, *1928 (17th impression, LMM's personal
        copy, signed, examined at Guelph), *1950 (23rd impression).

223.   -----. New York: A.L. Burt, 1929. 306 pp.

224.   -----. New York: Grosset and Dunlap, *1940. 306 pp.

225.   -----. Thrushwood Books. New York: Grosset and Dunlap, 1950.
        306 pp. Reprinted 1961.

226.   -----. An Anne of Green Gables Book. New York: Grosset and
        Dunlap, 1970. viii, 306 pp. Reprinted *1971, *1973 (ISBN
        0448025507).

Translations

Japanese:

227.   *Anne no tomodachi.* Tr. Hanako Muraoka. Tokyo: Mikasa Shobo,
        1956. 208 pp. Paperback.

228.   *Anne no tomodachi.* Tr. Hanako Muraoka. Tokyo: Mikasa Shobo,
        1956. 289 pp.

229.   *Anne no tomodachi.* Tr. Hanako Muraoka. Tokyo: Shincho Sha,
        1957. 294 pp. Paperback.

230.   *Anne no mura no hitobito.* Tr. Sakiko Nakamura. Tokyo: Kadoka-
        wa Shoten, 1965. 270 pp. Paperback.

231.   *Anne no tomodachi.* Tr. Hanako Muraoka. Tokyo: Kōdan Sha,
        *1966. 282 pp. Illustrated with one colour plate, many drawings,
        one photo. Reprinted 1973.

232.   *Anne no tomodachi.* Tr. Hanako Muraoka. Tokyo: Mikasa Shobo,
        1966. 211 pp. Illustrated with one colour plate, one photo of P.E.I.
        Reprinted *1969.

233.   *Anne no tomodachi.* Tr. Hanako Muraoka. Tokyo: Kaisei Sha,
        1967. 272 pp. Illustrated with one colour plate, many drawings.
        Reprinted *1971.

Korean:

234.   *Aeneui Chingudeul.* Tr. Ji-Shik Shin. Seoul: Changjosa, 1964.

235.   *Aeneui Chingudeul.* Anne Story series, vol. 4. Tr. Ji-Shik Shin.
        Seoul: Changjosa, *1985. 256 pp. Paperback. Illustrated with
        black line drawings.

Spanish:

236.   *Anne y su pequeño mundo.* Tr. Lydia and José García Díaz. Buenos
        Aires: Emecé Editores, 1953, 1969. 205 pp. Illustrated.

Swedish:

237.   *Grönkullagrannar.* Tr. Birger Bjerre. Lund: Gleerup, *1968. 225
        pp.

THE GOLDEN ROAD

First edition. Boston: Page, 1913.

Editions in English

Australia:

238.   *The Golden Road.* Sydney: Cornstalk Publishing Co., 1925. x, 328 pp. One colour plate.

239.   -----. Sydney: Angus and Robertson, 1954. vi, 250 pp.

240.   -----. [New ed.] Sydney: Angus and Robertson, 1982. vi, 250 pp.

Canada:

241.   *The Golden Road.* Toronto: McClelland and Goodchild, 1913. x, 369 pp. Coloured frontispiece.

242.   -----. Toronto: Ryerson, 1944. x, 369 pp. Reprinted *1947, *1954, *1962, *1967, *1972 (ISBN 0770000770).

Great Britain:

243.   *The Golden Road.* London: Cassell, 1914. 369 pp.

244.   -----. London: Harrap, 1925. 286 pp. Reprinted 1926, 1928, 1929, 1932, 1934, 1935, 1936, *1937, 1939, 1941.

245.   -----. London: Harrap, 1943. Reset from previous edition; reprinted 1946, 1948.

United States:

246.   *The Golden Road.* Boston: Page, *1913. x, 369 pp. With frontispiece and cover in colour by George Gibbs. First impression examined at Silver Bush, Park Corner, P.E.I. Reprinted *1913 (LMM's personal copy, signed, examined at Guelph), *1920 (5th impression, LMM's personal copy, signed, examined at Guelph), 1926.

247.   -----. New York: Grosset and Dunlap, *1913. x, 369 pp. With frontispiece and cover in colour by George Gibbs. This edition is identical to the original Page edition, except that the publisher's imprint has been changed.

248.   -----. New York: A.L. Burt, 1926.

249.   -----. Juveniles of Distinction series. New York: Grosset and Dun-
        lap, *1943. x, 369 pp. An edition by Grosset and Dunlap, printed
        during the Second World War, with this pagination, was examined;
        there were no illustrations, although the title page says there is a
        frontispiece by George Gibbs (which suggests that the original
        plates were used for this cheaper edition).

Translations

Japanese:

250.   Ōgon no michi. Vol. 1. Tr. Yuriko Kimura. Tokyo: Shinozaki Sho-
        rin, *1980. 186 pp. Illustrated.

251.   Ōgon no michi. Vol. 2. Tr. Yuriko Kimura. Tokyo: Shinozaki Sho-
        rin, *1980. 176 pp. Illustrated.

ANNE OF THE ISLAND

First edition. Boston: Page, 1915.

Editions in English

Australia:

252.   Anne of the Island. Bellbird series. Sydney: Cornstalk Publishing
        Co., 1925. 313 pp.

253.   -----. Platypus series. Sydney: Cornstalk Publishing Co., 1927.
        313 pp.

254.   -----. Sydney: Angus and Robertson, 1949. viii, 276 pp. Reprinted
        1950, 1965.

255.   -----. Sydney: Angus and Robertson, 1972. 221 pp. ISBN
        0207123527. Reprinted 1974, 1975, 1979, 1980, 1982.

Canada:

256.   Anne of the Island. Toronto: Ryerson, *1942. viii, 326 pp.
        Reprinted *1944, 1945, *1947, 1949, 1952, 1956, 1960, 1963, *1966.

257.   -----. Toronto: Ryerson, *1968. viii, 326 pp. Paperback.

258.   -----. Toronto: Seal Books, McClelland and Stewart-Bantam,
        *1981. 244 pp. Paperback. ISBN 0770416942. Frequently reprint-
        ed with new ISBN, no dates available.

259.   -----. Large print ed. London, Ont.: Gatefold Books, *1982. ISBN
        0919155065.

Great Britain:

260.   *Anne of the Island.* London: Pitman, 1915. viii, 326 pp. With fron-
        tispiece and cover in colour by H. Weston Taylor. This edition,
        printed in the U.S., is probably identical to the original Page edi-
        tion, except that the publisher's imprint has been changed.

261.   -----. London: Harrap, 1925. 288 pp. Reprinted 1926, 1927, 1928,
        1929, 1930, 1931, 1932, 1934 (twice), *1935, 1936, 1937, *1938,
        1939, 1940, *1941.

262.   -----. London: Harrap, 1943. 221 pp. Reset from previous edition.
        Reprinted 1944, 1945, 1948, 1950, 1952, *1953, 1955, 1956, 1959,
        1961, 1965, 1966, 1969, 1971, 1972, *1974 (ISBN 24555128X), 1975,
        1976, 1977, 1978, 1980.

United States:

263.   *Anne of the Island.* Boston: Page, *1915. viii, 326 pp. With fron-
        tispiece and cover in colour by H. Weston Taylor. Reprinted *1915
        (seven times; examined first reprint, autographed by LMM, at Park
        Corner, P.E.I.; examined seventh reprint, LMM's personal copy, at
        Guelph archives), 1916 (twice), 1917, *1918 (twice, the last one
        examined), 1919, *1920 (the 17th impression).

264.   -----. New York: Grosset and Dunlap, 1915. viii, 326 pp. With
        frontispiece and cover in colour by H. Weston Taylor. This is prob-
        ably identical to the original Page edition, but with the publisher's
        imprint changed from Page to Grosset and Dunlap.

265.   -----. New York: A.L. Burt, 1928.

266.   -----. Thrushwood Books. New York: Grosset and Dunlap, 1951.
        viii, 326 pp. Reprinted 1961. A copy bearing no date was exam-
        ined.

267.   -----. An Anne of Green Gables Book. New York: Grosset and
        Dunlap, *1970. x, 307 pp. ISBN 0448025477. Reprinted 1974.

268.   -----. New York: Bantam, 1976. 256 pp. Paperback. Ten printings
        through 1980. Published in Canada as a Seal-Bantam Book.

Translations

Dutch:

269.   *Anne van het eiland.* Tr. Betsy de Vries. Haarlem: Tjeenk Willink,
         *1916. 277 pp. Frontispiece and cover illustration in colour by H.
         Weston Taylor, as in the Page edition. Personal copy of LMM,
         signed, examined at Guelph. Reprinted 1920, 1925.

270.   *Anne gaat studeren.* Anne van het Groene Huis series, vol. 5. Tr.
         Martha Heesen. Baarn: De Fontein, *1980. 102 pp. Part One of
         Anne of the Island. ISBN 9026112386.

271.   *Anne en Gilbert.* Anne van het Groene Huis series, vol. 6. Tr.
         Martha Heesen. Baarn: De Fontein, *1980. 117 pp. Part Two of
         Anne of the Island. ISBN 9026112394.

Finnish:

272.   *Annan unelmavuodet.* Tr. Toini Kalima. Porvoo: Werner Söder-
         ström, *1921. 320 pp. Personal copy of LMM, signed, examined at
         Guelph. Reprinted, Porvoo and Helsinki, 1944, 1945, 1947, 1952,
         1958.

273.   *Annan unelmavuodet.* Tr. Toini Kalima. Porvoo: Werner Söder-
         ström, *1962. 225 pp. Reprinted, Porvoo and Helsinki, *1967, 1973
         (ISBN 9510043796).

Hebrew:

274.   *An Shirli.* Tr. Israel Fishman. Tel-Aviv: M. Newman, 1957. 220
         pp.

Icelandic:

275.   *Anna trúlofast.* Anna í Grænuhlíð series, vol. 3. Tr. Axel
         Guðmundsson. Reykjavík: Ólafur Erlingsson, 1935. 144 pp.
         Reprinted, Reykjavik: Iðunn, 1951-66, *[1965?], 149 pp. Condensed
         version.

Japanese:

276.   *Anne no Aijo.* Tr. Hanako Muraoka. Tokyo: Shincho Sha, 1956.
         376 pp. Paperback.

277.   *Anne ni Kon'yaku.* Tr. Sakiko Nakamura. Tokyo: Kadokawa Sho-
         ten, 1959. 313 pp. Paperback.

278.   *Anne no Aijo.* Tr. Hanako Muraoka. Tokyo: Kōdan Sha, *1964. 318
         pp. Illustrated with one colour plate, many drawings, two photos of
         LMM and family. Reprinted 1966, 1971, 1973.

279. *Anne no Aijo.* Tr. Hanako Muraoka. Tokyo: Mikasa Shobo, 1966. 217 pp. Illustrated with photo of P.E.I. Reprinted *1969.

280. *Anne no Aijo.* Tr. Hanako Muraoka. Tokyo: Kaisei Sha, 1967. 274 pp. Illustrated with one colour plate, many drawings. Reprinted *1970.

281. *Anne no Aijo.* Tr. Hanako Muraoka. Tokyo: Poplar Sha, 1967. 270 pp. Illustrated.

Korean:

282. *Aeneui Sarang.* Tr. Ji-Shik Shin. Seoul: Changjosa, 1964.

283. *Aeneui Sarang.* Anne Story series, vol. 3. Tr. Ji-Shik Shin. Seoul: Changjosa, *1985. 256 pp. Paperback. Illustrated with black line drawings.

Norwegian:

284. *Anne på college.* Tr. Elise Horn. Kristiania: H. Aschehoug, 1920. 176 pp.

285. *Anne på college.* Abridged ed. Tr. Jo Tenfjord. Oslo: Aschehoug, *1956. 144 pp. Reprinted 1974.

Polish:

286. *Ania z wyspy.* Tr. Andrzej Magórski. Łodź: Nakł. Księgarni Francuza, 1930. 288 pp. Reprinted 1935.

287. *Ania na uniwersytecie.* Tr. Janina Zawisza-Krasucka. Warsaw: Wydawnictwo Literatur Obcych, 1931. 300 pp.

288. *Ania z wyspy.* Tr. Andrzej Magórski [pseud. Tarnowski Marceli]. Palestine: Nakł. Sekcja Wydawn. Armii Polskiej na Wschodzie, 1944. 212 pp.

289. *Ania na uniwersytecie.* Tr. Janina Zawisza-Krasucka. Wrocław: M. Arcti Dom Książki Polskiej, 1948. 246 pp.

290. *Ania na uniwersytecie.* Tr. Janina Zawisza-Krasucka. Warsaw: Nasza Księgarnia, 1957. 271 pp. Illus. Bogdan Zieleniec.

291. *Ania na uniwersytecie; Wymarzony dom Ani.* Tr. Janina Zawisza-Krasucka and Stefan Fedyński. Warsaw: Nasza Księgarnia, *1968. 504 pp. Illus. Bogdan Zieleniec. Translation of both *Anne of the Island* and *Anne's House of Dreams.* Reprinted 1971, 1974.

292.   *Ania na uniwersytecie.* Tr. Janina Zawisza-Krasucka. Warsaw:
        Nasza Księgarnia, 1976. 316 pp. Illus. Bogdan Zieleniec, with
        black and white sketches, colour cover. Reprinted *1981. Bears
        copyright date of 1957. Paperback.

Slovak (Czechoslovakia):

293.   *Anna v Redmonde.* Tr. Jozef Šimo. Bratislava: Mladé léta, 1969.
        267 pp. Illus. Jozef Trepáč. Reprinted *1972, 1975.

Spanish:

294.   *Anne, la de la Isla.* Tr. José García Díaz. Buenos Aires: Emecé
        Editores, 1952.

Swedish:

295.   *Drömmens uppfyllelse.* Tr. Karin Lidforss Jensen. Lund: Gleerup,
        1916. [303 pp.?] Reprinted 1920, 1927, 1936 (twice), 1946, 1951,
        1953, 1956; (may have been reset in 1946 in an edition of 280 pp.).

296.   *Drömmens uppfyllelse.* Tr. Karin Lidforss Jensen. Lund: Gleerup,
        *1964. 296 pp. Reprinted 1971.

ANNE'S HOUSE OF DREAMS

First edition. New York: Stokes, 1917.

Editions in English

Australia:

297.   *Anne's House of Dreams.* Platypus series. Sydney: Cornstalk Pub-
        lishing Co., 1925. 321 pp. Frontispiece.

298.   -----. Bellbird series. Sydney: Angus and Robertson, 1932. 321 pp.

299.   -----. Sydney: Angus and Robertson, 1941. vi, 282 pp. Reprinted
        1949, 1953.

300.   -----. Sydney: Angus and Robertson, 1972. 224 pp. ISBN
        0207125473. Reprinted 1974, 1976, *1980, 1982.

Canada:

301.   *Anne's House of Dreams.* Toronto: McClelland, Goodchild and
        Stewart, *1917. viii, 346 pp. With frontispiece in colour by M.L.

Kirk. This is identical to the original Stokes edition, except that the publisher's imprint has been changed from Stokes to McClelland, Goodchild and Stewart. This edition was printed in the U.S., and bears the Stokes copyright. Reprinted *1922, but with the McClelland and Stewart copyright.

302.   -----. Toronto: McClelland and Stewart, *1922. 291 pp. Not illustrated. This is a new edition and bears the McClelland and Stewart copyright, as do all McClelland and Stewart editions from this point on. Reprinted *1947: two different versions using the same plates, but with different sizes and bindings have been examined; one is the Cavendish edition, with a letter "C" stamped on cloth cover and slightly larger dimensions than the standard edition. Reprinted 1962.

303.   -----. Canadian Children's Favourites series. Toronto: McClelland and Stewart, *1972. iv, 291 pp. Paperback. Reprinted in Canadian Favourites series, 1979, *1981. ISBN 077106196X.

304.   -----. Anne of Green Gables series, no. 5. Toronto: Seal Books, McClelland and Stewart-Bantam, *1981. 230 pp. Paperback. ISBN 0770416721. This edition reports 9 printings of this title, in unspecified editions, by McClelland and Stewart between 1962 and 1979. Reprinted *1983, ISBN 0770420761; frequently reprinted with new ISBN, no dates available.

Great Britain:

305.   *Anne's House of Dreams*. London: Constable, 1917. 346 pp. This edition was probably printed from the same plates as the original Stokes edition; it was, though, printed in England. Reprinted 1918, 1920.

306.   -----. London: Harrap, 1926. 352 pp. Reprinted 1927, 1928, 1929, 1930, 1931, 1933, 1934, 1935, 1936, 1937, 1938, 1940, 1941.

307.   -----. London: Harrap, 1943. 224 pp. Reset from the previous edition. Reprinted 1946, 1949, 1950, 1953, 1955, 1957, 1958, 1961, 1964, 1966, 1969, 1971, 1972, 1973, *1975 (ISBN 0245551301), 1977, 1980.

308.   -----. Harmondsworth: Penguin, Puffin Books, *1981. 297 pp. Paperback. ISBN 0140314709.

United States:

309.   *Anne's House of Dreams*. New York: Stokes, *1917. viii, 346 pp. With frontispiece in colour by M.L. Kirk.

310.   -----. New York: A.L. Burt, *1917. viii, 346 pp. With frontispiece
        in colour by M.L. Kirk. This is identical to the original Stokes edi-
        tion, except that the publisher's imprint has been changed from
        Stokes to Burt. It bears the Stokes copyright.

311.   -----. New York: Grosset and Dunlap, 1917. viii, 346 pp. With
        frontispiece in colour by M.L. Kirk. This edition is probably identi-
        cal to the original Stokes edition, except that the publisher's
        imprint has been changed from Stokes to Grosset and Dunlap.
        Reprinted 1938.

312.   -----. Thrushwood Books. New York: Grosset and Dunlap, 1951.
        viii, 245 pp. Reprinted 1961. A copy with this pagination, but not
        called a Thrushwood Book, and bearing no date, with the notice
        that it is published by arrangement with Lippincott, was examined.

313.   -----. An Anne of Green Gables Book. New York: Grosset and
        Dunlap, *1970. viii, 245 pp. Reprinted 1971, *1974 (ISBN
        0448025493).

314.   -----. New York: Bantam, *1981. 230 pp. Paperback. ISBN
        0553149954. Published in Canada as a Seal-Bantam Book.

Translations

Dutch:

315.   Het huis van Anne's droomen. Tr. Betsy de Vries. Haarlem: Tjeenk
        Willink, 1920. 284 pp. Reprinted 1926.

Finnish:

316.   Anna omassa kodissaan. Tr. Hilja Walldén. Porvoo: Werner Söder-
        ström, *1922. 317 pp. Personal copy of LMM, signed, examined at
        Guelph. Reprinted 1944, 1945, 1950, 1954.

317.   Anna omassa kodissaan. Tr. Hilja Walldén. Porvoo and Helsinki:
        Werner Söderström, 1963. 223 pp. Reset from the previous edi-
        tion. Reprinted *1968, 1976.

Icelandic:

318.   Anna giftist. Anna í Grænuhlíð series, vol. 4. Tr. Axel
        Guðmundsson. Reykjavík: Leiftur, 1945. 136 pp. Condensed ver-
        sion. Reprinted, Reykjavík: Iðunn, 1951-[1964?], *[1966?].

Japanese:

319.   *Anne no yume no ie.* Tr. Hanako Muraoka. Tokyo: Mikasa Shobo, 1958. 212 pp. Paperback.

320.   *Anne no yume no ie.* Tr. Hanako Muraoka. Tokyo: Shincho Sha, 1958. 358 pp. Paperback.

321.   *Anne no yume no ie.* Tr. Sakiko Nakamura. Tokyo: Kadokawa Shoten, *1962. 298 pp. Paperback.

322.   *Anne no yume no ie.* Tr. Hanako Muraoka. Tokyo: Kōdan Sha, *1965. 279 pp. Illustrated with one colour plate, many drawings, photo of LMM, map of P.E.I. Reprinted 1966, 1971, 1973.

323.   *Anne no yume no ie.* Tr. Hanako Muraoka. Tokyo: Mikasa Shobo, 1966. 213 pp. Illustrated with one colour plate, one photo of P.E.I. Reprinted *1969.

324.   *Anne no yume no ie.* Tr. Hanako Muraoka. Tokyo: Kaisei Sha, 1967. 282 pp. Illustrated with one colour plate, many drawings. Reprinted *1971.

325.   *Anne no yume no ie.* Tr. Hanako Muraoka. Tokyo: Poplar Sha, *1967. 274 pp. Illustrated with one colour plate, many drawings, several photos of P.E.I.

Korean:

326.   *Aeneui Ggumeui Jib.* Tr. Ji-Shik Shin. Seoul: Changjosa, 1964.

327.   *Aen.* Tr. Yeong-Hi Seo. Seoul: Pyeonghwa, 1972.

328.   *Aeneui Ggumeui Jib.* Anne Story series, vol. 6. Tr. Ji-Shik Shin. Seoul: Changjosa, *1985. 256 pp. Paperback. Illustrated with black line drawings.

Norwegian:

329.   *Annes drømmehjem.* Tr. Aagot Holst. Kristiania: H. Aschehoug, 1922. 202 pp.

330.   *Annes drømmehjem.* Tr. Jo Tenfjord. Oslo: Aschehoug, 1957. 176 pp. Reprinted 1974.

Polish:

331.   *Wymarzony dom Ani.* Tr. Stefan Fedyński. Warsaw: Wydawnictwo Arcydzieł Literatur Obcych, 1931. 329 pp.

332.   *Wymarzony dom Ani.* Tr. Stefan Fedyński. Warsaw: Nasza Księgarnia, 1959. 279 pp. Illus. Bogdan Zieleniec.

333.   *Ania na uniwersytecie; Wymarzony dom Ani.* Tr. Janina Zawisza-Krasucka and Stefan Fedyński. Warsaw: Nasza Księgarnia, *1968. 504 pp. Illus. Bogdan Zieleniec. Translation of *Anne of the Island* and *Anne's House of Dreams.* Reprinted 1971, 1974.

334.   *Wymarzony dom Ani.* Tr. Stefan Fedyński. Warsaw: Nasza Księgarnia, *1977. 333 pp. Illus. Bogdan Zieleniec. Reprinted *1982. ISBN 8310081022.

Swedish:

335.   *Drömslottet.* Tr. Karin Lidforss Jensen. Lund: Gleerup, 1920. 286 pp. Reprinted 1942, 1946, 1950, 1955, *1957, *1964, *1972. Reprinted, Lund: Liber Läromedel, 1978. 286 pp. ISBN 914004565X.

RAINBOW VALLEY

First edition. New York: Stokes, 1919.

Editions in English

Australia:

336.   *Rainbow Valley.* Platypus series. Sydney: Cornstalk Publishing Co., 1925. Reprinted 1929. 315 pp. Colour frontispiece.

337.   -----. Sydney: Angus and Robertson, 1947. vi, 312 pp. Reprinted 1955.

338.   -----. [New ed.] Sydney: Angus and Robertson, 1975. vi, 312 pp. ISBN 0207131732. Reprinted *1979.

Canada:

339.   *Rainbow Valley.* Toronto: McClelland and Stewart, *1919. viii, 341 pp. With frontispiece and cover in colour by M.L. Kirk. A copy of the first edition, inscribed by LMM, was examined at Park Corner, P.E.I. This edition is identical to the original Stokes edition, except that the publisher's imprint has been changed to McClelland and Stewart. It bears the Stokes copyright, and was printed in the U.S. Reprinted *1922, *1923 (on the 1923 edition, and all subsequent editions published by McClelland and Stewart, the copyright reads McClelland and Stewart).

340.   -----. Cavendish ed. Toronto: McClelland and Stewart, *[1940s?].
        viii, 341 pp.

341.   -----. Canadian Favourites series. Toronto: McClelland and Stew-
        art, *1973. x, 341 pp. Paperback. ISBN 0771063857.

Great Britain:

342.   *Rainbow Valley.* London: Constable, 1920. viii, 341 pp. Reprinted
        1922. This is probably identical to the original Stokes edition,
        except for a change in the publisher's imprint.

343.   -----. London: Harrap, 1926. viii, 341 pp. Reprinted 1927, 1929,
        1931, 1934, 1935, 1936, 1937, 1940, 1941, 1953, 1956, 1962.

344.   -----. New ed. London: Harrap, *1975. 341 pp. ISBN 245527982.
        Reprinted 1976, 1979.

United States:

345.   *Rainbow Valley.* New York: Stokes, *1919. viii, 341 pp. With
        frontispiece and cover in colour by M.L. Kirk. Personal copy of
        LMM, signed, examined at Guelph.

346.   -----. New York: A.L. Burt, *1919. viii, 341 pp. Reprinted 1922.
        This is identical to the original Stokes edition, except for a change
        in the publisher's imprint.

347.   -----. New York: Grosset and Dunlap, 1938. viii, 341 pp.

Translations

Dutch:

348.   *Het regenboogdal.* Tr. Betsy de Vries. Haarlem: Tjeenk Willink,
        *1921. 326 pp. Personal copy of LMM, signed, examined at
        Guelph.

Finnish:

349.   *Sateenkaarinotko.* Tr. Alli Wiherheimo. Porvoo: Werner Söder-
        ström, 1925. 318 pp. Reprinted, Porvoo and Helsinki: Werner
        Söderström, 1951, 1953, 1959.

350.   *Sateenkaarinotko.* Tr. Alli Wiherheimo. Porvoo and Helsinki: Wer-
        ner Söderström, *1964. 232 pp. Reprinted 1972.

Japanese:

351. *Niji no tani no Anne.* Tr. Hanako Muraoka. Tokyo: Shincho Sha, 1958. 180 pp.

352. *Niji no tani no Anne.* Tr. Hanako Muraoka. Tokyo: Shincho Sha, 1959. 204 pp. Paperback.

353. *Niji no tani no Anne.* Tr. Hanako Muraoka. Tokyo: Kōdan Sha, *1966. 262 pp. Illustrated with one colour plate, several drawings. Reprinted 1971, 1973.

354. *Niji no tani no Anne.* Tr. Hanako Muraoka. Tokyo: Mikasa Shobo, 1966. 202 pp. Illustrated with one colour plate and one photo of P.E.I. Reprinted *1969.

355. *Niji no tani no Anne.* Tr. Hanako Muraoka. Tokyo: Poplar Sha, 1967. 289 pp. Illustrated.

Korean:

356. *Mujigaegoljjageui Aen.* Tr. Ji-Shik Shin. Seoul: Changjosa, 1964.

357. *Mujigaegoljjageui Aen.* Anne Story series, vol. 8. Tr. Ji-Shik Shin. Seoul: Changjosa, *1985. 256 pp. Paperback. Illustrated with black line drawings.

Norwegian:

358. *Regnbuedalen.* Tr. Aagot Holst. Kristiania: H. Aschehoug, *1922. 202 pp. Paperback. Personal copy of LMM, signed, examined at Guelph.

359. *Anne og Regnbuedalen.* Tr. Jo Tenfjord. Oslo: Aschehoug, 1958. 160 pp. Reprinted 1974.

Polish:

360. *Dolina Tęczy.* Tr. Janina Zawisza-Krasucka. Warsaw: Wydawnicto Arcydziel Literatur Obcych, 1932. 285 pp.

361. *Dolina Tęczy.* Tr. Janina Zawisza-Krasucka. Warsaw: Nasza Księgarnia, *1959. 244 pp. Illus. Bogdan Zieleniec.

362. *Dolina Tęczy; Rilla ze Złotego Brzegu.* Tr. Janina Zawisza-Krasucka. Warsaw: Nasza Księgarnia, *1970. 475 pp. Illus. Bogdan Zieleniec. Translation of both *Rainbow Valley* and *Rilla of Ingleside.* Reprinted 1972, 1974.

363.   *Dolina Tęczy.* Tr. Janina Zawisza-Krasucka. Warsaw: Nasza Księgarnia, 1977. 288 pp. Illus. Bogdan Zieleniec.

Swedish:

364.   *Regnbågens dal.* Tr. Karin Lidforss Jensen. Lund: Gleerup, 1927.
314 pp. Reprinted 1931, 1943, 1948, 1951, 1953, 1956.

365.   *Regnbågens dal.* Tr. Karin Lidforss Jensen. Lund: Gleerup, 1963.
276 pp. Reset from previous edition. Reprinted *1967, and Lund:
Liber Läromedel, 1978 (ISBN 9140300161).

FURTHER CHRONICLES OF AVONLEA

First edition. Boston: Page, 1920.

Editions in English

Australia:

366.   *Further Chronicles of Avonlea.* Sydney: Angus and Robertson,
1953. xiii, 231 pp. Illustrated.

367.   -----. Sydney: Angus and Robertson, 1972.   220 pp.   ISBN
0207128669. Reprinted 1973, 1976, 1980.

Canada:

368.   *Further Chronicles of Avonlea.* Toronto: Doran, 1920. xi, 301 pp.
Illustrated, with frontispiece. This was probably identical to the
original Page edition, except for a change in the publisher's
imprint.

369.   -----. Toronto: Ryerson, *1953. vi, 301 pp. Reprinted *1956,
*1968, *1972.

Great Britain:

370.   *Further Chronicles of Avonlea.* London: Harrap, 1925. 254 pp.
Reprinted 1926.

371.   -----. Rev. ed. London: Harrap, *1954. vi, 220 pp. Revised and
reset from previous edition. Reprinted 1957, 1962, 1963, 1971,
*1975 (ISBN 245508066).

United States:

372.   *Further Chronicles of Avonlea.* Boston: Page, *1920. xi, 301 pp.
       Illus. John Goss. Introduction by Nathan Haskell Dole. Presenta-
       tion copy, with note in LMM's hand, dated 1928, examined at
       Guelph. Reprinted *1953.

373.   -----. Thrushwood Books. New York: Grosset and Dunlap, *1953.
       xi, 301 pp. Introduction by Nathan Haskell Dole.

374.   -----. An Anne of Green Gables Book. New York: Grosset and
       Dunlap, *1970. xi, 301 pp.

Translations

Japanese:

375.   *Anne o meguru hitobito.* Tr. Hanako Muraoka. Tokyo: Mikasa Sho-
       bo, 1958. 221 pp. Paperback.

376.   *Anne o meguru hitobito.* Tr. Hanako Muraoka. Tokyo: Shincho Sha,
       *1959. 304 pp.

377.   *Anne o meguru hitobito.* Tr. Hanako Muraoka. Tokyo: Kōdan Sha,
       *1966. 294 pp. Illustrated with one colour plate, many drawings.
       Reprinted 1973.

Korean:

378.   *Aengwa Maeulsaramdeul.* Tr. Ji-Shik Shin. Seoul: Changjosa, 1964.

379.   *Aengwa Maeulsaramdeul.* Anne Story series, vol. 9. Tr. Ji-Shik
       Shin. Seoul: Changjosa, *1985. 256 pp. Paperback. Illustrated
       with black line drawings.

Spanish:

380.   *Nuevas Crónicas de Avonlea.* Robin Hood series. Tr. J.J. Llobet.
       Buenos Aires: Acme, 1955. 270 pp. Illustrated.

RILLA OF INGLESIDE

First edition. Toronto: McClelland and Stewart, 1920.

Editions in English

Australia:

381.   *Rilla of Ingleside*. Sydney: Cornstalk Publishing Co., 1928. vi, 366 pp.

382.   -----. Sydney: Angus and Robertson, 1934. vi, 366 pp. Reprinted 1937, 1938, 1939.

383.   -----. Sydney: Angus and Robertson, 1973. vi, 303 pp. ISBN 0207126585. Reprinted 1974, *1977, 1980.

Canada:

384.   *Rilla of Ingleside*. Toronto: McClelland and Stewart, *1920. v, 370 pp. Reprinted *1922.

385.   -----. Toronto: McClelland and Stewart, *1921. vi, 370 pp. With cover and frontispiece in colour by M.L. Kirk.

386.   -----. Cavendish ed. Toronto: McClelland and Stewart, *1947. viii, 285 pp.

387.   -----. Canadian Favourites series. Toronto: McClelland and Stewart, *1973. x, 285 pp. Paperback. ISBN 0771064063.

Great Britain:

388.   *Rilla of Ingleside*. London: Hodder and Stoughton, 1921. 318 pp. Reprinted 1922, 1924.

389.   -----. London: Harrap, 1928. 318 pp. Reprinted 1930, 1933, 1936, 1938, 1940, 1941, 1953, 1954, 1958.

390.   -----. New ed. London: Harrap, *1975. 318 pp. ISBN 0245527990. Reprinted 1976, 1979.

United States:

391.   *Rilla of Ingleside*. New York: Stokes, *1921. v, 370 pp. With frontispiece and cover in colour by M.L. Kirk. This is identical to the McClelland and Stewart 1921 edition, except for the changes in publisher's imprint and copyright. Personal copy of LMM, signed, examined at Guelph. Reprinted 1921 (twice), 1922, 1923 (twice).

392.   -----. New York: A.L. Burt, *1921. v, 370 pp. With frontispiece
        and cover in colour by M.L. Kirk. Reprinted 1923. Published by
        arrangement with Stokes, in an identical edition, except for the
        publisher's imprint.

393.   -----. New York: Grosset and Dunlap, 1938. 370 pp.

Translations

Dutch:

394.   *Rilla van Ingleside.* Tr. Ida Haakman. Haarlem: Tjeenk Willink,
        *1922. 414 pp. Personal copy of LMM, signed, examined at
        Guelph.

Finnish:

395.   *Kotikunnaan Rilla.* Abridged ed. Tr. Kerttu Piskonen. Porvoo and
        Helsinki: Werner Söderström, 1962. 244 pp. Reprinted *1963,
        1970, 1978 (ISBN 951004380X), 1982.

Japanese:

396.   *Anne no musume Rilla.* Tr. Hanako Muraoka. Tokyo: Shincho Sha,
        1959. 430 pp. Paperback.

397.   *Anne no musume Rilla.* Tr. Hanako Muraoka. Tokyo: Kōdan Sha,
        *1966. 334 pp. Illustrated with one colour plate, several drawings,
        photos of LMM and translator. Reprinted 1973, 1974.

398.   *Anne no musume Rilla.* Tr. Hanako Muraoka. Tokyo: Mikasa Sho-
        bo, 1966. 272 pp. Illustrated with one colour plate, one photo of
        P.E.I. Reprinted *1969.

399.   *Anne no musume Rilla.* Tr. Hanako Muraoka. Tokyo: Poplar Sha,
        1967. 286 pp. Illustrated.

Korean:

400.   *Aeneui ddal Rilla.* Tr. Ji-Shik Shin. Seoul: Changjosa, 1964.

401.   *Aeneui ddal Rilla.* Anne Story series, vol. 10. Tr. Ji-Shik Shin.
        Seoul: Changjosa, *1985. 256 pp. Paperback. Illustrated with
        black line drawings.

Norwegian:

402.   *Anne og Marilla.* Abridged ed. Tr. Jo Tenfjord. Oslo: Aschehoug,
        *1959. 128 pp. Reprinted 1972.

Polish:

403. *Rilla ze Złotego Brzegu.* Tr. Janina Zawisza-Krasucka. Warsaw: Nakł. Księgarnia Kozłowskiego, 1933. 334 pp.

404. *Dolina Tęczy; Rilla ze Złotego Brzegu.* Tr. Janina Zawisza-Krasucka. Warsaw: Nasza Księgarnia, *1970. 475 pp. Illustrated. Translation of both *Rainbow Valley* and *Rilla of Ingleside.* Reprinted 1972, 1974.

405. *Rilla ze Złotego Brzegu.* Tr. Janina Zawsiza-Krasucka. Warsaw: Nasza Księgarnia, 1977. 327 pp. Illus. Bogdan Zieleniec. Reprinted 1983.

Swedish:

406. *Lilla Marilla.* Tr. A.G. son Söllberg. Lund: Gleerup, 1928. 348 pp.

407. *Lilla Marilla.* Tr. A.G. son Söllberg. Lund: Gleerup, 1942. 299 pp.

408. *Lilla Marilla.* Tr. A.G. son Söllberg. Lund: Gleerup, 1947. 271 pp. Reprinted 1952, 1956, *1961, 1970, 1974 (ISBN 9140022129).

409. *Lilla Marilla.* Tr. A.G. son Söllberg. Lund: Liber Läromedel, 1978. 271 pp. ISBN 9140045668.

EMILY OF NEW MOON

First edition. Toronto and New York: McClelland and Stewart, and Stokes, 1923.

Editions in English

Australia:

410. *Emily of New Moon.* Platypus series. Sydney: Cornstalk Publishing Co., 1925. 363 pp. Coloured frontispiece.

411. -----. Sydney: Angus and Robertson, 1948. ix, 304 pp.

412. -----. Sydney: Angus and Robertson, 1951. 279 pp.

413. -----. Sydney: Angus and Robertson, 1973. 304 pp. Reprinted 1981, 1982.

Canada:

414.   *Emily of New Moon.* Toronto: McClelland and Stewart, *1923. viii, 351 pp. With frontispiece and cover in colour by M.L. Kirk.

415.   -----. Toronto: McClelland and Stewart, *1925. viii, 351 pp. Not illustrated.

416.   -----. Cavendish ed. Toronto: McClelland and Stewart, *[1940s?]. viii, 351 pp.

417.   -----. Canadian Favourites series. Toronto: McClelland and Stewart, *1973. 351 pp. Paperback. ISBN 0771062389.

418.   -----. Toronto: Seal Books, McClelland and Stewart-Bantam, *1983. 339 pp. Paperback. ISBN 0770417984. Frequently reprinted with new ISBN but no change in date; current (1985) ISBN 0770017981.

Great Britain:

419.   *Emily of New Moon.* London: Hodder and Stoughton, *1923. viii, 299 pp. Personal copy of LMM, signed, examined at Guelph. This is a leather-bound presentation copy, with letter to LMM from Sir Ernest Hodder-Williams pasted inside. Bound by Sancorski and Sutcliffe, London. Reprinted 1924, 1925.

420.   -----. London: Harrap, 1928. xii, 299 pp. Reprinted 1930, 1933, 1937, 1939, 1941.

421.   -----. London: Harrap, *1977. xii, 299 pp. ISBN 0245531793. With foreword by Lady Mary Wilson, including the text of a letter written to her by LMM.

422.   -----. Large print ed. Leicester: Ulverscroft, *1980. 594 pp. ISBN 0708904017. With foreword by Lady Mary Wilson, as in Harrap 1977 edition.

United States:

423.   *Emily of New Moon.* New York: Stokes, *1923. viii, 351 pp. With frontispiece and cover in colour by M.L. Kirk. This is identical to the original McClelland and Stewart edition except for the change in the publisher's imprint. Personal copy of LMM, signed, examined at Guelph.

424.   -----. New York: A.L. Burt, 1925.

425.   -----. New York: Grosset and Dunlap, 1938. 351 pp.

Translations

Dutch:

426. *Emily van de nieuwe maan.* Tr. A.E. [Betsy] de Vries. Haarlem: Tjeenk Willink, *1924. 430 pp. Personal copy of LMM, signed, examined at Guelph.

Finnish:

427. *Pieni runotyttö.* Tr. I.K. Inha. Porvoo: Werner Söderström, 1928.

428. *Pieni runotyttö.* Tr. I.K. Inha. Porvoo and Helsinki: Werner Söderström, 1948. 450 pp. Reprinted 1955.

429. *Pieni runotyttö.* Rev. ed. Tr. I.K. Inha. Porvoo and Helsinki: Werner Söderström, 1961. 310 pp. Reprinted *1965, 1971, 1979 (ISBN 9510043818).

French:

430. *Emilie de la nouvelle lune.* Tr. Paule Daveluy. Montreal: Pierre Tisseyre, 1983. 318 pp. Cover illustration by Charles N. Vinh. Paperback.

Japanese:

431. *Kaze no Naka no Emily.* Tr. Hanako Muraoka. Tokyo: Akimoto Shobo, 1959. 179 pp. (May be part one of a two-volume set.)

432. *Ame no Utau Emily.* Tr. Hanako Muraoka. Tokyo: Akimoto Shobo, 1959. 179 pp. (May be part two of a two-volume set.)

433. *Kawaii Emily.* Tr. Hanako Muraoka. Tokyo: Shincho Sha, 1964. 500 pp. Paperback.

434. *Kawaii Emily.* Tr. Hanako Muraoka. Tokyo: Kōdan Sha, 1967. 324 pp.

Korean:

435. *"Emily" Yahng* (Phonetic transcription in Korean). Tr. Ji-Shik Shin. Seoul: Changjosa, 1967. 322 pp.

Norwegian:

436. *Emily på Manegarden.* Abridged ed. Tr. Jo Tenfjord. Oslo: Aschehoug, 1960. 153 pp. Part One of *Emily of New Moon.*

437. *Emily Reiser Bust.* Abridged ed. Tr. Jo Tenfjord. Oslo: Asche-
      houg, 1961. 134 pp. Part Two of *Emily of New Moon* and Part One
      of *Emily Climbs.*

Polish:

438. *Emilka ze Srebrnego Nowiu.* Tr. Maria Rafałowicz-Radwanowa.
      Warsaw: Księgarnia Popularna, *1936. 406 pp. Personal copy of
      LMM, signed, examined at Guelph.

Swedish:

439. *Emily.* Tr. Stina Hergin. Lund: Gleerup, 1955. 218 pp. Transla-
      tion of Part One of *Emily of New Moon.* Reprinted 1956.

440. *Emily och hennes vånner.* Tr. Stina Hergin. Lund: Gleerup, *1956.
      200 pp. Contains Part Two of *Emily of New Moon,* and Part One of
      Emily Climbs.

EMILY CLIMBS

First edition. Toronto and New York: McClelland and Stewart, and Stokes,
1925.

Editions in English

Australia:

441. *Emily Climbs.* Bellbird series. Sydney: Cornstalk Publishing Co.,
      1925.

442. -----. 6th ed. Platypus series. Sydney: Angus and Robertson,
      1930. 339 pp. Reprinted 1948.

443. -----. [New ed.] Sydney: Angus and Robertson, 1981. 339 pp.

Canada:

444. *Emily Climbs.* Toronto: McClelland and Stewart, *1925. vii, 312
      pp. With frontispiece and cover in colour by M.L. Kirk. Reprinted
      1925, *1925 (without frontispiece).

445. -----. Cavendish ed. Toronto: McClelland and Stewart, *[between
      1935 and 1942?]. vii, 312 pp.

446. -----. Canadian Favourites series. Toronto: McClelland and Stew-
      art, *1974. 312 pp. Paperback. ISBN 0771062991.

447.   -----. Toronto: Seal Books, McClelland and Stewart-Bantam,
        *1983. 325 pp. Paperback. Reprinted *1984. ISBN 077042032X.
        Frequently reprinted with new ISBN, no dates available.

Great Britain:

448.   *Emily Climbs.* London: Hodder and Stoughton, *1925. 317 pp.
        Personal copy of LMM, signed, examined at Guelph. This is a pres-
        entation copy, leather-bound by Sancorski and Sutcliffe, London.
        Reprinted 1929.

449.   -----. London: Harrap, 1928. 317 pp. Reprinted 1930, 1934, 1937,
        1941, 1942.

450.   -----. London: Harrap, *1979. 289 pp. ISBN 0245534113.

United States:

451.   *Emily Climbs.* New York: A.L. Burt, 1925. 312 pp. With frontis-
        piece in colour. This is probably identical to the original McClel-
        land and Stewart edition, except for a change in publisher's
        imprint. Reprinted 1927.

452.   -----. New York: Stokes, *1925. 312 pp. With frontispiece and
        cover in colour by M.L. Kirk. Personal copy of LMM, signed,
        examined at Guelph. This is identical to the McClelland and Stew-
        art edition except for the publisher's imprint. Copyright is Stokes.

453.   -----. New York: Grosset and Dunlap, 1939. 312 pp.

454.   -----. New York: Bantam, 1983. 325 pp. Paperback. Published in
        Canada as a Seal Book.

Translations

Dutch:

455.   *Emily bergopwaarts.* Tr. A.E. [Betsy] de Vries. Haarlem: Tjeenk
        Willink, 1926. 432 pp.

Finnish:

456.   *Runotyttö maineen polulla.* Tr. I.K. Inha. Helsinki: Werner Söder-
        ström, 1948. 415 pp. Reprinted, Porvoo and Helsinki: Werner
        Söderström, 1955.

457.   *Runotyttö maineen polulla.* Tr. I.K. Inha. Porvoo and Helsinki:
        Werner Söderström, *1964. 308 pp. Reprinted 1970, 1978 (ISBN
        9510043834), 1982.

Japanese:

458.   *Emily wa noboru.* Tr. Hanako Muraoka. Tokyo: Kōdan Sha, 1967.
       342 pp. Illustrated.

459.   *Emily wa noboru.* Tr. Hanako Muraoka. Tokyo: Shincho Sha,
       *1967. 476 pp. Paperback.

Norwegian:

460.   *Emily på egne veier.* Abridged ed. Tr. Jo Tenfjord. Oslo: Asche-
       houg, *1962. 147 pp. Part Two of *Emily Climbs.* (Part One of
       Emily Climbs appears as the last part of *Emily reiser bust.)*

Polish:

461.   *Emilka dojrzewa.* Tr. Maria Rafałowicz-Radwanowa. Warsaw:
       Księgarnia Popularna, *1936. 359 pp. Personal copy of LMM,
       signed, examined at Guelph.

Swedish:

462.   *Emily och hennes vänner.* Abridged ed. Tr. Stina Hergin. Lund:
       Gleerup, *1956. 200 pp. Abridged version of *Emily of New Moon*
       and *Emily Climbs.*

463.   *Emily på egna vagar.* Abridged ed. Tr. Stina Hergin. Lund: Gleer-
       up, *1957. vi, 215 pp.

THE BLUE CASTLE

First edition. Toronto and New York: McClelland and Stewart, and Stokes,
1926.

Editions in English

Australia:

464.   *The Blue Castle.* Sydney: Cornstalk Publishing Co., 1929. 321 pp.

465.   -----. 5th ed. Sydney: Angus and Robertson, 1932. 321 pp.

466.   -----. [New ed.] Sydney: Angus and Robertson, 1972. 321 pp.
       Reprinted *1980. ISBN 207143404.

Canada:

467.   *The Blue Castle*. Toronto: McClelland and Stewart, *1926. viii, 310 pp. Reprinted *1926 (different printer).

468.   -----. Cavendish ed. Toronto: McClelland and Stewart, *1947. iv, 265 pp.

469.   -----. Canadian Children's Favourites series. Toronto: McClelland and Stewart, *1972. iv, 265 pp. Paperback. ISBN 0771062176.

Great Britain:

470.   *The Blue Castle*. London: Hodder and Stoughton, 1926. 318 pp. Reprinted 1932.

471.   -----. London: Harrap, 1935. 318 pp. Reprinted 1936, 1941.

United States:

472.   *The Blue Castle*. New York: Grosset and Dunlap, *1926. 310 pp. Reprinted 1938.

473.   -----. New York: Stokes, *1926. 310 pp. Personal copy of LMM, signed, examined at Guelph. This is identical to the McClelland and Stewart edition, except that the publisher's imprint and the copyright read Stokes instead of McClelland and Stewart.

474.   -----. New York: A.L. Burt, 1928.

Translations

Dutch:

475.   *Valencia's droomslot*. Tr. A.E. [Betsy] de Vries. Haarlem: Tjeenk Willink, *1927. 312 pp. Personal copy of LMM, signed, examined at Guelph.

Finnish:

476.   *Sininen linna*. Tr. A.J. Salonen. Hämeenlinna: Karisto, 1930. 280 pp. Reprinted *1969 (three times), 1973, *1977 (ISBN 9512310651), 1978.

Japanese:

477.   *Aoi Shiro*. Tr. Yumiko Taniguchi. Tokyo: Shinozaki Shorin, *1980. 306 pp. Illustrated.

478.   *Aoi Shiro.* Tr. Yumiko Taniguchi. Tokyo: Shinozaki Shorin, *[1982]. 305 pp. Illustrated with 1 colour plate, and several line drawings.

Polish:

479.   *Błękitny zamek.* Warsaw: J. Kubicki, 1926. 229 pp.

480.   *Błękitny zamek.* Tr. Karol Borawski. Warsaw: Księgarnia Literacka, 1939. 271 pp.

EMILY'S QUEST

First edition. Toronto and New York: McClelland and Stewart, and Stokes, 1927.

Editions in English

Australia:

481.   *Emily's Quest.* Sydney: Cornstalk Publishing Co., 1927. 285 pp.

482.   -----. Sydney: Angus and Robertson, 1934. iv, 284 pp. Reprinted 1948.

483.   -----. [New ed.] Sydney: Angus and Robertson, 1972. 284 pp. Reprinted 1981.

Canada:

484.   *Emily's Quest.* Toronto: McClelland and Stewart, *1927. viii, 310 pp. Cover and frontispiece in colour by M.L. Kirk. Reprinted *1927 (no frontispiece).

485.   -----. Toronto: McClelland and Stewart, *[1940s?]. viii, 310 pp. (No illustrations.)

486.   -----. Cavendish ed. Toronto: McClelland and Stewart, *1947. vi, 262 pp.

487.   -----. Canadian Children's Favourites series. Toronto: McClelland and Stewart, *1972. vi, 262 pp. Paperback. ISBN 077106280X. Reprinted, Canadian Favourites series, 1974.

488.   -----. Toronto: Seal Books, McClelland and Stewart-Bantam, *1983. 228 pp. Paperback. ISBN 0770417973. Frequently reprinted with new ISBN, no dates available.

Great Britain:

489.   *Emily's Quest*. London: Hodder and Stoughton, 1927. 312 pp.
        Reprinted 1930.

490.   -----. London: Harrap, 1935. 312 pp. Reprinted 1936, 1940.

491.   -----. London: Harrap, *1979. 204 pp. ISBN 0245534121.

United States:

492.   *Emily's Quest*. New York: Stokes, *1927. 310 pp. Cover and fron-
        tispiece in colour by M.L. Kirk. Pers(al copy of LMM, signed,
        examined at Guelph. This is identical to the McClelland and Stew-
        art edition, except that the publisher's imprint and copyright read
        Stokes instead of McClelland and Stewart.

493.   -----. New York: A.L. Burt, 1929. 310 pp.

494.   -----. New York: Grosset and Dunlap, 1940. 310 pp.

495.   -----. New York: Bantam, 1983. 228 pp. Paperback. Published in
        Canada as a Bantam-Seal book.

Translations

Dutch:

496.   *Emily's eerzucht*. Tr. A.E. [Betsy] de Vries. Haarlem: Tjeenk Wil-
        link, *1928. 312 pp. Personal copy of LMM, signed, examined at
        Guelph.

Finnish:

497.   *Runotyttö etsii tähteäänn*. Tr. Laine Järventaus-Aav. Porvoo:
        Werner Söderström, 1949. 306 pp. Reprinted, Porvoo and Helsinki:
        Werner Söderström, 1954.

498.   *Runotyttö etsii tähteäänn*. New ed. Tr. Laine Järventaus-Aav.
        Porvoo and Helsinki: Werner Söderström, *1965. 215 pp. Reset
        from previous edition; reprinted 1970, *1982 (ISBN 9510043826).

Japanese:

499.   *Emily no motomeru mono*. Tr. Hanako Muraoka. Tokyo: Shincho
        Sha, 1969. 323 pp. Paperback.

Polish:

500. *Emilka na falach życia.* Tr. Maria Rafałowicz-Radwanowa. Warsaw: Księgarnia Popularna, *1936. 319 pp. Personal copy of LMM,
signed, examined at Guelph.

MAGIC FOR MARIGOLD

First edition. Toronto and New York: McClelland and Stewart, and Stokes,
1929.

Editions in English

Australia:

501. *Magic for Marigold.* Sydney: Cornstalk Publishing Co., 1929. vi,
308 pp.

502. -----. [New ed.] Sydney: Angus and Robertson, 1977. 308 pp.
Reprinted 1981. ISBN 0207143099.

Canada:

503. *Magic for Marigold.* Toronto: McClelland and Stewart, *1929. viii,
328 pp. With cover and frontispiece in colour by Edna Cooke Shoemaker.

504. -----. Toronto: McClelland and Stewart, *1929. viii, 328 pp.
Reprinted 1930, *[1940s?].

505. -----. Cavendish ed. Toronto: McClelland and Stewart, *[1940s?].
viii, 328 pp. In front matter are two erroneous statements:
"copyright 1927," and statement that edition has frontispiece and
cover by Edna Cooke Shoemaker (there is no frontispiece and cover
is standard Cavendish cover with small logo).

506. -----. Canadian Favourites series. Toronto: McClelland and Stewart, *1977. viii, 328 pp. Paperback.

Great Britain:

507. *Magic for Marigold.* London: Hodder and Stoughton, *1929. 346
pp. Personal copy of LMM, signed, examined at Guelph. This is a
presentation copy, leather-bound by Sancorski and Sutcliffe, London.

508. -----. London: Hodder and Stoughton, 1935. 318 pp.

509.   -----. London: Harrap, 1935. 325 pp. Reprinted 1937, 1941.

United States:

510.   *Magic for Marigold*. New York: A.L. Burt, 1929. 328 pp. Reprint-
          ed 1931.

511.   -----. New York: Stokes, *1929. vii, 328 pp. With cover and fron-
          tispiece in colour by Edna Cooke Shoemaker. Personal copy of
          LMM, signed, examined at Guelph. This is identical to the McClel-
          land and Stewart edition, except that the copyright reads L.M.
          Montgomery, and the publisher's imprint reads Stokes rather than
          McClelland and Stewart. Reprinted 1939.

512.   -----. New York: Grosset and Dunlap, 1941. vii, 328 pp.

Translations

Dutch:

513.   *Marigold's tooverland*. Tr. A.E. [Betsy] de Vries. Haarlem: Tjeenk
          Willink, *1929. 320 pp. Personal copy of LMM, signed, examined
          at Guelph.

Italian:

514.   *Marigold, la bimba dal cuore esultante*. Tr. Elisa Ferrero. Milan:
          Antonio Vallardi, *1939. 468 pp. Illus. Edvig Collin. Reprinted
          1941, 1948, 1951, 1953. Personal copy of LMM, signed, examined
          at Guelph.

515.   *Marigold, la bimba dal cuore esultante*. Tr. Elisa Ferrero. Milan:
          Vallardi, 1973. 425 pp. Illustrated.

Japanese:

516.   *Marigold no Maho*. Vol. 1. Tr. Tokiko Tanaka. Tokyo: Shinozaki
          Shorin, *1982. 204 pp. Illustrated.

517.   *Marigold no Maho*. Vol. 2. Tr. Tokiko Tanaka. Tokyo: Shinozaki
          Shorin, 1983. 224 pp. Illustrated.

A TANGLED WEB

First edition. Toronto and New York: McClelland and Stewart, and Stokes, 1931. In Great Britain, this book has been published as *Aunt Becky Began It*.

Editions in English

Australia:

518.   *A Tangled Web*. Sydney: Angus and Robertson, 1931. viii, 311 pp. Reprinted *1935, 1949.

519.   -----. [New ed.] Sydney: Angus and Robertson, 1982. 311 pp.

Canada:

520.   *A Tangled Web*. Toronto: McClelland and Stewart, *1931. ix, 324 pp. Reprinted *[1940s?].

521.   -----. Cavendish ed. Toronto: McClelland and Stewart, *[1940s?]. ix, 324 pp.

522.   -----. Canadian Children's Favourites series. Toronto: McClelland and Stewart, *1972. viii, 324 pp. Paperback. ISBN 0771064276.

Great Britain:

523.   *Aunt Becky Began It*. London: Hodder and Stoughton, *1931. 317 pp. Reprinted 1932, 1934.

United States:

524.   *A Tangled Web*. New York: Stokes, *1931. viii, 324 pp. Personal copy of LMM, signed, examined at Guelph. This edition is identical to the McClelland and Stewart edition, except that the publisher's imprint has been changed to Stokes, and the copyright is L.M. Montgomery.

525.   -----. New York: A.L. Burt, 1933. 324 pp.

526.   -----. New York: Grosset and Dunlap, 1939. 324 pp.

Translations

Italian:

527.   *Matassa ingarbugliata*. Tr. Mara Fabietti. Milan: Vallardi, 1953. 301 pp.

Japanese:

528.   *Motsureta Kumo-no-Su*. Vol. 1. Tr. Yumiko Taniguchi. Tokyo: Shinozaki Shorin, *1981. 204 pp. Illustrated.

529.   *Motsureta Kumo-no-Su*. Vol. 2. Tr. Yumiko Taniguchi. Tokyo: Shinozaki Shorin, *1981. 206 pp. Illustrated.

PAT OF SILVER BUSH

First edition. Toronto and New York: McClelland and Stewart, and Stokes, 1933.

Editions in English

Australia:

530.   *Pat of Silver Bush*. Sydney: Angus and Robertson, 1933. 335 pp.

531.   -----. Sydney: Angus and Robertson, 1949. vi, 281 pp. Illustrated. Reprinted 1956.

532.   -----. [New ed.] Sydney: Angus and Robertson, 1974. Reprinted 1981. ISBN 0207143013.

Canada:

533.   *Pat of Silver Bush*. Toronto: McClelland and Stewart, *1933. viii, 329 pp. With frontispiece in colour by Edna Cooke. Reprinted *[1930s or 1940s?], no frontispiece.

534.   -----. Cavendish ed. Toronto: McClelland and Stewart, *[1940s?]. viii, 329 pp. Personal copy of LMM, signed, examined at Guelph. Reprinted *[1950s?].

535.   -----. Canadian Favourites series. Toronto: McClelland and Stewart, 1974. 329 pp. Paperback. Reprinted 1982. ISBN 0771063644.

Great Britain:

536.   *Pat of Silver Bush.* London: Hodder and Stoughton, 1933. 320 pp. Reprinted 1936.

537.   -----. London: Harrap, 1935. 320 pp. Reprinted 1936, 1940.

United States:

538.   *Pat of Silver Bush.* New York: A.L. Burt, 1933. 329 pp. Reprinted 1936.

539.   -----. New York: Stokes, *1933. 329 pp. With frontispiece in colour by Edna Cooke. This is identical to the 1933 McClelland and Stewart edition, except for a change in the publisher's imprint.

540.   -----. New York: Grosset and Dunlap, 1939. 329 pp.

Translations

Japanese:

541.   *Shirakaba yashiki no shojo.* Tr. Tokiko Tanaka. Tokyo: Iwasaki Shoten, 1974. 243 pp.

542.   *Gin no Mori no Pat.* Vol. 1. Tr. Tokiko Tanaka. Tokyo: Shinozaki Shorin, *1980. 232 pp. Illustrated.

543.   *Gin no Mori no Pat.* Vol. 2. Tr. Tokiko Tanaka. Tokyo: Shinozaki Shorin, *1981. 252 pp. Illustrated.

MISTRESS PAT

First edition. Toronto and New York: McClelland and Stewart, and Stokes, 1935.

Editions in English

Australia:

544.   *Mistress Pat.* Sydney: Angus and Robertson, 1935. viii, 304 pp. Reprinted 1937, 1938.

545.   -----. [New ed.] Sydney: Angus and Robertson, 1982. 304 pp.

Canada:

546. *Mistress Pat*. Toronto: McClelland and Stewart, *1935. xii, 338 pp. With frontispiece in colour by Marie Lawson.

547. -----. Toronto: McClelland and Stewart, *[1935?]. xii, 338 pp. Reprinted *[1939?].

548. -----. Cavendish ed. Toronto: McClelland and Stewart, *[late 1930s or early 1940s; publication date precedes death of LMM in 1942]. xii, 338 pp.

549. -----. Canadian Favourites series. Toronto: McClelland and Stewart, *1977. x, 338 pp.

Great Britain:

550. *Mistress Pat*. London: Harrap, 1935. 348 pp. With frontispiece in colour by Marie Lawson. This is probably identical to the McClelland and Stewart edition, except for a change in publisher's imprint. Reprinted with no frontispiece, 1937, 1940, 1941.

United States:

551. *Mistress Pat*. New York: Stokes, *1935. 338 pp. With frontispiece in colour by Marie Lawson. This is identical to the McClelland and Stewart edition, except for a change in publisher's imprint.

552. -----. New York: A.L. Burt, 1937. 338 pp.

553. -----. New York: Grosset and Dunlap, 1939. 338 pp.

Translations

Japanese:

554. *Zoku Pat ojosan*. Tr. Hanako Muraoka. Tokyo: Hobun-do, 1960. 248 pp.

555. *Patto ojosan*. Tr. Hanako Muraoka. Tokyo: Shincho Sha, *1965. 497 pp. Paperback.

ANNE OF WINDY POPLARS

First edition. Toronto and New York: McClelland and Stewart, and Stokes, 1936. In Australia and Great Britain, this book has been published with the title *Anne of Windy Willows.*

Editions in English

Australia:

556.   *Anne of Windy Willows.* Sydney: Angus and Robertson, 1936. viii, 277 pp. Reprinted 1939, 1947, 1954.

557.   -----. Sydney: Angus and Robertson, 1966. 224 pp.

558.   -----. [New ed.] Sydney: Angus and Robertson, *1972. 224 pp. Reprinted 1974, 1975, 1979, 1980, 1982. ISBN 0207125457.

Canada:

559.   *Anne of Windy Poplars.* Toronto: McClelland and Stewart, *1936. viii, 301 pp.

560.   -----. Cavendish ed. Toronto: McClelland and Stewart, *1939. viii, 301 pp.

561.   -----. Canadian Favourites series. Toronto: McClelland and Stewart, *1973. 301 pp. Paperback. ISBN 0771061757.

562.   -----. Toronto: Seal Books, McClelland and Stewart-Bantam, *1981. viii, 258 pp. Paperback. ISBN 077041673X. Frequently reprinted with new ISBN but no change in date; current (1985) ISBN 077042077X.

Great Britain:

563.   *Anne of Windy Willows.* London: Harrap, *1936. 296 pp. Reprinted 1936, 1938 (twice), 1940, 1941 (twice).

564.   -----. London: Harrap, 1943. 224 pp. Reset from previous edition. Reprinted 1945, 1948, 1949 (twice), 1951, 1954, 1956, 1958, 1960, 1964, 1966, 1968, 1971, 1973, 1974, 1975, *1977 (ISBN 0245551298), 1979, 1981.

United States:

565.   *Anne of Windy Poplars.* New York: Stokes, *1936. viii, 301 pp. This is identical to the McClelland and Stewart edition except that the publisher's imprint has been changed. Personal copy of LMM, signed, examined at Guelph.

566.   -----. New York: Grosset and Dunlap, *1938. 301 pp. Publisher's note explains that this edition is available for sale at a lower price than previous ones because the author has agreed to a reduced royalty.

567.   -----. Madison Square Books. New York: Grosset and Dunlap, 1940. 312 pp.

568.   -----. New York: Pocket Books Inc., 1940. Paperback.

569.   -----. Thrushwood Books. New York: Grosset and Dunlap, 1951. 246 pp. Reprinted 1961.

570.   -----. An Anne of Green Gables Book. New York: Grosset and Dunlap, *1971. 246 pp. Paperback.

571.   -----. New York: Bantam, [1970s?]. 240 pp. Paperback. Published in Canada as a Seal Book.

Translations

Dutch:

572.   *Ank van "De ruischende peppels."* Tr. Ko van de Laan. Laren: n.p., [1938?]. 246 pp.

Japanese:

573.   *Akage no Anne no kohuku.* Tr. Hanako Muraoka. Tokyo: Kōdan Sha, 1956. 302 pp.

574.   *Anne no kohuku.* Tr. Hanako Muraoka. Tokyo: Mikasa Shobo, 1956. 289 pp. Paperback. Reprinted 1957. A cloth-bound version, believed to be of this edition (published by Mikasa Shobo, with 289 pp.) was examined.

575.   *Anne no kohuku.* Tr. Hanako Muraoka. Tokyo: Mikasa Shobo, 1957. 256 pp. Paperback.

576.   *Anne no kohuku.* Tr. Hanako Muraoka. Tokyo: Shincho Sha, *1958. 399 pp. Paperback.

577.   *Anne no kohuku.* Tr. Sakiko Nakamura. Tokyo: Kadokawa Shoten, 1961. 344 pp. Paperback.

578.   *Anne no kohuku.* Tr. Hanako Muraoka. Tokyo: Kōdan Sha, *1964. 318 pp. Illustrated with one colour plate, many drawings. Reprinted 1966, 1971, 1973.

579.   *Anne no kohuku.* Tr. Hanako Muraoka. Tokyo: Mikasa Shobo, 1966.
        258 pp. Illustrated with one colour plate, photo of Green Gables.
        Reprinted *1969.

Korean:

580.   *Aeneui Haengbok.* Tr. Ji-Shik Shin. Seoul: Changjosa, 1964.

581.   *Aeneui Haengbok.* Anne Story series, vol. 5. Tr. Ji-Shik Shin.
        Seoul: Changjosa, *1985. 256 pp. Paperback. Illustrated with
        black line drawings.

Polish:

582.   *Ania z Szumiących Topoli.* Tr. Maria Rafałowicz-Radwanowa.
        Warsaw: Księgarnia Popularna, 1939. 329 pp.

583.   *Ania z Szumiacych Topoli.* Tr. Aleksandra Kowalak-Bojarczuk.
        Warsaw: Nasza Księgarnia, *1977. 295 pp. Illus. Leonia Janecka.
        Reprinted 1981.

Swedish:

584.   *Anne på egen hand.* Tr. Stina Hergin. Lund: Gleerup, 1954. 210
        pp. Reprinted *1966, 1971, 1974 (ISBN 9140300153), and reprinted
        Lund: Liber Läromedel, 1978.

JANE OF LANTERN HILL

First edition. Toronto and New York: McClelland and Stewart, and Stokes,
1937.

Editions in English

Australia:

585.   *Jane of Lantern Hill.* Sydney: Angus and Robertson, 1937. vi, 268
        pp. Reprinted 1950.

586.   -----. [New ed.] Sydney: Angus and Robertson, 1977. 268 pp. ISBN
        020714348X. Reprinted *1980.

Canada:

587.   *Jane of Lantern Hill.* Toronto: McClelland and Stewart, *1937. iv,
        297 pp. With frontispiece in colour, probably by Louise Costello.

588.   -----. Cavendish ed. Toronto: McClelland and Stewart, *[1938?].
         iv, 297 pp.

589.   -----. Toronto: McClelland and Stewart, [no date except copyright
         date]. vi, 297 pp. Not a Cavendish edition; no frontispiece.

590.   -----. Canadian Favourites series. Toronto: McClelland and Stew-
         art, *1977. 297 pp. Paperback. ISBN 0771063016.

Great Britain:

591.   *Jane of Lantern Hill.* London: Harrap, 1937. 271 pp. Reprinted
         1937, 1941, 1954.

United States:

592.   *Jane of Lantern Hill.* New York: Stokes, *1937. iv, 297 pp. With
         frontispiece in colour by Louise Costello. Personal copy of LMM,
         signed, examined at Guelph. This is identical to the McClelland
         and Stewart edition except that the publisher's imprint and copy-
         right have been changed to Stokes.

593.   -----. New York: Grosset and Dunlap, *1937. iv, 297 pp. Reprint-
         ed 1938.

Translations

Dutch:

594.   *Jane van Lantern Hill.* Tr. J.D.A. van Gumster. Laren: A.G.
         Schoonderbeek, 1938. 221 pp.

Japanese:

595.   *Oka no ie no Jane.* Tr. Hanako Muraoka. Tokyo: Mikasa Shobo,
         *1959. 205 pp. Paperback.

596.   *Oka no ie no Jane.* Tr. Hanako Muraoka. Tokyo: Shincho Sha,
         *1960. 340 pp. Paperback.

597.   *Jane no negai.* Tr. Hanako Muraoka. Tokyo: Kōdan Sha, 1966. 314
         pp.

ANNE OF INGLESIDE

First edition. Toronto and New York: McClelland and Stewart, and Stokes, 1939.

Editions in English

Australia:

598.   *Anne of Ingleside.* Sydney: Angus and Robertson, 1939. 312 pp. Reprinted 1947.

599.   -----. Sydney: Angus and Robertson, 1965. 252 pp.

600.   -----. [New ed.] Sydney: Angus and Robertson, 1972. 252 pp. ISBN 0207125465. Reprinted 1974, 1977, 1980, 1982.

Canada:

601.   *Anne of Ingleside.* Toronto: McClelland and Stewart, *1939. iv, 323 pp. With frontispiece in colour by Charles V. John. Copy autographed by LMM, examined at Park Corner (copy makes reference to the frontispiece by John, but does not have one).

602.   -----. Cavendish ed. Toronto: McClelland and Stewart, *[1940s?]. iv, 323 pp.

603.   -----. Canadian Children's Favourites series. Toronto: McClelland and Stewart, *1972. iv, 323 pp. Paperback. ISBN 0771061544. Reprinted 1974, 1975, *1977 (Canadian Favourites).

604.   -----. Toronto: Seal Books, McClelland and Stewart-Bantam, *1981. vi, 277 pp. Paperback. ISBN 0770416713. Frequently reprinted with new ISBN but no change in date; current (1985) ISBN 0770420230.

Great Britain:

605.   *Anne of Ingleside.* London: Harrap, 1939. 323 pp. Reprinted 1940 (twice).

606.   -----. London: Harrap, 1943. iv, 252 pp. Reset from previous edition. Reprinted 1946, 1949 (twice), 1951, 1953, 1954, 1957, 1960, 1962, 1965, 1967, 1971, 1972, 1973, *1975 (ISBN 024555131X), 1977, 1980.

United States:

607.   *Anne of Ingleside.* New York: Stokes, *1939. iv, 323 pp. With frontispiece in colour by Charles V. John. Personal copy of LMM, signed, examined at Guelph. This is identical to the McClelland and Stewart edition, except for a change in publisher's imprint and copyright.

608.   -----. New York: Grosset and Dunlap, 1940. 323 pp.

609.   -----. Thrushwood Books. New York: Grosset and Dunlap, 1951. 247 pp. With frontispiece in colour by Charles V. John. Reprinted 1961.

610.   -----. An Anne of Green Gables Book. New York: Grosset and Dunlap, *1970. viii, 247 pp. Reprinted *1971, *1973 (ISBN 0448025469).

611.   -----. New York: Bantam, *1981. 277 pp. Paperback. ISBN 0553200046. Published in Canada as a Seal Book.

Translations

Japanese:

612.   *Anne no tanoshi katei.* Tr. Hanako Muraoka. Tokyo: Mikasa Shobo, 1958. 252 pp. Paperback.

613.   *Rohen-so no Anne.* Tr. Hanako Muraoka. Tokyo: Shincho Sha, *1958. 439 pp. Paperback.

614.   *Anne no ai no katei.* Tr. Hanako Muraoka. Tokyo: Kōdan Sha, 1965. 278 pp. Reprinted 1971, 1973.

615.   *Rohen-so no Anne.* Tr. Hanako Muraoka. Tokyo: Mikasa Shobo, 1966. 252 pp. Illustrated with one photo of P.E.I. Reprinted *1969.

Korean:

616.   *Eomeoniga Doen Aen.* Tr. Ji-Shik Shin. Seoul: Changjosa, 1964.

617.   *Eomeoniga Doen Aen.* Anne Story series, vol. 7. Tr. Ji-Shik Shin. Seoul: Changjosa, *1985. 256 pp. Paperback. Illustrated with black line drawings.

Part 2

OTHER BOOKS BY LUCY MAUD MONTGOMERY

Items in Part 2 marked with an asterisk have been personally examined.

COLLECTED POEMS

The Watchman, and Other Poems

First edition: Toronto: McClelland, Goodchild and Stewart, 1916.

618.   *The Watchman, and Other Poems.* Toronto: McClelland, Goodchild
       and Stewart, *1916. xii, 159 pp. This book contains poems previ-
       ously published in various Canadian and American periodicals. Per-
       sonal copy of LMM, signed, examined at Guelph.

619.   -----. London: Constable, 1920. xii, 159 pp. This edition is prob-
       ably identical to the McClelland, Goodchild and Stewart edition,
       except for a change in publisher's imprint. It was printed in Toron-
       to.

620.   -----. New York: Stokes, *[1917]. xii, 159 pp. This edition is iden-
       tical to the McClelland, Goodchild and Stewart edition except for a
       change in the publisher's imprint. It was printed in Toronto, and
       bears no date or copyright page.

NON-FICTION

621.   *Courageous Women.* By LMM, Marian Keith, and Mabel Burns
       McKinley. Toronto: McClelland and Stewart, *1934. 203 pp. This
       contains brief biographies of 21 women notable for their achieve-
       ments in many fields; 15 of the women are Canadian.

AUTOBIOGRAPHY

The Alpine Path: the Story of My Career

Editions in English

622.   *The Alpine Path: the Story of My Career.* Toronto: Fitzhenry and
        Whiteside, *1975. 96 pp. ISBN 0889020191. Originally published in
        Everywoman's World, in six installments, June, July, August, Sep-
        tember, October, November 1917.

Translations

Japanese:

623.   *Kewashii michi.* Tr. Masako Yamaguchi. Tokyo: Shinozaki Shorin,
        1979. 154 pp. Paperback. Illustrated with two photos and two
        maps.

LETTERS

The Green Gables Letters: From L. M. Montgomery to Ephraim Weber,
1905–1909

624.   *The Green Gables Letters: From L. M. Montgomery to Ephraim
        Weber, 1905–1909.* Edited and with General Introduction (pp.1-22)
        by Wilfrid Eggleston. Toronto: Ryerson, *1960. ix, 102 pp.

625.   -----. 2nd ed. Ottawa: Borealis Press, *1981. ix, 102 pp. With
        new five-page "Preface to the Second Edition" by Eggleston.

626.   -----. Edited and with General Introduction (pp.1-22) by Wilfrid
        Eggleston. London, England: Bailey Brothers, 1960. This edition is
        probably identical to the Ryerson edition, except for a change in
        publisher's imprint.

My Dear Mr. M.: Letters to G.B. MacMillan from L. M. Montgomery

Editions in English

627.   *My Dear Mr. M.: Letters to G.B. MacMillan from L. M. Montgom-
        ery.* Eds. Francis W. P. Bolger and Elizabeth R. Epperly. Toronto:
        McGraw-Hill Ryerson, *1980. 212 pp. Four leaves of plates. ISBN
        007092399X.

Translations

Japanese:

628.   *Montgomery Shokan-Shu 1*. Tr. Junzo Miyatake and Noriko Miya-
        take. Tokyo: Shinozaki Shorin, *1981. 274 pp. Six leaves of
        plates.

PUBLISHED JOURNALS

629.   *Selected Journals of L. M. Montgomery*, vol. 1 (1889-1910). Eds.
        Mary Rubio and Elizabeth Waterston. Toronto: Oxford University
        Press, 1985. 424 pp. Illustrated with photographs.

POSTHUMOUS COLLECTED STORIES

The Road to Yesterday

Editions in English

630.   *The Road to Yesterday*. Toronto: McGraw-Hill Ryerson, *1974. x,
        251 pp. ISBN 0070777217. The manuscript for this collection of
        stories, originally titled by LMM "The Blythes are Quoted," was
        found among LMM's papers by her son Stuart. Some material,
        including poems, was deleted, and the stories were reorganized for
        this edition.

631.   -----. London, England: Angus and Robertson, *1975. x, 251 pp.
        ISBN 0207956464. This edition was printed from the same plates as
        the original McGraw-Hill Ryerson edition, but with a different cov-
        er, on different stock, and with a new title page.

632.   -----. Sydney, Australia: Angus and Robertson, 1975. This is prob-
        ably identical to the Angus and Robertson, London, edition, except
        for a change in locale.

Translations

Finnish:

633.   *Tie eiliseen.* Tr. Marja Helanen-Ahtola. Hameenlinna: Karisto,
        *1976. 343 pp. ISBN 9512310147.

Japanese:

634.   *Anne no mura no hibi.* Tr. Masanori Kamitsubo. Tokyo: Shinozaki
        Shorin, *1977. 246 pp. Illustrated.

635.   *Zoku Anne no mura no hibi.* Tr. Masanori Kamitsubo and Yoshiko
        Yamada. Tokyo: Shinozaki Shorin, *1979. 220 pp. Illustrated.

Spanish:

636.   *Historias de Avonlea.* Tr. Dora Delfino de Lorenti. Buenos Aires:
        Emecé Editores, *1980. 334 pp. Paperback.

The Doctor's Sweetheart and Other Stories

Editions in English

637.   *The Doctor's Sweetheart and Other Stories.* Selected and with an
        introduction by Catherine McLay. Toronto: McGraw-Hill Ryerson,
        *1979. 192 pp. ISBN 0070927902. This is a collection of stories
        originally published by LMM in various periodicals.

638.   -----. Selected and with an introduction by Catherine McLay.
        London, England: Harrap, *1979. 190 pp. ISBN 245534547. This is
        identical to the McGraw-Hill Ryerson edition, except for some
        changes in the preliminary pages and a different dust jacket. It
        was printed in Canada.

Translations

Finnish:

639.   *Tiedan salaisuuden.* Tr. Marja Helanen-Ahtola. Hameenlinna: Kar-
        isto, *1981. 227 pp. ISBN 9512317249.

Japanese:

640.   *Lucy no Yakusoku.* Tr. Keizaburo Yamaguchi and Masako Yamagu-
        chi. Tokyo: Shinozaki Shorin, *1979. 308 pp.

Part 3

ADAPTATIONS FOR OTHER MEDIA

Items marked with an asterisk in Part 3 have been personally examined.

FILM

641. *Anne of Green Gables.* Taylor, William Desmond, dir. With Mary Miles Minter, Frederick Burton, Marcia Harris, Leila Romer, Russell Hewitt. Realart, 1919.

642. *Anne of Green Gables.* Nicholls, George, Jr., dir. Produced by Kenneth Macgowan; screenplay by Sam Mintz; with Anne Shirley, Tom Brown, O.P. Heggie, Helen Westley. RKO Pictures, 1934 (79 minutes, black and white).

643. *Anne of Windy Poplars.* Hively, Jack, dir. Produced by Cliff Reid; screenplay by Michael Kanin and Jerry Cady; with Anne Shirley, James Ellison, Henry Travers, Patric Knowles. RKO Productions, 1940. Released in the United Kingdom in 1940 under the title *Anne of Windy Willows* (86 minutes).

644. *I Know A Secret.* Pittman, Bruce, dir.; screenplay by Amy Jo Cooper. Toronto, Atlantis Films Ltd., *1982 (24 minutes, 48 seconds). Adaptation of a short story, published in *Good Housekeeping*, August 1935, pp. 22-25.

STAGE (PUBLISHED VERSIONS)

645. *Anne of Green Gables.* By Wilbur Braun [pseud. Alice Chadwicke]. New York and Toronto: Samuel French, 1937. 139 pp. Dramatization in 3 acts.

646. *Anne of Avonlea.* By James Reach [pseud. Jeanette Carlisle]. New York, Los Angeles, London, and Toronto: Samuel French, *1940. 89 pp. A comedy in 3 acts.

647. *Anne of Green Gables.* A musical, by Norman Campbell and Donald Harron. New York and London: Samuel French, *1972. 92 pp. ISBN 573080399. Adapted from the novel by Donald Harron. Lyrics by Donald Harron and Norman Campbell. Additional lyrics by Mavor Moore and Elaine Campbell.

648.   *Anne of Green Gables.* A musical by Norman Campbell and Donald
        Harron. London: Chappel, 1973. 156 pp. A new edition of the pre-
        ceding item.

TELEVISION

649.   *Anne de Green Gables.* Gauthier, Jacques, dir. Adapted and trans-
        lated by Jean Hamelin. Théâtre populaire. CBFT, 8 Sept. 1957
        (59 minutes). (French translation of *Anne of Green Gables.)*

650.   *Anne of Green Gables.* Craft, Joan, dir. Produced by John McRae;
        dramatized by Julia Jones; with Kim Braden (Anne), Elliott Sullivan
        (Matthew), Barbara Hamilton (Marilla). BBC TV serialization in 5
        parts: 20 Feb. 1972 (44 minutes), 27 Feb. 1972 (44 minutes), 5 Mar.
        1972 (44 minutes), 12 Mar. 1972 (44 minutes), 19 Mar. 1972 (44
        minutes); broadcast repeated 5 Aug. 1973-2 Sept. 1973.

651.   *Anne of Avonlea.* Craft, Joan, dir. Produced by John McRae;
        dramatized by Elaine Morgan; with Kim Braden (Anne), Barbara
        Hamilton (Marilla), Jan Francis (Diana), Christopher Blake (Gil-
        bert). BBC TV serialization in 6 parts (all approximately 52 min-
        utes): 26 Jan. 1975, 2 Feb. 1975, 9 Feb. 1975, 16 Feb. 1975, 23
        Feb. 1975, 2 Mar. 1975; broadcast repeated 2 Jan. 1977-6 Feb.
        1977.

652.   *Anne of Green Gables.* Sullivan, Kevin, dir. Adapted and produced
        by Kevin Sullivan; with Megan Follows (Anne), Colleen Dewhurst
        (Marilla), Richard Farnsworth (Matthew). Anne of Green Gables
        Productions, Inc. Distributed by Sullivan Films, Toronto (198 min-
        utes). CBC serialization in two two-hour parts, broadcast on
        CBC-TV network, 1, 2 Dec. *1985.

SOUND RECORDINGS

653.   *Anne of Green Gables.* From the production of the musical by Nor-
        man Campbell and Donald Harron. Directed by Alan Lund, pro-
        duced by Henry Borden. Columbia Records, *WELS 354. Featuring
        Polly James, Barbara Hamilton and Hiram Sherman. Music super-
        vision by John Fenwick; Music Director Martin Goldstein.

Part 4

STORIES, POEMS, MISCELLANEOUS PIECES, SELECTED ANTHOLOGIZED WORKS

Unless otherwise indicated, all items in Parts 4, 5 and 6 have been personally examined.

STORIES

The following stories are listed primarily from the collection of scrapbooks kept by LMM, in which she pasted stories, and sometimes wrote the bibliographical details on the clipping.[5] This information has been supplemented by information found in LMM's ledger list of stories and poems, and by research in libraries.[6] All reprintings of a story are listed after the first publication, including revised versions, and revised titles. When the first publication, identified in the scrapbook, has not been found, but subsequent publications of the same story have been found, the story is listed under the date of the first verified publication. The pseudonym used, or the indication "[anon.]" is given when the item does not appear under LMM's name. A scrapbook reference number is given when the story is found in the scrapbooks; thus "Scbk. 7" means the story is found in scrapbook 7; "Scbk. 10 (2)" means that the second published version listed is found in scrapbook 10; "Scbks. 11 and 10" means that the first published version is found in scrapbook 11, the second publication is found in scrapbook 10. When the story has been reprinted in a collection or in a novel, this is indicated by an abbreviated title reference, as follows: *Anne of Avonlea (AA); Anne of Ingleside (AIn); Anne of the Island (AIs); Anne of Windy Poplars (AWP); Anne's House of Dreams (AHD); Chronicles of Avonlea (CA); The Doctor's Sweetheart (DS); Emily Climbs (EC); Emily of New Moon (ENM); Further Chronicles of Avonlea (FCA); The Golden Road (GR); Magic for Marigold (MM); Rainbow Valley (RV); Rilla of Ingleside (RI); The Road to Yesterday (RY); The Story Girl (SG); A Tangled Web (TW).* A separate listing is given

---

[5] For details on the scrapbooks, see items 1729-42, below.

[6] See Rea Wilmshurst, "L.M. Montgomery's Short Stories: A Preliminary Bibliography," *Canadian Children's Literature*, No. 29 (1983), pp. 25-42, for further details on the scrapbooks and ledger list. A detailed study of this material has been carried out by Ms. Wilmshurst subsequent to this article, supported by a separate grant from the Social Sciences and Humanities Research Council of Canada. The details which we give here on the stories and poems are drawn from this later study. See Rea Wilmshurst, "A Bibliography of Lucy Maud Montgomery's Short Stories, Poems, and Miscellaneous Articles" (unpublished research report, copies of which are held by the author, and by the National Library, Ottawa).

at the end of stories found only in the scrapbooks, followed by a separate
listing of titles from the ledger list of stories which have not been found.

654.   "A Baking of Gingersnaps." By Maud Cavendish. *Ladies' Journal*,
        July 1895. Scbk. 7.

655.   "Our Charivari." By Maud Cavendish. *Golden Days*, 9 May 1896, p.
        396. Scbk. 7.

656.   "In Spite of Myself." By M.L. Cavendish. *Chicago Inter Ocean*, 5
        July 1896, pp. 37-38. Scbk. 7.

657.   "Our Practical Joke." *Golden Days*, 8 Aug. 1896, pp. 604-5. Also in
        Churchman, 21 May 1910, p. 730. Scbk. 1.

658.   "The Missing Pony." *Golden Days*, 17 Sept. 1896, pp. 764-65. Scbk.
        7.

659.   "The Prize in Elocution." By L.W.[sic] Montgomery. *Philadelphia
        Times*, 7 Mar. 1897, p. 26. Scbk. 7.

660.   "The Goose Feud." By Maud Cavendish. *Arthur's Home Magazine*,
        Apr. 1897, pp. 225-30. Scbk. 7.

661.   "Extra French Examination." *Philadelphia Times*, 16 May 1897, p.
        30. Scbk. 7.

662.   "Detected by the Camera." *Philadelphia Times*, 27 June 1897, p.
        30. Scbk. 7.

663.   "A Strayed Allegiance." By Maud Cavindish [sic]. *Arthur's Home
        Magazine*, July 1897, pp. 422-31. Scbk. 7.

664.   "A Case of Trespass." *Golden Days*, 24 July 1897, pp. 561-62. Also
        in *King's Own*, 15 May 1909, p. 79. Scbks. 7 and 9.

665.   "The Violet Challie Dress." *Philadelphia Times*, 15 Aug. 1897, p.
        28. Scbk. 7.

666.   "The Gold-Link Bracelet." *Philadelphia Times*, 26 Sept. 1897, p.
        30. Scbk. 7.

667.   "Our Uncle Wheeler." *Golden Days*, 22 Jan. 1898, pp. 145-46. Scbk.
        7.

668.   "The Brothers' Queer Ruse." *Philadelphia Times*, 23 Jan. 1898, p.
        30. Scbk. 7.

669.   "A Pastoral Call." *Christian Herald*, 13 and 20 Apr. 1898, pp. 331
        and 356-57. Scbk. 2.

670. "Old Hector's Dog." *Golden Days*, 4 June 1898, pp. 449-50. Scbk. 2.

671. "A Real Test of Friendship." *Philadelphia Times*, 26 June 1898, p. 32. Scbk. 2.

672. "The Red Room." *Waverley Magazine*, 23 July 1898, pp. 50-52.

673. "Courage for the Occasion." *Philadelphia Times*, 24 July 1898, p. 32. Also as "Ruth's Raspberrying," *Churchman*, 24 July 1909, pp. 137-38. Scbk. 2.

674. "A New-Fashioned Flavoring." *Golden Days*, 27 Aug. 1898, pp. 640-41. Scbk. 2.

675. "Margaret Ann's Mother." *Springfield Republican*, 28 Aug. 1898, p. 14. Also in *Farm and Fireside*, 10 Sept. 1910, p. 14. Scbk. 2.

676. "The Story of a Ruby Ring." *Philadelphia Times*, 25 Sept. 1898, p. 28. Also as "The Ruby Ring," *Churchman*, 22 Oct. 1910, pp. 636-37. Scbk. 2.

677. "Jen's Device." *Family Herald*, 15 Nov. 1898, p. 5. Also in *Congregationalist*, 26 Nov. 1910, p. 802. Scbk. 2.

678. "A Little Accident." *Illustrated Youth and Age*, Dec. 1898. Scbk. 2.

679. "A Double Joke." *Golden Days*, 21 Jan. 1899, pp. 145-46. Also in *Children's Visitor*, 3 Apr. 1910, pp. 5-6. Scbk. 2.

680. "Her Pretty Golden Hair." *Philadelphia Times*, 26 Mar. 1899, p. 22. Scbk. 2.

681. "Which Dear Charmer?" *Ladies' Home Journal*, May 1899. Also in *Waverley Magazine*, 1 July 1899, p. 410. Scbk. 2.

682. "Kismet." *Canadian Magazine*, July 1899, pp. 228-32. Rpt. *DS*. Scbk. 2.

683. "Miss Marietta's Jersey." *Household*, July 1899, pp. 5-6. Adapted for chap. 2 of *AA*. Scbk. 2.

684. "John Vanderey." *Waverley Magazine*, 5 July 1899, pp. 69-70. Scbk. 2.

685. "A Brave Girl." *Family Herald*, 19 July 1899, p. 5. Scbk. 2.

686. "A Lesson in Behavior." *Philadelphia Times*, 20 Aug. 1899, p. 34. Scbk. 2.

687. "The Way of the Winning of Anne." *Springfield Republican*, 10 Dec. 1899, p. 18. Also as [anon.] "The Winning of Anne," *Family Herald*, 30 May 1900, p. 22. Scbk. 2.

688. "A Christmas Mistake." *Family Herald*, 20 Dec. 1899, p. 5. Scbk. 2.

689. "The Knuckling Down of Mrs. Gamble." *Good Housekeeping*, Jan. 1900, pp. 3-8. Also in *Waverley Magazine*, 20 Jan. 1900, pp. 35-36; and in *Presbyterian Banner*, 23 June 1910, pp. 78-80. Scbk. 2.

690. "An Invitation Given on Impulse." *Philadelphia Times*, 22 Apr. 1900, p. 32. Scbk. 2.

691. "The Courtship of Sherman Craig." *Springfield Republican*, 27 May 1900, p. 14. Also in *Westminster*, Aug. 1910, pp. 154-58. Rpt. *CA*. Scbk. 2.

692. "A Helping Hand." *Zion's Herald*, 4 July 1900, p. 849. Scbk. 2.

693. "Francoise." *Waverley Magazine*, 14 July 1900, pp. 25-26. Scbk. 2.

694. "A Wedding at Four-Winds Farm." *Springfield Republican*, 2 Sept. 1900, p. 14. Also in *American Messenger*, May 1910, pp. 94-95. Scbk. 1.

695. "The Glenns' Light." *Good Cheer*, Oct. 1900, pp. 37-38. Scbk. 1.

696. "The Adventures of A Story." *Philadelphia Times*, 28 Oct. 1900, p. 32. Also in *Churchman*, 5 Feb. 1910, pp. 203-4. Scbk. 1.

697. "Lilian's Business Venture." *Advocate and Guardian*, 1 Nov. 1900, pp. 335-37.

698. "Of Miss Calista's Peppermint." *Springfield Republican*, 11 Nov. 1900, p. 14. Also as "Miss Calista's Peppermint," *Westminster*, Nov. 1910, pp. 321-24. Scbk. 1.

699. "A Home-Sick Heart." *Family Herald*, 28 Nov. 1900, p. 5. Also as "How Grandma Ran Away," *American Agriculturist*, 27 Mar. 1909, pp. 432-34; and in *New England Homestead*, 27 Mar. 1909, pp. 416-18. Scbk. 1.

700. "Sadie's Hint." *Chicago Record*, 16 Feb. 1901, p. 10. Also in *Children's Visitor*, 23 May 1909, p. 5. Scbk. 1.

701. "When Friend Helps Friend." *Philadelphia Times*, 14 Apr. 1901, p. 36.

702.   "A Chapter of Accidents." *Waverley Magazine*, 4 May 1901, pp. 276-77.

703.   "Miriam's Lover." *Waverley Magazine*, 29 June 1901, pp. 403-4. Scbk. 1.

704.   "Lilian's Roses." *Zion's Herald*, 10 July 1901, p. 881. Scbk. 1.

705.   "A Holiday Adventure." *American Boy*, Aug. 1901, p. 290. Scbk. 1.

706.   "Young Si." *Waverley Magazine*, 3 Aug. 1901, pp. 65-66. Scbk. 1.

707.   "The Courtship of Josephine." *Springfield Republican*, 11 Aug. 1901, p. 14. Also as "Akin to Love," *Canadian Magazine*, Dec. 1909, pp. 143-52. Rpt. *DS*. Scbk. 1.

708.   "The Story of an Invitation." *Philadelphia Times*, 18 Aug. 1901, pp. 28-29. Also in *Children's Visitor*, 13 Feb. 1910, p. 5. Scbk. 1.

709.   "The Waking of Helen." *Waverley Magazine*, 31 Aug. 1901, pp. 129-30. Scbk. 1.

710.   "Two Summers." *Waverley Magazine*, 5 Oct. 1901, pp. 209-12. Scbk. 6.

711.   "The Setness of Theodosia." *Springfield Republican*, 27 Oct. 1901, p. 18. Also in *Westminster*, Jan. 1910, pp. 17-23. Scbk. 1.

712.   "There Were Two Loyal Hearts." *Springfield Republican*, 8 Dec. 1901, p. 18. Also as "A Loyal Heart," *Westminster*, June 1910, pp. 461-65. Scbk. 1.

713.   "Uncle Chatterton's Gingerbread." *What To Eat*, Jan. 1902, pp. 26-27. Also in *Housewife*, Mar. 1912, p. 27. Scbk. 6.

714.   "A Double Birthday." *Zion's Herald*, 1 Jan. 1902, p. 17. Scbk. 1.

715.   "Margaret's Books." *Forward* and *Wellspring*, 18 Jan. 1902, pp. 18-19. Scbk. 2.

716.   "A Case of Mistaken Identity." *American Boy*, Feb. 1902, p. 105. Scbk. 6.

717.   "Cyriac's Pony." *Star Monthly*, Feb. 1902, pp. 10-12. Scbk. 6.

718.   "Diana's Wedding-Dress." *Farm and Fireside*, 1 Mar. 1902, p. 16. Also in *Holland's Magazine*, Aug. 1912, pp. 52-53. Scbk. 6.

719.   "A Long Delayed Wedding." *Springfield Republican*, 30 Mar. 1902, p. 18. Scbk. 6.

720.   "The Second-Hand Travel Club." *Forward* and *Wellspring*, 12 Apr. 1902, pp. 118-19. Scbk. 6.

721.   "Patty's Mistake." *Zion's Herald*, 16 Apr. 1902, p. 494. Scbk. 6.

722.   "Davenport's Story." *Waverley Magazine*, 19 Apr. 1902, p. 244. Scbk. 6.

723.   "The Romance of Aunt Beatrice." *Springfield Republican*, 20 Apr. 1902, p. 18. Scbk. 6.

724.   "What Came of a Dare." *Designer*, May 1902, pp. 94-95. Scbk. 6.

725.   "The Merryweather Flower Beds." *Zion's Herald*, 21 May 1902, p. 656. Scbk. 6.

726.   "Teddy's Mother." *American Messenger*, June 1902, p. 126. Also in *Waverley Magazine*, 27 Sept. 1902, pp. 195-96. Scbk. 6.

727.   "The Peterkins' Rose-Jars." *Zion's Herald*, 9 July 1902, p. 881. Scbk. 6.

728.   "The Story of a Camping-Out." *Springfield Republican*, 20 July 1902, p. 18. Scbk. 6.

729.   "Mock Sunshine." *Waverley Magazine*, 2 Aug. 1902, pp. 67-68. Also in *New York Home Journal* and in *Holland's Magazine*, Apr. 1911, pp. 17-18. Scbk. 2 (2).

730.   "When Hearts Are Trumps." *Waverley Magazine*, 16 Aug. 1902, pp. 97-98. Scbk. 6.

731.   "The Visit of Geoffrey's Wife." *Springfield Republican*, 7 Sept. 1902, p. 18. Scbk. 6.

732.   "Aunt Nan's Garden." *Zion's Herald*, 10 Sept. 1902, pp. 1168-69. Scbk. 6.

733.   "The Curtain Island Mystery." *Star Monthly*, Oct. 1902, pp. 3-4. Scbk. 6.

734.   "The Quest of a Story." *Youth*, Oct. 1902, pp. 292-96. Also in *East and West*, 28 Sept. 1907, pp. 305-6. Scbks. 6 and 12.

735.   "Mabel's Cookies." *Zion's Herald*, 3 Dec. 1902, p. 1561. Scbk. 6.

736.   "The Martyrdom of Estella." *Waverley Magazine*, 20 Dec. 1902, pp. 385-86. Scbk. 6.

737. "Ned's Stroke of Business." *Farm and Fireside*, 15 Jan. 1903, p. 17. Scbk. 6.

738. "Brenton Kennedy's Monument." *American Agriculturist*, 24 Jan. 1903, p. 117. Also in *New England Homestead*, 24 Jan. 1903, p. 117. Scbk. 6.

739. "How Trudy and Prudy Made Up." *Christian Advocate*, 5 Mar. 1903, p. 373. Scbk. 6.

740. "After Many Days." *Ram's Horn*, 21 Mar. 1903, pp. 9-10. Scbk. 6.

741. "The Old Cooky Woman." *Good Cheer*, Apr. 1903, pp. 13-14. Scbk. 6.

742. "A Patent Medicine Testimonial." *Star Monthly*, Apr. 1903, pp. 7-8. Scbk. 6.

743. "An Unconventional Confidence." *Designer*. Also in *New Idea Woman's Magazine*, Apr. 1903, pp. 20-22; and in *Canadian Courier*, 20 Apr. 1912, pp. 32-33. Scbk. 6.

744. "Mother's Vacation." *Forward* and *Wellspring*, 9 May 1903, pp. 149-50. Scbk. 6.

745. "The Night of the Party." *Waverley Magazine*, 27 June 1903, p. 409. Scbk. 6.

746. "The Cake That Prissy Made." *Congregationalist*, 11 July 1903, p. 59. Also in *Advocate and Guardian*, 15 Aug. 1903, pp. 245-46; and in *Christian Advocate*, 26 Mar. 1909, pp. 204-5. Scbk. 6.

747. "The Unhappiness of Miss Farquhar." *Springfield Republican*, 12 July 1903, p. 18. Scbk. 6.

748. "The Little Three-Cornered Lot." *Zion's Herald*, 29 July 1903, pp. 954-55. Scbk. 6.

749. "A Sandshore Wooing." *Designer*, Aug. 1903, pp. 396-99. Scbk. 3.

750. "Uncle Dick's Little Girl." *American Agriculturist*, 15 Aug. 1903, pp. 136-37. Also in *New England Homestead*, 15 Aug. 1903, pp. 136-37. Scbk. 6.

751. "The Minister's Daughter." *What To Eat*, Sept. 1903, pp. 75-79. Scbk. 11.

752. "What Happened to Mark Antony." *Boys' World*, 5 Sept. 1903, pp. 1-2. Scbk. 3.

753.   "A Pioneer Wooing." *Farm and Fireside*, 15 Sept. 1903, pp. 14-15. Also in *Canadian Courier*, 20 May 1911, pp. 8, 26-28. Adapted for chap. 7 of *SG*. Scbk. 3.

754.   "The Strike at Putney." *Western Christian Advocate*, 16 Sept. 1903, pp. 14-15. Also in *National Magazine*, May 1909, pp. 193-96; and in *Westminster*, May 1914, pp. 467-72. Scbk. 4 (3).

755.   "The Old Chest at Wyther Grange." *Waverley Magazine*, 19 Sept. 1903, pp. 185-86. Adapted for chaps. 12 and 32 of *SG*. Scbk. 9.

756.   "The Magical Bond of the Sea." *Springfield Republican*, 20 Sept. 1903, p. 18. Also as "The Bond of the Sea," *Blue Book Magazine*, Jan. 1911, pp. 524-31. Scbk. 3.

757.   "Dorothy's Birthday." *American Messenger*, Oct. 1903, p. 200. Scbk. 3.

758.   "Our Runaway Kite." *New Idea Woman's Magazine*, Oct. 1903, pp. 44-45. Scbk. 3.

759.   "The Bride Roses." *Christian Endeavor World*, 1 Oct. 1903, pp. 5-6. Scbk. 3.

760.   "In the Pantry." *Congregationalist*, 3 Oct. 1903, p. 475. Scbk. 3.

761.   "Daphne North's Two Lovers." *Springfield Republican*, 4 Oct. 1903, p. 18. Also as "The Love Story of Daphne North," *Westminster*, Mar. 1911, pp. 209-15. Scbk. 3.

762.   "Janie's Visitor." *Advocate and Guardian*, 15 Oct. 1903, pp. 309-10. Scbk. 11.

763.   "The Schoolma'm's Donation Party." *Ram's Horn*, 24 Oct. 1903, pp. 9-10.

764.   "Dixie." *Children's Visitor*, 25 Oct. 1903, p. 6. Also in *Churchman*, 25 Sept. 1909, pp. 456-57. Scbk. 8.

765.   "Emily's Husband." *Canadian Magazine*, Nov. 1903, pp. 78-82. Also in *Presbyterian Banner*, 20 Feb. 1913, pp. 1215-17; and as "Emily Fair and Her Husband," *Springfield Republican*, 18 Apr. 1909, p. 26. Rpt. *DS*. Scbk. 3.

766.   "Kenneth's Treasure Trove." *Good Cheer*, Nov. 1903, pp. 42-43. Scbk. 8.

767.   "Patchwork." *Classmate*, 14 Nov. 1903, pp. 362-63.

768. "The Running Away of Chester." *Boys' World*, 14 Nov.-26 Dec. 1903, p. 4 *passim*. Scbk. 9.

769. "The Bitterness in the Cup." *American Home*, Dec. 1903 and Jan. 1904, pp. 3-8 and 6-8. Also as "Schooled with Briars," *Everywoman's World*, May [n/a] and June 1916, pp. [n/a] and 10, 25. Scbks. 9 and 12.

770. "Min." *American Home*, Dec. 1903, pp. 12-14.

771. "Ted's Double." *Men of Tomorrow*, Dec. 1903, pp. 706-11. Also in *Boys' World*, 28 Aug. 1909, pp. 1, 6. Scbk. 4.

772. "The Osbornes' Christmas." *Zion's Herald*, 16 Dec. 1903, pp. 1604-5. Scbk. 11.

773. "A Friendship Won." *Boys and Girls*, 26 Dec. 1903, pp. 205-6. Also in *East and West*, 26 Feb. 1910, p. 67.

774. "The Brook's Story." *Pure Words*, Jan. 1904, p. 3. Scbk. 11.

775. "The Girl and the Wild Race." *Era*, Jan. 1904, pp. 65-69. Also as "A Race for a Wife," *Westminster*, Sept. 1909, pp. 206-10. Rpt. *DS*. Scbk. 4.

776. "At the Bay Shore Farm." *Forward* and *Wellspring*, 9 Jan. 1904, pp. 9-10. Scbk. 12.

777. "A Fortunate Mistake." *Girls' Companion*, 23 Jan. 1904, p. 4. Scbk. 10.

778. "The Spelling-Match at Albury." *Days of Youth*, 24 Jan. 1904, p. 2. Scbk. 11.

779. "A Platonic Experiment." *Housewife*, Feb. 1904, pp. 3-4. Scbk. 12.

780. "The Promise of Lucy Ellen." *Delineator*, Feb. 1904, pp. 268-71. Also in *Canadian Courier*, 3 May 1913, pp. 8-9, 25. Rpt. *DS*. Scbks. 11 and 10.

781. "Polly Patterson's Autograph Square." *Zion's Herald*, 3 Feb. 1904, pp. 146-47. Adapted for chap. 23 of *GR*. Scbk. 11.

782. "Mrs. March's Revenge." *Western Christian Advocate*, 17 Feb. 1904, pp. 14-15. Scbk. 11.

783. "Penelope's Party Waist." *Designer*, Mar. 1904, pp. 530-31. Scbk. 11.

784. "The Son of His Mother." *Canadian Magazine*, Mar. 1904, pp. 469-78. Rpt. *FCA*.

785. "The Losing of Dot." *Pure Words*, 27 Mar. 1904, pp. 1, 3. Scbk. 11.

786. "Tannis of the Flats." *Criterion*, Apr. 1904, pp. 11-15. Also in *Canadian Magazine*, Jan. 1914, pp. 275-82. Rpt. *FCA*. Scbk. 4.

787. "Their Trip to Town." *Sunday School Times*, 30 Apr. 1904, p. 249. Also in *Presbyterian*, 28 May 1904, p. 697. Scbk. 9.

788. "The Pursuit of the Ideal." *What To Eat*, May 1904, pp. 145-47. Scbk. 11.

789. "Sara's Way." *Criterion*, May 1904, pp. 39-41. Rpt. *FCA*. Scbk. 4.

790. "Victor from Vanquished Issues." *Springfield Republican*, 22 May 1904, p. 22. Also in *Maclean's*, Aug. 1915, pp. 17-19, 81-85. Scbk. 11 (2).

791. "The Chiffon Dress." *Sunday School Advocate*, 4 June 1904, pp. 220-21.

792. "Aunt Rose's Girl." *American Agriculturist*, 18 June 1904, pp. 680-81. Also in *New England Homestead*, 18 June 1904, pp. 684-85. Scbk. 10 (2).

793. "How Don Was Saved." *Boys' World*, 18 June 1904, pp. 1-2. Scbk. 10.

794. "Ted's Celebration." *Boys' World*, 25 June 1904, pp. 1-2. Scbk. 10.

795. "How Nan Went to the Party." *Children's Visitor*, 17 July 1904, p. 1.

796. "The Softening of Miss Cynthia." *Living Church*, 30 July 1904, pp. 457-58. Also in *Advocate and Guardian*, 1 Oct. 1904, pp. 297-98: "from *Living Church*." Scbk. 4 (2).

797. "Aunt Cyrilla's Golden Birthday." *American Messenger*, Aug. 1904, p. 154. Scbk. 10.

798. "Bessie's Dream." *American Thresherman*, Aug. 1904, p. 78. Also in *Churchman*, 8 Jan. 1910, p. 67.

799. "Eunice Holland's Sacrifice." *Springfield Republican*, 7 Aug. 1904, p. 22. Rpt. as "In Her Selfless Mood," *FCA*.

800. "Debby's Day Off." *Boys and Girls*, 13 Aug. 1904, pp. 141-42. Scbk. 10.

801.   "Natty of Blue Point." *Forward* and *Wellspring*, 13 Aug. 1904, pp.
        265-66. Scbk. 12.

802.   "Dimple's Flowers." *Congregationalist*, 20 Aug. 1904, pp. 257-58.
        Scbk. 11.

803.   "Aunt Cynthia's Persian Cat." *Reader*, Sept. 1904, pp. 392-98. Also
        in *Canadian Courier*, 17 Jan. 1914, pp. 8-9, 16. Rpt. *FCA*. Scbk. 9
        (2).

804.   "Miss Madeline's Proposal." *Modern Women*, Sept. 1904, pp. 103-4.
        Also in *Westminster*, Dec. 1913, pp. 633-36. Scbk. 10.

805.   "Little Joscelyn." *Christian Endeavor World*, 1 Sept. 1904, pp.
        988-89. Rpt. *CA*.

806.   "Freda's Adopted Grave." *Zion's Herald*, 7 Sept. 1904, pp. 1138-39.
        Scbk. 11.

807.   "Popsy's Day at School." *Christian Advocate*, 8 Sept. 1904, pp.
        1461-62. Also in *Holland's Magazine*, Dec. 1911, p. 48. Scbk. 11.

808.   "Mackereling out in the Gulf." *Springfield Republican*, 8 Oct. 1905,
        p. 22. Scbk. 8.

809.   "The Nuisance of Women." *American Agriculturist*, 15 Oct. 1904,
        p. 335. Also in *New England Homestead*, 15 Oct. 1904, pp. 336, 339.
        Scbk. 9 (2).

810.   "The Man on the Train." *Ram's Horn*, 29 Oct. 1904, pp. 9-10. Also
        in *Canadian Courier*, 11 July 1914, pp. 7, 21; and as "The Man That
        Was on the Train," *Springfield Republican*, 6 Mar. 1910, p. 26.
        Scbks. 11 and 9.

811.   "Miss Sally's Company." *Forward* and *Wellspring*, 29 Oct. 1904, pp.
        258-59.

812.   "Elizabeth's Thanksgiving Dinner." *Western Christian Advocate*, 16
        and 23 Nov. 1904, pp. 15-16 and 15-16. Scbk. 11.

813.   "Why Not Ask Miss Price." *Girls' Companion*, 19 Nov. 1904, p. 4.
        Scbk. 10.

814.   "Aunt Ethelinda's Monument." *Christian Advocate*, 1 Dec. 1904,
        pp. 1940-41. Adapted for part of chap. 11 in *AIs*. Scbk. 11.

815.   "What Teddy and Gordon Saw in the Lane." *Churchman*, 10 Dec.
        1904, p. 1094. Scbk. 11.

816. "Elizabeth's Child." *Young People*, 17 Dec. 1904, pp. 407-8. Scbk. 12.

817. "Aunt Felicia's Preserve-Jars." *Western Christian Advocate*, 18 Jan. 1905, pp. 15-16. Scbk. 10.

818. "Aunt Susanna's Birthday Celebration." *New Idea Woman's Magazine*, Feb. 1905, pp. 30-31. Scbk. 11.

819. "Lavender's Room." *East and West*, 11 Feb. 1905, pp. 41-42. Scbk. 12.

820. "The Shyness of Cissy Emmeline." *Congregationalist*, 18 Mar. 1905, p. 362. Scbk. 11.

821. "Aunt Polly's Rose Party." *Pure Words*, Apr. 1905, pp. 1-2. Scbk. 11.

822. "The Jewel of Consistency." *Ladies' World*, Apr. 1905, pp. 3-5. Also in *American Agriculturist*, [7 and 14 Aug. 1909, issue n/a]; and in *New England Homestead*, 7 and 14 Aug. 1909, pp. 117-18 and 134. Scbk. 9 (3).

823. "The Fraser Scholarship." *Boys' World*, 15 Apr. 1905, pp. 1-2. Scbk. 10.

824. "The Hurrying of Ludovic." *Canadian Magazine*, May 1905, pp. 67-71. Rpt. *CA*.

825. "Frank's Wheat Series." *Western Christian Advocate*, 10 May 1905, p. 15. Also in *East and West*, 9 Sept. 1905, p. 282. Scbk. 11.

826. "A Soldier of the Queen." *Classmate*, 20 May 1905, pp. 157-58. Scbk. 12.

827. "Frank's Revenge." *Children's Visitor*, 21 May 1905, pp. 2, 7.

828. "Why People Liked Amy." *Zion's Herald*, 31 May 1905, p. 688.

829. "Aunt Olivia's Beau." *Designer*, June 1905, pp. 196-200. Rpt. *CA*.

830. "By the Grace of Sarah Maud." *Modern Women*, June 1905, pp. 4-5. Also as "By the Grace of Sarah May," *Maclean's*, Aug. 1916, pp. 27-28. Scbks. 9 and 11.

831. "The Schoolmaster's Letters." *Sunday Magazine*, 4 June 1905, pp. 7-8, 12-13. Also in *Holland's Magazine*, Aug. 1914, pp. 14, 39. Scbks. 9 and 10.

832.   "Ol' Man Reeves' Girl." *Farm and Fireside*, 15 June 1905, pp. 14-15. Rpt., revised, as "Old Man Shaw's Girl," *CA*.

833.   "A Fence and a Lesson." *Zion's Herald*, 21 June 1905, pp. 784-85. Scbk. 11.

834.   "The Love Story of an Awkward Man." *Springfield Republican*, 25 June 1905, p. 22. Scbk. 8.

835.   "At Five O'Clock in the Morning." *National Magazine*, July 1905, pp. 405-11. Also in *Maclean's*, Sept. 1914, pp. 8-9, 132-34. Scbks. 4 and 11.

836.   "The Girl with the Red Scarf." *Sunday School Advocate*, 15 July 1905, pp. 217-18. Scbk. 11.

837.   "The Jenkinson Grit." *Boys and Girls*, 15 July 1905, pp. 117-18. Scbk. 10.

838.   "A Butterfly Queen." *New Idea Woman's Magazine*, Aug. 1905, pp. 46-48. Also in *Western Christian Advocate*, 14 Oct. 1914, pp. 1177-78. Scbk. 11 (1 and 2).

839.   "Her Own People." *American Messenger*, Aug. 1905, pp. 154-55. Scbk. 10.

840.   "The Understanding of Sister Sara." *Pilgrim*, Aug. 1905, pp. 11-12. Also in *Holland's Magazine*, Oct. 1907, pp. 20-21. Scbk. 9 (2).

841.   "Discontented Dorothy." *Children's Visitor*, 6 Aug. 1905, p. 3. Also in *Presbyterian Banner*, 11 Nov. 1909, p. 736.

842.   "The Daughter of Ben-Ithiel." *Epworth Herald*, 19 and 26 Aug. 1905, pp. 292-93 and 318-19. Scbk. 11.

843.   "A Correspondence and a Climax." *Sunday Magazine*, 20 Aug. 1905, pp. 13-14, 17. Also in *Family Herald*, 27 Sept. and 4 Oct. 1905, pp. 6 and 6: "reprinted from New York Tribune." Scbk. 10.

844.   "Between the Hill and the Valley." *Springfield Republican*, 27 Aug. 1905, p. 18. Also as "The Hill and the Valley," *Maclean's*, Apr. 1915, pp. 28-30. Scbk. 8.

845.   "Miss Juliana's Wedding Dress." *New Idea Woman's Magazine*, Sept. 1905, pp. 25-26. Also in *Westminster*, Jan. 1916, pp. 83-86. Scbk. 11.

846.   "Aunt Mary's Day." *Boys' World*, 2 Sept. 1905, pp. 1-2. Scbk. 10.

847.   "Ronald's Scoop." *Forward* and *Wellspring*, 9 Sept. 1905, pp. 290-91. Scbk. 12.

848.   "Dora's Gingerbread." *Zion's Herald*, 20 Sept. 1905, pp. 1200-1201. Scbk. 11.

849.   "When Jack and Jill Took a Hand." *Gunter's Magazine*, Oct. 1905, pp. 370-78. Also in *Maclean's*, Mar. 1915, pp. 20-22, 91-94. Scbks. 4 and 11.

850.   "One of the Juniors." *East and West*, 28 Oct. 1905, pp. 337-38. Scbk. 12.

851.   "A Case of Atavism." *Reader*, Nov. 1905, pp. 658-66. Rpt., revised, as "The Winning of Lucinda," *CA*.

852.   "The Story of a Pumpkin Pie." *American Thresherman*, Nov. 1905, p. 42. Also in *Zion's Herald*, 18 Nov. 1914, p. 1456. Scbks. 10 and 11.

853.   "The Bartletts' Thanksgiving." *Ram's Horn*, 18 Nov. 1905, pp. 7-8. Also as "The Bartletts' Thanksgiving Day," *New England Homestead*, 21 Nov. 1914, pp. 3, 27. Scbks. 11 and 9.

854.   "Cyrilla's Inspiration." *Epworth Herald*, 25 Nov. 1905, pp. 673-75. Scbk. 11.

855.   "Millicent's Double." *East and West*, 16 Dec. 1905, pp. 397-98. Scbk. 12.

856.   "The Pink and Gold Heart." *Zion's Herald*, 20 Dec. 1905, p. 1617. Scbk. 11.

857.   "The Christmas Surprise at Enderly Road." *King's Own*, 23 Dec. 1905, pp. 201-2. Scbk. 10.

858.   "Bertie's New Year." *Pittsburgh Christian Advocate*, 28 Dec. 1905, pp. 10-12. Scbk. 11.

859.   "Ida's New Year Cake." *Days of Youth*, 31 Dec. 1905, pp. 2-3, 7. Scbk. 11.

860.   "A Night in the Cold." *Pure Words*, 31 Dec. 1905, pp. 1-2, 4. Scbk. 11.

861.   "A Little Golden Head." *American Agriculturist*, 6 Jan. 1906, pp. 21-22. Also in *New England Homestead*, 6 Jan. 1906, pp. 22, 25. Scbk. 9 (2).

862.   "Elvira's Rebellion." *East and West*, 20 Jan. 1906, p. 22. Also in *Presbyterian Banner*, 13 Oct. 1910, pp. 608-9. Scbk. 12.

863.   "The Dissipation of Miss Ponsonby." *Housewife*, Feb. 1906, pp. 1-2. Scbk. 9.

864.   "Elizabeth's Pumpkin Pie." *King's Own*, 3 Feb. 1906, pp. 18-19. Scbk. 10.

865.   "The Tide at Golden Gate." *Churchman*, 10 Feb. 1906, pp. 229-30. Scbk. 10.

866.   "Pa Rudge's Purchase." *Christian Endeavor World*, 22 Feb. 1906, pp. 421-22. Rpt. as "Pa Sloane's Purchase," *CA*.

867.   "Dot's World." *Zion's Herald*, 28 Feb. 1906, p. 274.

868.   "The Box of Violets." *Pilgrim*, Mar. 1906, pp. 15-16. Also in *Holland's Magazine*, Aug. 1907, pp. 15-16. Scbk. 10 (2).

869.   "Light on the Big Dipper." *Churchman*, 17 Mar. 1906, pp. 429-30. Scbk. 11.

870.   "The Education of Sally." *Gunter's Magazine*, Apr. 1906, pp. 297-306. Also in *Canadian Courier*, 21 June 1913, pp. 9-10, 25-26. Rpt. as "The Education of Betty," *FCA*. Scbk. 4.

871.   "The Wooing of Bessy." *Trotwood's Monthly*, Apr. 1906, pp. 367-71. Scbk. 4.

872.   "The Blue North Room." *East and West*, 21 Apr. 1906, pp. 121-22. Scbk. 12.

873.   "Prodigal Brother." *Ram's Horn*, 5 May 1906, pp. 7-8. Also in *Holland's Magazine*, Mar. 1914, pp. 38-39. Scbk. 11.

874.   "Aunt Meg's Reporter." *Boys' World*, 12 May 1906, pp. 1-2. Scbk. 10.

875.   "How Shanky Saved the Day." *Star Monthly*, June 1906, pp. 3-4. Scbk. 11.

876.   "The Redemption of John Churchill." *American Messenger*, June 1906, pp. 114-15. Scbk. 9.

877.   "The Lady of the Spring." *King's Own*, 21 and 28 July 1906, pp. 113-14 and 119. Scbk. 10.

878.   "The Story of Uncle Dick." *American Agriculturist*, 28 July 1906, pp. 76-77. Also in *New England Homestead*, 28 July 1906, pp. 79-80. Scbk. 9 (2).

879.   "The Girl at the Gate." *National Magazine*, Aug. 1906, pp. 539-40.
       Scbk. 4.

880.   "Betty's Visit." *Congregationalist*, 25 Aug. 1906, pp. 242-43. Scbk.
       11.

881.   "The Pot of Gold at Rainbow's End." *Boys' World*, 25 Aug. 1906, pp.
       1, 5.

882.   "The Indecision of Margaret." *Gunter's Magazine*, Sept. 1906, pp.
       156-65. Also, with slightly revised ending, in *Maclean's*, Jan. 1915,
       pp. 9-11, 90-92. Later version adapted in *AIs, passim*. Scbks. 4 and
       11.

883.   "The Girls' Impromptu Party." *Springfield Republican*, 2 Sept.
       1906, p. 18. Scbk. 8.

884.   "In the Old Valley." *American Agriculturist*, 8 Sept. 1906, pp.
       199-200. Also in *New England Homestead*, 8 Sept. 1906, pp. 212,
       214; and as "The Old Valley," *Holland's Magazine*, Mar. 1910, pp.
       15-16. Scbk. 10.

885.   "The Little Fellow's Photograph." *Classmate*, 8 Sept. 1906, pp.
       281-82. Adapted for pt. 2, chaps. 2-3 of *AWP*. Scbk. 5.

886.   "Jane Lavinia." *Zion's Herald*, 26 Sept. 1906, pp. 1230-32. Scbk. 11.

887.   "The Burton Girls' Patch Party." *East and West*, 27 Oct. 1906, pp.
       337-38. Also in *Epworth Herald*, 29 Jan. 1910, pp. 131-33. Scbk.
       12.

888.   "Miss Pridey." *Pure Words*, 28 Oct. 1906, pp. 1-2. Scbk. 11.

889.   "The Story of a Love." *Holland's Magazine*, Nov. 1906, p. 24. Also
       in *Canadian Magazine*, Mar. 1911, pp. 487-89. Scbk. 12.

890.   "Janie's Prize." *King's Own*, 3 Nov. 1906, pp. 173-74. Scbk. 10.

891.   "Aunt Nancy." *Boys' World*, 10 Nov. 1906, pp. 1-2. Scbk. 10.

892.   "Evangeline's Father." *Forward* and *Wellspring*, 10 Nov. 1906, pp.
       366-67. Scbk. 12.

893.   "The Wisdom of the Heart." *Watson's Magazine*, Dec. 1906, pp.
       257-61. Also as "The Doctor's Sweetheart," *Canadian Magazine*,
       June 1908, pp. 154-58. Rpt. *DS*. Scbk. 4.

894.   "An Adventure on Island Rock." *Boys' World*, 1 Dec. 1906, pp. 1-2.
       Scbk. 10.

895. "Harry's Adventure." *King's Own*, 1 Dec. 1906, pp. 189-90. Scbk. 10.

896. "Dorinda's Desperate Deed." *Days of Youth*, 9 Dec. 1906, pp. 2-3, 7. Scbk. 11.

897. "A Brave Boy." *Boys' World*, 15 Dec. 1906, p. 1. Scbk. 9.

898. "Clorinda's Gifts." *Epworth Herald*, 15 Dec. 1906, pp. 731-32. Scbk. 11.

899. "A Christmas of Long Ago." *Western Christian Advocate*, 19 Dec. 1906, p. 15. Scbk. 11.

900. "The Unforgotten One." *Zion's Herald*, 19 Dec. 1906, pp. 1619-20. Also in *Canadian Courier*, 18 Dec. 1909, pp. 15, 23; and as "She Was the Forgotten One," *Springfield Republican*, 22 Dec. 1907, p. 24. Scbk. 11.

901. "Jane's Baby." *Christian Endeavor World*, 20 Dec. 1906, pp. 249, 260-61. Rpt. *FCA*.

902. "The Falsoms' Christmas Dinner." *East and West*, 22 Dec. 1906, p. 401-2. Scbk. 12.

903. "The Pursuit of Pirate Gold." *Children's Visitor*, 30 Dec. 1906, pp. 5, 7. Scbk. 9.

904. "Aunt Julietta Talks to Nora May." *Holland's Magazine*, Jan. 1907, p. 17. Scbk. 9.

905. "The Luck of the Tremaynes." *American Home*, Jan. and Feb. 1907, pp. 3-4, 14, 15, 19, and [issue n/a]. Scbk. 9.

906. "A Chip of [sic] the Old Block." *Springfield Republican*, 6 Jan. 1907, p. 22. Also in *Canadian Courier*, 8 Feb. 1913, pp. 8, 21-22. Adapted for chap. 16 of *RV*. Scbk. 8.

907. "Dottie and Tottie." *Zion's Herald*, 9 Jan. 1907, p. 48. Scbk. 11.

908. "The Parting of the Ways." *Canadian Magazine*, Feb. 1907, pp. 335-36. Rpt. *DS*. Scbk. 4.

909. "In a Garden of Old Delights." *National Magazine*, Mar. 1907, pp. 554-56. Scbk. 4.

910. "Paul, Shy Man." *Housekeeper*, Mar. 1907, pp. 5, 6, 39. Adapted for chap. 25 of *GR*. Scbk. 10.

911.   "A Substitute Journalist." *Forward* and *Wellspring*, 9 Mar. 1907,
        pp. 73-74. Scbk. 12.

912.   "The Easter Solo." *East and West*, 30 Mar. 1907, p. 99. Scbk. 12.

913.   "Mehitible Jane's Call." *Classmate*, 30 Mar. 1907, pp. 97-98. Scbk.
        12.

914.   "The Old Fellow's Letters." *Blue Book Magazine*, Apr. 1907, pp.
        1246-49.

915.   "The Quarantine at Alexander Abraham's." *Everybody's*, Apr. 1907,
        pp. 495-503. Rpt. *CA*.

916.   "Freda's Picnic." *King's Own*, 6 Apr. 1907, p. 55. Scbk. 10.

917.   "Patty's Guest." *King's Own*, 27 Apr. 1907, p. 67. Scbk. 10.

918.   "An Unpremeditated Ceremony." *Gunter's Magazine*, May 1907,
        pp. 392-97. Also in *Canadian Courier*, 5 Feb. 1910, pp. 16, 21.
        Scbk. 4.

919.   "The Tollivers' Picnic." *Congregationalist*, 4 May 1907, pp. 598-99.
        Scbk. 11.

920.   "The Word of a Kennedy." *East and West*, 11 May 1907, pp. 145-46.

921.   "In the Sweet o' the Year." *Housekeeper*, June 1907, pp. 5-6. Scbk.
        12.

922.   "The Lost Knife." *Boys' World*, 8 June 1907, p. 3.

923.   "The Little Brown Book of Miss Emily." *Farm and Fireside*, 10
        June 1907, p. 11. Also in *Maclean's*, Jan. 1917, pp. 31-32. Rpt.
        FCA. Scbk. 11 (2).

924.   "The Deferment of Hester." *Blue Book Magazine*, July 1907, pp.
        625-31. Adapted for chaps. 31-34 of *AIs*. Scbk. 4.

925.   "The Materializing of Cecil." *Home Magazine*, July 1907, pp. 8-9,
        26. Also in *Canadian Courier*, 13 July 1912, pp. 12, 27-28. Rpt.
        FCA. Scbk. 9.

926.   "Missy's Room." *Zion's Herald*, 3 July 1907, pp. 847-49. Scbk. 11.

927.   "The End of a Quarrel." *American Agriculturist*, 20 July 1907, pp.
        56, 58-59. Also in *New England Homestead*, 20 July 1907, pp.
        56-57. Rpt. *CA*.

928.   "Ted's Afternoon Off." *King's Own*, 3 Aug. 1907, pp. 122-23. Scbk. 10.

929.   "A Girl and a Picture." *Farm and Fireside*, 10 Aug. 1907, pp. 13, 17. Also as "The Girl and the Photograph," *Maclean's*, May 1915, pp. 36-38. Scbk. 10.

930.   "Marcella's Reward." *Zion's Herald*, 28 Aug. 1907, pp. 1104-6. Scbk. 11.

931.   "The Luck of Four-Leaved Clover." *Congregationalist*, 31 Aug. 1907, pp. 281-82. Scbk. 11.

932.   "Aunt Caroline's Silk Dress." *East and West*, 7 Sept. 1907, pp. 285-86. Scbk. 12.

933.   "Fair Exchange and No Robbery." *Springfield Republican*, 15 Sept. 1907, p. 20.

934.   "Mrs. Skinner's Story." *Westminster*, Oct. 1907, pp. 255-58. Adapted for chap. 30 of *AIs*. Scbk. 4.

935.   "Aunt Susanna's Thanksgiving Dinner." *Housewife*, Nov. 1907, pp. 5, 14. Also as "Aunt Elmira's Thanksgiving Dinner," *Family Herald*, 7 Oct. 1936, pp. 24, 27. Scbk. 12.

936.   "The Old Fowler Clock." *Boys' World*, 9 and 16 Nov. 1907, pp. 4 and 4. Scbk. 9.

937.   "The Genesis of the Doughnut Club." *Epworth Herald*, 23 Nov. 1907, pp. 659-61. Scbk. 11.

938.   "In Place of Queen Mab." *Zion's Herald*, 4 Dec. 1907, p. 1553.

939.   "The End of the Young Family Feud." *Epworth Herald*, 14 Dec. 1907, pp. 743-45. Scbk. 11.

940.   "Her Father's Daughter." *Christian Endeavor World*, 26 Dec. 1907, pp. 269, 275-77. Rpt. *FCA*.

941.   "Anna's Love Letters." *National Magazine*, Jan. 1908, pp. 441-45. Scbk. 4.

942.   "By Grace of Julius Caesar." *Red Book Magazine*, Jan. 1908, pp. 402-5. Also in *Canadian Magazine*, Sept. 1908, pp. 412-16. Rpt. *DS*. Scbk. 4.

943.   "The Old South Orchard." *Outing Magazine*, Jan. 1908, pp. 413-16. Adapted in *SG*, *passim*. Scbk. 4.

944.   "Only a Common Fellow." *American Agriculturist*, 11 Jan. 1908,
        pp. 50-51. Also in *New England Homestead*, 11 Jan. 1908, pp.
        54-55; and in *Canadian Courier*, 6 Sept. 1913, pp. 6-7, 21. Rpt.
        FCA.

945.   "For the Honor of the Club." *Children's Visitor*, 16 Jan. and 2 Feb.
        1908, pp. 5 and 2, 7. Scbk. 10.

946.   "Margaret's Patient." *East and West*, 15 Feb. 1908, p. 49. Scbk. 9.

947.   "The Locket That Was Baked." *Congregationalist*, 7 Mar. 1908, p.
        318. Also in *Christian Advocate*, 22 May 1908, pp. 650-51. Adapted
        for chap. 20 of *GR*. Scbk. 11.

948.   "The Winning of Frances." *East and West*, 25 Apr. 1908, pp.
        133-34.

949.   "The Twins and a Wedding." *Holland's Magazine*, May 1908, pp.
        12-13. Also in *Maclean's*, Sept. 1915, pp. 22-24, 84; and as "The
        Twins and a Pretty Wedding," *Springfield Republican*, 8 May 1910,
        p. 26. Scbks. 9 and 11.

950.   "A Double Surprise." *Blue Book Magazine*, June 1908, pp. 341-46.
        Scbk. 4.

951.   "By the Rule of Contrary." *Farm and Fireside*, 10 July 1908, p. 15.

952.   "The Proving of Russell." *Sabbath-School Visitor*, 1 Aug. 1908, p.
        138. Scbk. 10.

953.   "A Will, a Way and a Woman." *American Agriculturist*, 15 and 22
        Aug. 1908, pp. 136 and 157-58. Also in *New England Homestead*, 15
        and 22 Aug. 1908, pp. 141 and 161-62. Adapted for chap. 2 of *GR*.
        Scbk. 10.

954.   "Nurse Friedrich." *Holland's Magazine*, Sept. 1908, pp. 20-21. Scbk.
        10.

955.   "Ted Williams, Sneak." *Children's Visitor*, 20 and 27 Sept. 1908, pp.
        5 and 2, 7.

956.   "The Growing Up of Cornelia." *Pictorial Review*, Oct. 1908, pp.
        8-9, 15, 65. Scbk. 9.

957.   "By Way of the Brick Oven." *East and West*, 3, 10, 17, 24 Oct. and
        7, 14 Nov. 1908, pp. 313-14, 325; 330-31; 337-38; 346-47; 353-54;
        361-62. Scbk. 12.

958.   "Four Winds." *Housewife*, Oct. and Nov. 1908, pp. 3-5, 9, and 3-4,
        7-8. Also as "Windy Willows," *Family Herald*, 30 Oct. and 6, 13, 20
        Nov. 1935, pp. 20, 43; 20, 43; 18; 18-19. Scbk. 12.

959.   "The Girl Who Drove the Cows." *Presbyterian Banner*, 15 Oct. 1908, pp. 14-15. Scbk. 11.

960.   "The Revolt of Mary Isabel." *Blue Book*, Dec. 1908, pp. 318-25. Scbk. 4.

961.   "An After-Thanksgiving Story." *Epworth Herald*, 12 Dec. 1908, pp. 749-51. Scbk. 11.

962.   "The Punishment of the Twins." *Blue Book*, Feb. 1909, pp. 814-21. Scbk. 4.

963.   "A Redeeming Sacrifice." *Holland's Magazine*, Feb. 1909, pp. 7-8. Scbk. 12.

964.   "Miss Mattie's Birthday Gift." *Philadelphia Times*. Also in *Churchman*, 13 Feb. 1909, pp. 245-46; and in *Zion's Herald*, 19 July 1911, p. 915: "Reprinted from *Congregationalist*." Scbk. 1.

965.   "A Soul That Was Not at Home." *Springfield Republican*, 21 Mar. 1909, p. 22. Scbk. 8.

966.   "Miss Judith's Peonies." *Christian Endeavor World*, 22 Apr. 1909, pp. 633-34. Scbk. 9.

967.   "The Conscience Case of David Staunton." *Westminster*, May 1909, pp. 325-30. Rpt. as "The Conscience Case of David Bell," *FCA*.

968.   "The Return of Hester." *Canadian Magazine*, May 1909, pp. 73-77. Rpt. *FCA*.

969.   "The Dream Child." *Christian Endeavor World*, 6 May 1909, pp. 669-70. Rpt. *FCA*.

970.   "Robert Turner's Revenge." *Springfield Republican*, 9 May 1909, p. 26. Scbk. 8.

971.   "A Golden Wedding." *American Messenger*, June 1909, p. 114.

972.   "Jessamine." *Household Dealer*. Also in *Farm and Fireside*, 10 June 1909, pp. 14-15. Scbk. 1.

973.   "The Courting of Prissy Strong." *Housewife*, July 1909, pp. 12-13. Rpt. *CA*.

974.   "The Great Actor's Part." *Canadian Courier*, 17 July 1909, pp. 14, 20. Scbk. 9.

975.   "The Life-Book of Uncle Jesse." *Housekeeper*, Aug. 1909, pp. 8-9. Adapted in *AHD*, *passim*. Scbk. 12.

976.   "The Little Black Doll." *Zion's Herald*, 11 Aug. 1909, pp. 1012-13.
        Scbk. 11.

977.   "The Fillmore Elderberries." *East and West*, 18 Sept. 1909, pp. 299,
        302.

978.   "A Narrow Escape." *Zion's Herald*, 6 Oct. 1909, p. 1266.

979.   "Meeting with My Lady Jane." *Springfield Republican*, 24 Oct.
        1909, p. 26. Also as "My Lady Jane," *Maclean's*, Feb. 1915, pp.
        12-14. Rpt. *DS*. Scbk. 8.

980.   "Miracle at Mayfield." *Christian Endeavor World*, 28 Oct. 1909, pp.
        69-70. Rpt. as "Miracle at Carmody," *CA*.

981.   "The Neighbors at Sunny Brae." *Springfield Republican*, 14 Nov.
        1909, p. 26.

982.   "Our Thanksgiving Day." *Churchman*, 20 Nov. 1909, pp. 763, 765.

983.   "The Thorny Rose." *Holland's Magazine*, Dec. 1909, pp. 20-22.

984.   "Mary Ethel's Apology." By L. Montgomery. *Household Guest*.
        Also as "As to Mary Ethel's Apology," *Springfield Republican*, 5
        Dec. 1909, p. 26. Scbk. 6.

985.   "A Christmas Inspiration." *Family Herald*. Also in *Churchman*, 19
        Dec. 1909, pp. 918-20. Scbk. 1.

986.   "Christmas at Red Butte." *East and West*, 25 Dec. 1909, pp.
        409-10. Scbk. 12.

987.   "The Brother Who Failed." *The Globe* [Christmas Number], 1909,
        pp. 18-19. Rpt. *FCA*.

988.   "Uncle Richard's New Year's Dinner." *Congregationalist*, 1 Jan.
        1910, pp. 19-20. Also in *East and West*, 31 Dec. 1910, p. 419.

989.   "Bertha's Decision." *[Children's] Visitor*, 30 Jan. 1910, pp. 3, 6.

990.   "Gossip of Valley View." *National Magazine*, Feb. 1910, pp. 534-38.

991.   "A Valentine Mistake." *Days of Youth*. Also in *Churchman*, 12
        Feb. 1910, pp. 240-41. Scbk. 11.

992.   "A Garden of Old Delights." *Canadian Magazine*, June 1910, pp.
        154-60. Adapted for *SG*, *passim*. Scbk. 4.

993.   "A Passing Confidence." *Ladies' World*. Also in *Canadian Courier*,
        20 Aug. 1910, pp. 12, 25-26. Scbk. 6.

994.   "Each in His Own Tongue." *Delineator*, Oct. 1910, pp. 247, 324.
        Rpt. *CA*.

995.   "The Letters." *National Magazine*, Nov. 1910, pp. 119-26. Also in
        Maclean's, Dec. 1915, pp. 23-25, 89-91. Scbks. 4 and 11.

996.   "Aunt Sally's Letters." *Canadian Courier*, 26 Nov. 1910, pp. 13,
        24-25.

997.   "Charlotte's Ladies." *Epworth Herald*, 25 Feb. 1911, pp. 246-48.
        Scbk. 11.

998.   "The Jest That Failed." *Household Guest*. Also in *Presbyterian
        Banner*, 16 Mar. 1911, pp. 1330-31. Scbk. 1.

999.   "The Romance of Jedediah." *Housewife*, Sept. 1912, pp. 3-5. Scbk.
        12.

1000.   "The Finished Story." *Longman's Magazine*. Also in *Boston Post
        Sunday Magazine*, pp. 5-6; and in *Canadian Magazine*, Dec. 1912,
        pp. 108-12. Rpt. *DS*. Scbk. 12.

1001.   "Josephine's Husband." *Clover Magazine*. Also in *Housewife*, Jan.
        1913, pp. 3, 24. Scbk. 3.

1002.   "How We Went to the Wedding." *Housewife*, Apr. and May 1913,
        pp. 3-5, 31 and 12-13, 28. Also in *Family Herald*, 20, 27 Feb. and 6
        Mar. 1935, pp. 22, 34; 27; 23. Adapted for chap. 31 of *RI*. Scbks.
        12 and 5.

1003.   "The Five-thirty Train." *Household Guest*. Also in *New England
        Homestead*, 16 Aug. 1913, p. 114. Scbk. 1.

1004.   "The Promissory Note." *Zion's Herald*, 20 Sept. 1913, pp. 1170-72.
        Scbk. 11.

1005.   "Bessie's Doll." *Western Christian Advocate*, 11 Feb. 1914, pp.
        12-14. Scbk. 11.

1006.   "Aunt Philippa and the Men." *Red Book Magazine*, Jan. 1915, pp.
        518-24. Adapted for chap. 8 of *AHD*. Scbk. 4.

1007.   "The Beaton Family Group." *Springfield Republican*. Also in *Canadian Courier*, 9 Jan. 1915, p. 6. Sbcks. 8 and 9.

1008.   "Their Girl Josie." *American Home*, [1906]. Also in *Maclean's*, July
        1915, pp. 17-19. Scbk. 10.

1009.   "Abel and His Great Adventure." *Canadian Magazine*, Feb. 1917,
        pp. 355-63. Rpt. *DS*. Scbk. 4.

1010.   "Garden of Spices." *Maclean's*, Mar. 1918, pp. 28-30, 93, 95-96, 98-100. Rpt. *DS*. Scbk. 11.

1011.   "White Magic." *Woman's Century*, June and July 1921, pp. 4, 5, and 14. Scbk. 10.

1012.   "The Tryst of the White Lady." *Maclean's*, 1 Aug. 1922, pp. 28-29, 52.

1013.   "Enter, Emily." *Delineator*, Jan. 1925, pp. 10-11, 56-57. Chaps. 1-4 of *ENM*.

1014.   "Too Few Cooks." *Delineator*, Feb. 1925, pp. 10, 78, 81-82. Adapted for chaps. 6-8 of *ENM* and chap. 17 of *MM*.

1015.   "Night Watch." *Delineator*, Mar. 1925, pp. 10-11, 96-97. Chap. 3 of *EC*.

1016.   "Her Dog Day." *Delineator*, Apr. 1925, pp. 10, 30-83. Used as chaps. 22-24 of *MM*.

1017.   "Magic for Marigold." *Delineator*, May 1926, pp. 10-11, 82, 85. Adapted as chaps. 1 and 2 of *MM*.

1018.   "Lost--a Child's Laughter." *Delineator*, June 1926, pp. 15, 68, 70. Adapted as chap. 7 of *MM*.

1019.   "Bobbed Goldilocks." *Delineator*, July 1926, pp. 10, 70-71. Chap. 10 of *MM*.

1020.   "Playmate." *Delineator*, Aug. 1926, pp. 15, 66. Chap. 21 of *MM*.

1021.   "A Dinner of Herbs." *Chatelaine*, Oct. 1928, pp. 10-11, 40.

1022.   " 'It.' " *Chatelaine*, Apr. 1929, pp. 21, 56, 58. Chap. 8 of *MM*.

1023.   "A Question of Acquaintance." *Maclean's*, 1 Oct. 1929, pp. 12-13, 81-83.

1024.   "A House Divided Against Itself." *Canadian Home Journal*, Mar. 1930, pp. 3-5, 70, 72. Adapted for part of *TW*. Scbk. 5.

1025.   "The Price." *Chatelaine*, Mar. 1930, pp. 10-11, 39-42.

1026.   "Some Fools and a Saint." *Family Herald*, 20, 27 May, and 3, 10 June 1931, pp. 19-20; 19-20, 41; 19-20; 21-22.

1027.   "The Man Who Forgot." *Family Herald*, 6 and 13 Jan. 1932, pp. 23-24 and 41, 45.

1028.   "The Bride Is Waiting." *Canadian Magazine,* Apr. 1932, pp. 3-4, 33-34, 37. Rpt. *DS.*

1029.   "The House." *Chatelaine,* May 1932, pp. 10-11, 45.

1030.   "Charlotte's Quest." *Family Herald,* 4, 11, 18, 25 Jan. 1933, all on page 45.

1031.   "Fool's Errand." *Family Herald,* 22 Feb. 1933, pp. 19, 38. Rpt. *RY.* Scbk. 5.

1032.   "An Afternoon with Mr. Jenkins." *Family Herald,* 2 Aug. 1933, pp. 17, 20. Rpt. *RY.* Scbk. 5.

1033.   "From Out the Silence." *Family Herald,* 10 Jan. 1934, pp. 26-27.

1034.   "The Closed Door." *Family Herald,* 20 June 1934, pp. 18-19.

1035.   "For a Dream's Sake." *Family Herald,* 2 Jan. 1935, pp. 26, 40. Scbk. 5.

1036.   "Miss Curtis Comes." *Family Herald,* 15 May 1935, p. 19. Scbk. 5.

1037.   "What Aunt Marcella Would Have Called It." *Family Herald,* 19 June 1935, p. 19. Scbk. 5.

1038.   "House Party at Smoky Island." *Weird Tales Magazine,* Aug. 1935. Typescript in Guelph collection.

1039.   "I Know a Secret." *Good Housekeeping,* Aug. 1935, pp. 22-25, 137-39. Rpt. *DS.* Adapted for chaps. 30-31 of *AIn.*

1040.   "The Man Who Wouldn't Talk." *Family Herald,* 6 May 1936, pp. 22-23, 30. Adapted for *AWP,* pt. 1, chaps. 9-11.

1041.   "The Wedding at Poplar Point." *Family Herald,* 13 May 1936, pp. 22-23, 30. Adapted for *AWP,* pt. 1, chaps. 16-17.

1042.   "The Gift of a Day." *Family Herald,* 20 May 1936, pp. 20-21, 30. Adapted for *AWP,* pt. 1, chaps. 12-15.

1043.   "Everybody is Different." *Family Herald,* 27 May 1936, pp. 20-21. Adapted for *AWP,* pt. 2, chaps. 10-12.

1044.   "Miss Much-Afraid." *Family Herald,* 3 June 1936, pp. 20-21. Adapted for *AWP,* pt. 2, chaps. 8-9.

1045.   "The Westcott Elopement." *Family Herald,* 10 June 1936, pp. 20-21. Adapted for *AWP,* pt. 3, chaps. 5-8.

1046.   "A Tragic Evening." *Family Herald*, 24 June 1936, pp. 20-21.
         Adapted for *AWP*, pt. 3, chaps. 9-11.

1047.   "A Day Off." *Family Herald*, 1 July 1936, pp. 20-21. Adapted for
         AWP, pt. 3, chaps. 1-4.

Stories Found Only in Scrapbooks and Story Collections

This list includes stories for which further bibliographical identification has
not been found. "Rpt." before a story collection abbreviation indicates that
the title has been found in the ledger list.

1048.   "Affair of the Shy Professor." *Springfield Republican*. Scbk. 8.

1049.   "Aunt Cyrilla's Christmas Basket." *Young People*. Scbk. 6.

1050.   "Brother Beware." *RY*.

1051.   "The Cheated Child." Rpt. *RY*.

1052.   "The Children's Garden." *Ladies' Journal*. Scbks. 6 and 11.

1053.   "A Commonplace Woman." Rpt. *RY*.

1054.   "A Dream Come True." *RY*.

1055.   "Ethel's Victory." *Illustrated Youth and Age*. Scbk. 2.

1056.   "Fancy's Fool." Rpt. *RY*.

1057.   "Here Comes the Bride." Rpt. *RY*.

1058.   "The Joseph's Christmas." *Sunday School Visitor*. Scbk. 6.

1059.   "The Letter Patricia Wrote." Scbk. 8.

1060.   "Lives of Elmview." *Days of Youth*. Scbk. 11.

1061.   "A Millionaire's Proposal." *Amulet Magazine*. Scbk. 4.

1062.   "Miss Cordelia's Accommodation." *American Young People*. Scbk.
         6.

1063.   "Mrs. Lawrence's White Rose." *Young People*. Scbk. 6.

1064.   "Nan." Scbk. 12.

1065.   "Old Lady Lloyd." Rpt. *CA*.

1066.   "One Mother's Opinions." *Ladies' Journal*. Scbk. 6.

1067.   "Penelope Struts Her Theories." *RY.*

1068.   "The Penningtons' Girl." *Ladies' Journal.* Scbk. 1.

1069.   "The Pot and the Kettle." *RY.*

1070.   "The Powers That Wait." *Bluenose.* Scbk. 1.

1071.   "The Reconciliation." *RY.*

1072.   "Retribution." *RY.*

1073.   "The Road to Yesterday." Rpt. *RY.*

1074.   "Rosamond's Opportunity." *Days of Youth.* Scbk. 11.

1075.   "St. Valentine to the Rescue." *People's Magazine.* Scbk. 4.

1076.   "Spotty." *Household Guest.* Scbk. 2.

1077.   "The Springhill Picnic." *Young People.* Scbk. 12.

1078.   "A Thanksgiving Partnership." *Family Herald.* Scbk. 1.

1079.   "The Touch of Fate." *Unique Monthly.* Scbk. 6.

1080.   "Trouble in the Bend Choir." *Household Guest.* Scbk. 6.

1081.   "The Twins Pretend." Rpt. *RY.*

1082.   "Two Women." *Household Guest.* Scbk. 1.

1083.   "Where There Is a Will There Is a Way." Scbk. 5.

1084.   "Why Faith Spoke First." *Household Guest.* Scbk. 6.

1085.   "Why Mr. Cropper Changed His Mind." *Household Guest.* Scbk. 6.

1086.   "Winnie's Happy Days." *Nova Scotia Observer.* Scbk. 3.

1087.   "The Worst Girl in School." *Days of Youth.* Scbk. 11.

Unverified Ledger Titles

The following titles appear in LMM's ledger list of stories, but no further bibliographic details have been found:

1088.   "An Affair of Honor."

1089.   "Bertha's New Dress."

1090.   "The Biters Bit."

1091.   "The Bloom of May."

1092.   "Bobby's Picnic."

1093.   "By Proxy."

1094.   "The Cats of Tansy Patch."

1095.   "Christmas at Little Red House."

1096.   "Christmas Denials of [illegible]."

1097.   "Coco."

1098.   "A Counsel of Perfection" (probably chap. 11 of *MM*).

1099.   "Elsie's Necklace."

1100.   "The First of April."

1101.   "For the Good of Antony."

1102.   "Ghost at Barclay's."

1103.   "Gyp."

1104.   "Her Satanic Majesty."

1105.   "Her Triumph."

1106.   "Hill 'o Winds."

1107.   "The Home of Her Mother."

1108.   "House Party."

1109.   "How It Came to Pass" (probably chap. 19 of *MM*).

1110.   "Ingleside Stories" (8 separate entries).

1111.   "The Interception of Elizabeth."

1112.   "Janet's Rebellion."

1113.   "Janie's Bouquet."

1114.   "Jean's Party."

1115.   "Jim's House."

1116.   "The Law of Necessity."

1117.   "Leslie's Mother."

1118.   "The Lost MSS."

1119.   "Maggie's Kilter."

1120.   "The Matchmaker."

1121.   "Miriam's Choice."

1122.   "The Mirror."

1123.   "Miss C's Encore."

1124.   "Miss M's Rose Jar."

1125.   "Miss Prissy."

1126.   "Miss S's Caller."

1127.   "Miss Steinmetz' Article."

1128.   "A Needed Lesson."

1129.   "Neighbors at Tansy Patch."

1130.   "The New Girl."

1131.   "A Night Hunt."

1132.   "One Clear Call" (probably chap. 15 of *MM*).

1133.   "One of Us" (probably chap. 16 of *MM*).

1134.   "Our Christmas Divine."

1135.   "Our Hired Man."

1136.   "The Patch on the Sole."

1137.   "Patty's Scarf."

1138.   "Peter."

1139.   "Philippa."

1140.   "The Pineapple Apron."

1141.   "The Punishment of Billy" (probably chap. 20 of *MM*).

1142.   "Red Ink or --" (probably chap. 18 of *MM*).

1143.   "Roy's Chum."

1144.   "The Royal Family."

1145.   "Sam Scudder."

1146.   "The Schoolmaster's Bride."

1147.   "The Self Denial of Edith."

1148.   "South Hill Maples."

1149.   "Tomorrow Comes."

1150.   "Uncle L's Horn."

1151.   "You Can't Be up to Them."

POEMS

The poems are listed by the first known date of publication; frequently a poem was published in several periodicals, and the poem is listed under the date of the first verified publication. The reference is given to the scrapbook source, as was done for "Stories," above. As well, the first words of the poem are quoted. A separate listing is given of poems reprinted in *The Watchman* but for which no other source is known, apart from their presence in either the scrapbooks or on the ledger list. Similarly, a separate listing is given of the poems found only in the scrapbooks or in the manuscript "The Blythes Are Quoted" (BQ), for which no confirmed bibliographical details have been found. A final listing gives all the titles from LMM's ledger list which have not been found in print.

1152.   "On Cape Le Force." *Daily Patriot*, 26 Nov. 1890, p. 1. Scbk. 7. "One evening when . . ."

1153.   "June!" *Daily Patriot*, 12 June 1891, p. 4. Scbk. 7. " 'Wake up,' the robins . . ."

1154.   "Farewell." *The Saskatchewan*, 2 Sept. 1891, p. 1. Scbk. 6. "Sunset: and all the . . ."

1155.   "The Wreck of the 'Marco-Polo' -- 1883." *Daily Patriot*, 29 Aug. 1892. Scbk. 7. " 'Twas a wild day! . . ."

1156.   "The Last Prayer." *College Record*, Mar. 1894. Scbk. 7. "The carnage of the . . ."

1157. "The Violet's Spell." *Ladies' World*, July 1894, p. 5. Scbk. 7. "Only a violet in the . . ."

1158. "On the Gulf Shore." By Maud Eglington [sic]. *Ladies' Journal*, Feb. 1895, p. 2. Scbk. 7. "Lap softly on the . . ."

1159. "When the Apple-Blossoms Blow." By Maud Cavendish. *Ladies' Journal*, June 1895. Also in *American Messenger*, May 1910, p. 83. Scbk. 7. See also item 1211. "When the wheat . . . "

1160. "The Land of Some Day." *College Observer*, Apr. 1896. Scbk. 7. "Across the river of . . ."

1161. "Fisher Lassies." By M.L. Cavendish. *Youth's Companion*, 30 July 1896, p. 388. Scbk. 7. "The wind blows up . . ."

1162. "I Wonder." *Ladies' Journal*, Sept. 1896. Scbk. 7. "The sun has set . . ."

1163. "The Apple-Picking Time." By M.L. Cavendish. *Golden Days*, 3 Oct. 1896, p. 728. Also [anon.] in *Farm Journal*, Oct. 1901, p. 314; and in *East and West* [1905]. Scbks. 7 and 8 (3). "When September's purple asters . . ."

1164. "Home from Town." *American Agriculturist*, 28 Nov. 1896, p. 508. Scbk. 7. "There, I can draw . . ."

1165. "The New Moon." *Ladies' Journal*, Jan. 1897. Scbk. 7. "The air is dusk . . ."

1166. "Riding to Church." *American Agriculturist*, 20 Feb. 1897, p. 250. Also in *New England Homestead*, 20 Feb. 1897, p. 250; and in *Zion's Herald*, 5 May 1915, p. 558. Scbk. 7. "Jim, Hal and I sat at . . ."

1167. "The Gable Window." *Ladies' Journal*, Apr. 1897. Scbk. 7. "It opened on a world . . ."

1168. "Love and Lacework." *Ladies' Journal*, May 1897. Scbk. 7. "Marion there by the . . ."

1169. "Apple-Blossoms." *Ladies' World*, May 1897, p. 5. Scbk. 7. "White as the snows . . ."

1170. "In Haying Time." *Ladies' World*, July 1897, p. 5. Scbk. 7. "Wide meadows under . . ."

1171. "The Marked Door." *Ladies' Journal*, Aug. 1897. Scbk. 7. "Long ago, when the . . ."

1172. "At the Dance." *Ladies' Journal*, Sept. 1897. Scbk. 7. "Rythmic [sic] beating . . ."

1173. "When I Go Home." *Congregationalist*, 11 Nov. 1897, p. 693. Also in *Holland's Magazine*, Jan. 1913, p. 16. Scbk. 7. "When I go home -- a simple spell . . ."

1174. "If Love Should Come." *Munsey's*, Dec. 1897, p. 369. Scbk. 2. "If love should come / I wonder if my . . ."

1175. "Wanted -- A Little Girl." *Portland Transcript*, 15 Dec. 1897, p. 437. Scbk. 7. "Wanted -- a little girl / Of the good old-fashioned . . ."

1176. "An Old Letter." *The Home*, Jan. 1898. Also as "The Old Letter," *Children's Visitor*, 12 Oct. 1910, p. 5. Scbks. 7 and 8. "I found it to-day . . ."

1177. "A Country Boy." *Golden Days*, 8 Jan. 1898, p. 120. See also item 1571. Scbk. 7. "That's just what I am . . ."

1178. "Dressing for the Ball." *Family Story Paper*, 26 Feb. 1898, p. 8. Scbk. 7. "Marguerite to the ball . . ."

1179. "In Church." *Ladies' Journal*, Mar. 1898, p. 26. Scbk. 7. "The wind blew in . . ."

1180. "Wading in the Brook." *Portland Transcript*, 27 Apr. 1898, p. 38. Also in *Zion's Herald*, 15 July 1915, p. 374. Scbk. 7. "Say, Jim, do you . . ."

1181. "The Tree Lovers." *Ladies' Journal*, May 1898. Scbk. 2. "They grew in the fringe . . ."

1182. "The Perfume of Roses." *Family Story Paper*, 7 May 1898, p. 8. Scbk. 7. "Float back on the . . ."

1183. "The Afterlight." *Congregationalist*, June 1898. Scbk. 2. "When the sun has . . ."

1184. "The Poplars at the Gate." *Pilgrim of Our Lady of the Martyrs*, June 1898, p. 161. Scbk. 2. "Softly they murmur . . ."

1185. "I've Something to Tell You, Sweet." *Family Story Paper*, 30 July 1898, p. 3. Scbk. 7. "I've something to tell you, sweet, / That only you may . . ."

1186. "In Untrod Woods." *Churchman*, 10 Sept. 1898, p. 355. Also in *East and West*, 10 July 1909, p. 217. Scbk. 2. "Lonely, think you . . ."

1187.   "The Pot of Gold at the Rainbow's End." By S. M. Montgomery. *Portland Transcript*, 28 Sept. 1898, p. 305. Scbk. 7. "The sun shone out . . ."

1188.   "Night in the Pastures." *New England Farmer*, Oct. 1898. Scbk. 2. "The night wind steals . . ."

1189.   "The Song of the Winds." *Ladies' Journal*, Oct. 1898. Scbk. 7. "From the purple gates . . ."

1190.   "Irrevocable." *Congregationalist*, Nov. 1898. Scbk. 2. "Once on a time I spoke . . ."

1191.   "Forever." *Family Story Paper*, 12 Nov. 1898, p. 6. See also item 1502. Scbk. 2. "She sings a song . . ."

1192.   "Good-by." *Family Story Paper*, 10 Dec. 1898, p. 7. Scbk. 2. " 'Tis not the first time . . ."

1193.   "Christmas Morning." *American Agriculturist*, 24 Dec. 1898, p. 675. Also in *New England Homestead*, 24 Dec. 1898, p. 675; and in *Orange Judd Farmer*, Dec. 1899. Scbk. 2. "I tell you, our house . . ."

1194.   "The Light in Mother's Eyes." *Family Story Paper*, 31 Dec. 1898, p. 8. Also in *Farm Journal*, Jan. 1909, p. 35. Scbk. 2. "Dear beacon of my . . ."

1195.   "When the Fishing Boats Come In." *Weekly Bouquet*, Jan. 1899. Also in *East and West*, 1 Oct. 1910, p. 317. Scbks. 2 and 8. "The sea dusks shrouds . . ."

1196.   "The Popular Boy." *Good Cheer*, Apr. 1899. Scbk. 2. "A sunny smile has he . . ."

1197.   "An April Brook." *Home Guard*, Apr. 1899. Scbk. 2. "Full-fed from melted . . ."

1198.   "Up in the Poplars." *Portland Transcript*, 26 Apr. 1899, p. 39. Scbk. 2. "Up in the poplars altogether / Five of . . ."

1199.   "Sweet Summer Days." *Family Story Paper*, 27 May 1899, p. 5. Also in *Zion's Herald*, 14 Jan. 1914, p. 47. Scbk. 2. "Sweet summer days / When purple-misted . . ."

1200.   "Buttercups." By Maud Cavendish. *Mayflower*, July 1899, p. 292. Also in *Farm Journal*, May 1910, p. 311. Scbk. 7. "Like showers of gold . . ."

1201. "Blueberry Hill." *Ladies' World*, Aug. 1899, p. 4. Scbk. 2. "Warm blow the winds . . ."

1202. "Rain in the Woods." *Sports Afield*, Aug. 1899. Scbk. 2. "Just a hush among . . ."

1203. "The Trysting Spring." *Portland Transcript*, 2 Aug. 1899, p. 206. Scbk. 2. "I pause upon its placid . . ."

1204. "When the Fishing Boats Go Out." *Youth's Companion*, 14 Sept. 1899, p. 452. Rpt. *Watchman*. Scbk. 2. "When the pearly skies . . ."

1205. "When She Was Here." By M. M. *Family Story Paper*, 7 Oct. 1899, p. 7. Scbk. 2. "When she was here / Earth smiled . . ."

1206. "The Golden Dawn." *Messenger of the Sacred Heart*, Nov. 1899, p. 1041. Scbk. 2. "Silent arises the . . ."

1207. "When Ma's Away." *New England Homestead*, 11 Nov. 1899, p. 493. Also in *Vick's Magazine [Home & Flowers]*, Sept. 1903, p. 20; and in *Waverley Magazine*, 3 Oct. 1903, p. 221. Scbk. 2. "Tell you what, . . ."

1208. "A Winter Dawn." *Munsey's*, Dec. 1899, p. 432. Rpt. *Watchman*. Scbk. 2. "Above the marge of . . ."

1209. "A Wonderful Garden." *Good Cheer*, Jan. 1900, p. 4. Scbk. 2. "There's a wonderful garden I know of . . ."

1210. "Assurance." *Family Story Paper*, 10 Mar. 1900, p. 8. "Well, we have parted . . ."

1211. "When the Apple Blossoms Blow." *Ladies' World*, May 1900, p. 5. See also item 1159. Scbk. 2. "The winds are sweet . . ."

1212. "Night Watches." *Family Story Paper*, 28 July 1900, p. 8. Scbk. 2. "Oh, darkness and . . ."

1213. "Could We But Know." *Union Signal*, 9 Aug. 1900, p. 467. Scbk. 2. "Could we but know how often . . ."

1214. "At Sunset Hour." *Messenger of the Sacred Heart*, Sept. 1900, p. 817. Scbk. 2. "From out unbarred . . ."

1215. "The Prisoner." *Portland Transcript*, 10 Oct. 1900, p. 326. Also, illus. A. Lismer, in *Maclean's*, Mar. 1916, p. 41. Rpt. *Watchman*. Scbks. 2 and 5. "I lash and writhe . . ."

1216.   "Golden Rod." *Youth's Companion*, 25 Oct. 1900, p. 526. Rpt. *Watchman* as "In the Days of the Golden Rod." Scbk. 2. "Across the meadow . . ."

1217.   "The Only Way." *Good Cheer*, Jan. 1901, p. 2. See also item 1608. "So you want to learn . . ."

1218.   "Requiem." *Sports Afield*, Jan. 1901, p. 13. See also item 1370. Scbk. 2. "To-night, when the . . ."

1219.   "The Mayflower's Message." *Mayflower*, Mar. 1901, p. 153. Scbk. 2. "Here, on the gray old . . ."

1220.   "Your Influence." By Joyce Cavendish. *Family Story Paper*, 2 Mar. 1901, p. 6. Scbk. 2. "I met you -- and my . . ."

1221.   "A Little Soldier." *Sunday School Advocate*, 23 Mar. 1901, p. 45. Also in *Sunday School Advocate*, 4 Oct. 1902, p. 157. Scbk. 1. "My blue-eyed lad . . ."

1222.   "Comparisons." *Munsey's*, Apr. 1901, p. 16. Rpt. *Watchman* as "My 'longshore Lass." Scbk. 1. "Far in the gracious . . ."

1223.   "Come, Rest Awhile." *Home and Flowers*, June 1901, p. 13. Rpt. *Watchman*. Scbk. 1. "Come, rest awhile, and let us idly . . ."

1224.   "A Duet." *Sports Afield*, Aug. 1901, p. 126. Also in *Zion's Herald*, 23 Aug. 1916, p. 1066. Scbk. 1. "The pines bent down to . . ."

1225.   "Harbor Dawn." *Criterion*, Aug. 1901, p. 8. Also in *Current Literature*, Sept. 1901, p. 288. Rpt. *Watchman*. Scbk. 1. "There's a hush and . . ."

1226.   "The Two Guests." *Messenger of the Sacred Heart* [Supplement], Aug. 1901, p. 246. Scbk. 6. "Came on a time . . ."

1227.   "Come Where Violets Blow." By Joyce Cavendish. *Family Story Paper*, 24 Aug. 1901, p. 5. Scbk. 2. "Come where violets blow . . ."

1228.   "The Cross-Lots Road." *Children's Visitor*, 25 Aug. 1901, p. 7. Scbk. 1. "They do not know its . . ."

1229.   "An Old-Fashioned Woman." *Congregationalist*, 31 Aug. 1901, p. 314. Also in *Western Christian Advocate*, 2 Oct. 1901, p. 14; in *Christian Advocate*, 7 Aug. 1902, p. 1278; in *Morning Star*, 4 Sept. 1902, p. 567; and in *Western Christian Advocate*, 27 June 1903, p. 15. Scbk. 1. "No clever, brilliant . . ."

1230.   "Too Late." *Ram's Horn*, 31 Aug. 1901, p. 6. Scbk. 6. "When she was dead . . ."

1231.   "A Country Lane." [anon.] *Farm Journal*, Sept 1901, p. 276. Scbk.
        1. "Between the fences it . . ."

1232.   "The Gulls." *Criterion*, Sept. 1901, p. 30. Also in *Waverley Maga-
        zine*, 19 July 1902, p. 38. Rpt. *Watchman*. Scbk. 6 (2). "Soft is
        the sky . . ."

1233.   "Three Days." *National*, Sept. 1901, pp. 688-89. Scbk. 1. "Three
        days have I in my heart . . ."

1234.   "Southernwood." *Zion's Herald*, 4 Sept. 1901, p. 1136. Scbk. 1.
        "What is it you have . . ."

1235.   "The Words I Did Not Say." *Ram's Horn*, 14 Sept. 1901, p. 3. Also
        in *Advocate and Guardian*, 1 Oct. 1901, p. 289; and in *Classmate*,
        14 Dec. 1901, p. 395: "from *Ram's Horn*." Scbk. 1. "Many a word
        my tongue . . ."

1236.   "Do Not Forget." *American Messenger*, Oct. 1901, p. 154. Also in
        Christian Advocate, 15 May 1902, p. 771. Scbk. 1. "Do not forget
        as you go on your way . . ."

1237.   "Worth While." *Advocate and Guardian*, 1 Oct. 1901, p. 289. Also
        in *American Messenger*, Sept. 1906, p. 174. Scbk. 8. "It is worth
        while / To live in . . ."

1238.   "The Cure of the Fields." *Sunday School Times*, 4 Oct. 1901, p.
        638. Scbk. 1. "I went adown the great . . ."

1239.   "The Four Rules." *Children's Visitor*, 6 Oct. 1901, p. 2. Scbk. 1.
        "Little student, with . . ."

1240.   "I Have Buried My Dead." *Family Story Paper*, 12 Oct. 1901, p. 6.
        Scbk. 1. "I have buried my dead / And so I come . . ."

1241.   "A Smile." By Joyce Cavendish. *Family Story Paper*, 26 Oct. 1901,
        p. 5. Scbk. 1. "What is a smile? . . ."

1242.   "Sunrise along Shore." *Youth's Companion*, 28 Nov. 1901, p. 630.
        Rpt. *Watchman*. Scbk. 1. "Athwart the harbor . . ."

1243.   "Two Loves." *Canadian Magazine*, Dec. 1901, p. 147. Rpt. *Watch-
        man*. Scbk. 6. "One said, 'Lo, I would . . ."

1244.   "The Quest of Lazy-Lad." *Congregationalist*, 7 Dec. 1901, p. 905.
        Also in *Ram's Horn*, 22 Mar. 1902, p. 12; in *Christian Advocate*, 1
        May 1902, p. 694; in *Presbyterian*, 13 June 1903, p. 765; and in
        Advocate and Guardian, 1 Feb. 1904, p. 39. Scbk. 1. "Have you
        heard the tale . . ."

1245. "Harbor Sunset." *Ainslee's*, Jan. 1902, p. 490. Also in *Current Literature*, Mar. 1902, p. 321; in *Waverley Magazine*, 8 Mar. 1902, p. 149; and in *Christian Advocate*, 23 June 1904, p. 1021. Scbk. 6. "Beyond the bar the sun . . ."

1246. "A New Day." *Good Cheer*, Jan. 1902, p. 4. Scbk. 6. "Through the wide-open . . ."

1247. "To My Enemy." *Smart Set*, Jan. 1902, p. 92. Rpt. *Watchman*. Scbk. 6. "Let those who will . . ."

1248. "The Star thro' the Pines." By Joyce Cavendish. *Family Story Paper*, 4 Jan. 1902, p. 5. Scbk. 1. "White the moonbeams' . . ."

1249. "The Law." *Christian Advocate*, 9 Jan. 1902, p. 55. Scbk. 6. "Who stoops to lift . . ."

1250. "What Are We Here For?" *Forward*, 25 Jan. 1902, p. 29. Also in *American Messenger*, Apr. 1915, p. 76. Scbk. 1. "What are we here for, you and I . . ."

1251. "Wanted -- A Boy." *Good Cheer*, Feb. 1902, p. 8. Scbk. 6. "Wanted -- a boy who is pure and . . ."

1252. "When Ted's Away." *Ram's Horn*, 8 Feb. 1902, p. 3. Scbk. 6. "When Teddy has gone . . ."

1253. "In Twilight Land." *Churchman*, 22 Feb. 1902, p. 249. Scbk. 6. "In twilight land there are beautiful . . ."

1254. "Another Legend." *Home and Flowers*, Mar. 1902, p. 12. Scbk. 6. "Beside the sepulchre . . ."

1255. "The Sea-Spirit." *Criterion*, Apr. 1902, p. 12. Rpt. *Watchman*. Scbk. 1. "I smile o'er the . . ."

1256. "Milking Time." *Farm Journal*, May 1902, p. 161. Scbk. 6. "Dusking fields that . . ."

1257. "In Planting Time." *Children's Visitor*, 15 June 1902, p. 7. Scbk. 6. "When the winter snows . . ."

1258. "Grandmother's Garden." *Zion's Herald*, 23 July 1902, p. 942. Scbk. 6. " 'Twas the dearest spot . . ."

1259. "In August Days." *Criterion*, Aug. 1902, p. 16. Scbk. 6. "Soft blows the breath . . ."

1260. "It Is Best." *Boys and Girls* [Aug. 1902]. Scbk. 6. "It is best, my laddie, with . . ."

1261. "What Know We?" *Churchman.* Also in *First Baptist Monthly,* and in *Christian Advocate,* 21 Aug. 1902, p. 1336: "reprinted from *First Baptist Monthly.*" Scbk. 6. "What know we of the gnawing grief . . ."

1262. "The Good-Night Angel." *American Agriculturist.* Also in *Christian Endeavor World,* 4 Sept. 1902, p. 947; in *King's Own,* 11 July 1903, p. 110; and in *Sunday School Advocate,* 29 Aug. 1903, p. 342. Scbk. 8. "The good-night angel comes at eve . . ."

1263. "All Aboard for Dreamland." *Farm Journal,* Oct. 1902, p. 333. Scbk. 6. "The stars are a-wink . . ."

1264. "Indian Summer." *Farm Journal,* Oct. 1902, p. 305. Scbk. 6. "In the sun-warm valleys . . ."

1265. "The Best Way." *Good Cheer,* Oct. 1902, p. 40. Scbk. 6. "When promises are . . ."

1266. "Invitation." *Christian Advocate,* 2 Oct. 1902, p. 1577. Scbk. 6. "Lay now aside all toil . . ."

1267. "The Lullaby." *Classmate,* 11 Oct. 1902, p. 325. Scbk. 6. "To-day I walked on the . . ."

1268. "The Home-Sick Flower's Soliloquy." *Sports Afield,* Nov. 1902, p. 406. Scbk. 6. "They brought me to . . ."

1269. "Shall I Remember?" By Joyce Cavendish. *Family Story Paper,* 1 Nov. 1902, p. 8. Scbk. 6. "When on my spirit eyes . . ."

1270. "Coasting Song." *Good Cheer,* Dec. 1902, p. 46. Scbk. 6. "Adown the gleaming . . ."

1271. "The Christmas Night." *Ladies' World,* Dec. 1902, p. 5. Rpt. *Watchman.* Scbk. 6. "Wrapped was the world . . ."

1272. "The Wind." *Era,* Jan. 1903, p. 98. Rpt. *Watchman.* See also item 1633. Scbk. 6. "O wind! what saw you . . ."

1273. "Omega." *Waverley Magazine,* 31 Jan. 1903, p. 68. Scbk. 6. "I am to die to-night! . . ."

1274. "The Way, the Truth and the Life." *Congregationalist,* 7 Feb. 1903, p. 202. Scbk. 6. "He is the Way. Through . . ."

1275. "Farewell and Welcome." By Joyce Cavendish. *Family Story Paper,* 14 Feb. 1903, p. 8. "Farewell, Old Year! . . ."

1276.   "If I Had Known." *Zion's Herald*, 18 Feb. 1903, p. 206. Scbk. 6. "If I had known how much of lasting . . ."

1277.   "A Boy's Sister." *Children's Visitor*, 22 Feb. 1903, p. 7. Scbk. 6. "Of all the girls . . ."

1278.   "The New Day." *Classmate*, 7 Mar. 1903, p. 77. Also in *Wellspring*. Scbk. 6 (2). "The day lies open . . ."

1279.   "Sis." *American Agriculturist*, 14 Mar. 1903, p. 326. Also in *New England Homestead*, 14 Mar. 1903, p. 318. Scbk. 6. "Sis is just the girl . . ."

1280.   "The Old Church." *Zion's Herald*, 29 Apr. 1903, p. 526. Scbk. 6. "I'm free to say there's . . ."

1281.   "The Brown Seed." *Pilgrim Teacher*, May 1903, p. 254. Scbk. 6. "Tiny and brown and . . ."

1282.   "In Port." *Era*, May 1903, p. 468. Rpt. *Watchman*. Scbk. 6. "Out of the fires of . . ."

1283.   "Failure." *Ram's Horn*, 16 May 1903, p. 3. Scbk. 6. "I would not count it . . ."

1284.   "The Gray Silk Gown." By Joyce Cavendish. *Family Story Paper*, 23 May 1903, p. 8. Scbk. 6. "Folded away in the . . ."

1285.   "While I May." *Children's Visitor*, 24 May 1903, p. 7. Scbk. 6. "I must share my joy . . ."

1286.   "In the Fernland." *Churchman*, 6 June 1903, p. 767. Also in *Advocate and Guardian*, 15 June 1903, p. 179. Scbk. 6. "A bluebird is perched . . ."

1287.   "In Lovers' Lane." *Delineator*, July 1903, p. 16. Rpt. *Watchman*. Scbk. 6. "I know a place for . . ."

1288.   "A Prairie Lake." *Sports Afield*, July 1903, p. 10. Scbk. 6. "Across it blow the . . ."

1289.   "Trouble in the Kitchen." *American Agriculturist*, 25 July 1903, p. 78. Also in *New England Homestead*, 25 July 1903, p. 78. Scbk. 6. "The dinner was all . . ."

1290.   "A Little Sin." *Ram's Horn*, 25 July 1903, p. 3. Also in *Advocate and Guardian*, 2 Apr. 1906, p. 101: "from *Ram's Horn.*" Scbk. 6. "Oh, when it came it was . . ."

1291.   "The Brothers." *Children's Visitor*, 26 July 1903, p. 6. Scbk. 6. "Work and wait are . . ."

1292.   "Little Words." *American Messenger*, Aug. 1903, p. 158. Scbk. 6. "Just a little word . . ."

1293.   "The Old Garden." *Home and Flowers*. Also in *American Thresherman*, Aug. 1903, p. 56; and in *Zion's Herald*, 1 June 1910, p. 687. See also item 1475. Scbk. 8. "Here are the sweet old . . ."

1294.   "A Summer Day." *Criterion*, Aug. 1903, p. 23. Rpt. *Watchman*. Scbk. 6. "The dawn laughs out . . ."

1295.   "Down Stream." *Era*, Sept. 1903, p. 230. Rpt. *Watchman*. Scbk. 3. "Comrades, up! Let us . . ."

1296.   "How Easy." *American Messenger*, Sept. 1903, p. 168. Scbk. 6. "How easy it is to say a . . ."

1297.   "The Charm." By Joyce Cavendish. *Family Story Paper*, 19 Sept. 1903, p. 6. Scbk. 6. "The day was a glory . . ."

1298.   "Unconquered." *Christian Advocate*, 15 Oct. 1903, p. 1666. Scbk. 3. "It may not be for me . . ."

1299.   "My Library." *American Agriculturist*, 21 Nov. 1903, p. 450. Also in *New England Homestead*, 21 Nov. 1903, p. 454. Scbk. 6. "It is small and dim . . ."

1300.   "Twilight in an Old Farmhouse." *Congregationalist*, 21 Nov. 1903, p. 732. Rpt. *Watchman* as "In an Old Farmhouse." Scbk. 6. "Outside the afterlight . . ."

1301.   "Stick To It." *Good Cheer*, Dec. 1903, p. 47. Also in *Advocate and Guardian*, 16 Nov. 1903, p. 343: "reprinted from *Good Cheer*." "Stick to it . . ."

1302.   "The First Snowfall." *Sports Afield*, Dec. 1903, p. 499. Scbk. 3. "A bitter chill has . . ."

1303.   "Let Us Forget." *Children's Visitor*, 27 Dec. 1903, p. 1. Scbk. 3. "Some things 'twere wiser . . ."

1304.   "The Winter Wind." *Farm Journal*, Jan. 1904, p. 449. Scbk. 6. "I am the gladdest of . . ."

1305.   "The Choice." By Joyce Cavendish. *Family Story Paper*, 9 Jan. 1904, p. 7. See also item 1346. Scbk. 6. "What rose shall I . . ."

1306.   "If I Were Home." *Waverley Magazine*, 16 Jan. 1904, pp. 46-47. Scbk. 6. "If I were home on those dear green . . ."

1307.   "A Day of Days." *Era*, Feb. 1904, p. 160. Scbk. 3. "All other days were . . ."

1308.   "An Afternoon Nap." *New Idea Woman's Magazine*, Mar. 1904, p. 47. Scbk. 8. "Bless his sleepy . . ."

1309.   "Jealousy." By Joyce Cavendish. *Family Story Paper*, 5 Mar. 1904, p. 5. Scbk. 3. "I'm jealous of the wind . . ."

1310.   "The Upland Hill." *Zion's Herald*, 6 Apr. 1904, p. 417. Scbk. 8. "I know a path our . . ."

1311.   "The Old Mirror." *New England Magazine*, May 1904, p. 384. Scbk. 3. "Dim-gleaming in the . . ."

1312.   "A Life and a Living." *Children's Visitor*, 8 May 1904, p. 2. Scbk. 3. "A life and a living are two different . . ."

1313.   "The Time of the Clover Blossom." *Farm Journal*, June 1904, p. 223. Scbk. 3. "The wind from the . . ."

1314.   "On the Bridge." By Joyce Cavendish. *Family Story Paper*, 11 June 1904, p. 5. Scbk. 3. "She's standing on the . . ."

1315.   "Vacation Song." *Boys' World*, 25 June 1904, p. 5. See also item 1367. Scbk. 3. "We've put our books . . ."

1316.   "Midnight in Camp." *Criterion*, July 1904, p. 41. Also in *Waverley Magazine*, June 1905, p. 111. Rpt. *Watchman*. Scbk. 8. "Night in the . . ."

1317.   "When the Frogs are Singing." By Joyce Cavendish. *Family Story Paper*, 2 July 1904, p. 5. Scbk. 3. "Softly across the . . ."

1318.   "Pastures on the Hill." *Classmate*, 9 July 1904, p. 220. Scbk. 8. "In the long days of . . ."

1319.   "Garden Talk." *Classmate*. Also in *Sunday School Advocate*, 23 July 1904, p. 292. Scbk. 3. "I heard the blossoms . . ."

1320.   "The Pond Pasture." *Zion's Herald*, 27 July 1904, p. 944. Scbk. 8. "It is purely fair . . ."

1321.   "The Old Red Barn." *American Agriculturist*, 30 July 1904, p. 93. Also in *New England Homestead*, 30 July 1904, p. 93. Scbk. 8. "There's an old red barn . . ."

1322.   "Dorothy's Garden." *What To Eat*, Aug. 1904, p. 72. Scbk. 8.
        "Dorothy's garden is shady and sweet . . ."

1323.   "Watering the Cows." *Children's Visitor*, 7 Aug. 1904, p. 7. Scbk.
        8. "Every night at the end . . ."

1324.   "Rain Song." *Forward.* Also in *East and West*, 27 Aug. 1904, p.
        280; and in *Christian Advocate*, 1 Sept. 1904, p. 1418. Scbk. 3.
        "The summer drought is . . ."

1325.   "The Hill Maples." *Zion's Herald*, 31 Aug. 1904, p. 1089. Rpt.
        Watchman. Scbk. 8. "Here on a hill . . ."

1326.   "Fulfilment." *Munsey's*, Sept. 1904, p. 830. Scbk. 8. "She dreamed
        of many . . ."

1327.   "An Old Love Letter." *American Agriculturist*, 10 Sept. 1904, p.
        212. Also in *New England Homestead*, 10 Sept. 1904, p. 212. Scbk.
        8. "I found it as I searched . . ."

1328.   "Air Castles." By Joyce Cavendish. *Family Story Paper*, 24 Sept.
        1904, p. 5. Scbk. 8. "When I am tired . . ."

1329.   "Night in the Country." *Farm Journal*, Oct. 1904, p. 332. Scbk. 8.
        "In the city the night . . ."

1330.   "November Dusk." *Farm Journal*, Nov. 1904, p. 372. Scbk. 8. "A
        weird and dreamy . . ."

1331.   "The Purple Hills of Far Away." *Sports Afield*, Nov. 1904, p. 395.
        Scbk. 8. "They shut us round . . ."

1332.   "Off to the Fishing Ground." *Youth's Companion*, 3 Nov. 1904, p.
        556. Also in *East and West*, 29 July 1905, p. 238. Rpt. *Watchman.*
        Scbk. 8. "There's a piping wind . . ."

1333.   "The Fir Lane." *Bick's Magazine.* Also in *Vick's Magazine [Home
        and Flowers]*, Dec. 1904, p. 5; and in *Zion's Herald*, 6 Sept. 1916, p.
        1137. Scbk. 8. "We lingered there . . ."

1334.   "The New Year's Book." *Children's Visitor*, 1 Jan. 1905, p. 7. Scbk.
        8. "The book of the New Year . . ."

1335.   "Winter Dusk in the Firs." *Zion's Herald*, 11 Jan. 1905, p. 46. Scbk.
        8. "Afar there is a fair . . ."

1336.   "Snowshoe Song." *American Agriculturist*, 14 Jan. 1905, p. 46.
        Also in *New England Homestead*, 14 Jan. 1905, p. 52. Scbk. 8.
        "Heigh-ho for a tramp . . ."

1337.   "In Winter Woods." *Zion's Herald*, 1 Feb. 1905, p. 142. Scbk. 8.
        "When summer went away . . ."

1338.   "The Three." *Sunday School Times*. Also in *Advocate and Guardi-
        an*, 1 Feb. 1905, p. 33. Scbk. 3. "One walked the ways . . ."

1339.   "A Garden." *American Messenger*, Mar. 1905, p. 46. Scbk. 8. "I
        know a garden on an . . ."

1340.   "At Sundown." *What To Eat*, Mar. 1905, p. 95. Also in *Zion's Her-
        ald*, 13 Oct. 1915, p. 1292. Scbk. 8. "The hills are scarfed . . ."

1341.   "The Name Tree." By Joyce Cavendish. *Family Story Paper*, 11
        Mar. 1905, p. 5. "Tall and green at the . . ."

1342.   "The Water Nymph." By Joyce Cavendish. *Family Story Paper*, 15
        Apr. 1905, p. 5. Scbk. 8. "Here on glimmering waves . . ."

1343.   "Rain along Shore." *Ladies' World*, May 1905, p. 5. Rpt. *Watch-
        man*. Scbk. 8. "Wan white mists upon . . ."

1344.   "In an Old Town Garden." *Christian Endeavor World*, 4 May 1905,
        p. 607. Rpt. *Watchman*. Scbk. 8. "Shut from the clamor . . ."

1345.   "Song of the Mountain Cascade." *Classmate*, 13 May 1905, p. 149.
        Scbk. 8. "I was born the where [sic] . . ."

1346.   "The Choice." *Sunday School Times*, 20 May 1905, p. 277. Rpt.
        Watchman. See also item 1305. Scbk. 8. "Life, come to me . . ."

1347.   "I Wonder if She Knows." By Joyce Cavendish. *Family Story
        Paper*, 10 June 1905, p. 3. Scbk. 8. "It's a year ago this . . ."

1348.   "When the Cowbells Ring." *American Agriculturist*, 22 July 1905,
        p. 76. Also in *New England Homestead*, 22 July 1905, p. 82. Scbk.
        8. "When drowsy sweet . . ."

1349.   "The Silent House." By Joyce Cavendish. *Family Story Paper*, 19
        Aug. 1905, p. 6. Scbk. 8. "Not a note of boyish . . ."

1350.   "A Summer Shower." *American Agriculturist*, 19 Aug. 1905, p. 153.
        Also in *New England Homestead*, 19 Aug. 1905, p. 161. Scbk. 8.
        "Sweet is the rain . . ."

1351.   "August Dower." *Zion's Herald*, 23 Aug. 1905, p. 1072. Scbk. 8. "I
        have the joy . . ."

1352.   "An Autumn Shower." *Zion's Herald*, 11 Oct. 1905, p. 1294. Scbk.
        8. "Upon the russet fringes . . ."

1353.   "The Love Potion." *Family Story Paper*, 20 Jan. 1906, p. 5. Scbk. 8. "By the temple's inner . . ."

1354.   "The Singer." *Ram's Horn*, 27 Jan. 1906, p. 3. Scbk. 8. "A song, a song of . . ."

1355.   "The Master Speaks." *Zion's Herald*, 31 Jan. 1906, p. 129. Also as "The Master Knows," *Springfield Republican*, 11 Feb. 1906, p. 22. Scbk. 8. "Art tired, My child? . . ."

1356.   "Twilight." *Everybody's*, Feb. 1906, p. 190. Rpt. *Watchman*. Scbk. 8. "From vales of dawn . . ."

1357.   "The Bridal." *Lippincott's*, Mar. 1906, p. 346. Rpt. *Watchman*. Scbk. 8. "Last night a pale . . ."

1358.   "The Call of the Winds." *Christian Endeavor World*, 8 Mar. 1906, p. 459. Rpt. *Watchman*. Scbk. 8. "Ho, come out with the . . ."

1359.   "To Phyllis." By Joyce Cavendish. *Family Story Paper*, 31 Mar. 1906, p. 7. "Love me, sweetheart . . ."

1360.   "My Pictures." *Farm Journal*, May 1906, p. 160. Scbk. 8. "My pictures? Why yes; I will . . ."

1361.   "When the Spring Calls." *Zion's Herald*, 9 May 1906, p. 590. Scbk. 8. "I weary of the hungry . . ."

1362.   "Work-with-a-Will and Lazy-bones." *King's Own*, 23 June 1906, p. 100. Scbk. 8. "Have you ever heard of . . ."

1363.   "My Legacy." *Zion's Herald*, 27 June 1906, p. 815. Rpt. *Watchman*. Scbk. 8. "My friend has gone . . ."

1364.   "Down in the Pastures." *Farm Journal*, July 1906, p. 234. Scbk. 8. "Down in the pastures, . . ."

1365.   "Midsummer." *Outing Magazine*, July 1906, p. 486. See also item 1509. Scbk. 8. "The world is in its . . ."

1366.   "In the Hayloft." *American Agriculturist*, 7 July 1906, p. 17. Also in *New England Homestead*, 7 July 1906, p. 17. Scbk. 8. "It's the jolliest spot . . ."

1367.   "Vacation Song." *Boys' World*, 7 July 1906, p. 8. See also item 1315. Scbk. 8. "School is ended and . . ."

1368.   "A Thanksgiving." *Zion's Herald*, 8 Aug. 1906, p. 1008. Scbk. 8. "Father, I thank Thee . . ."

1369.   "The Grumble Family." *King's Own*, 18 Aug. 1906, p. 132. Scbk. 8;
         BQ, pp. 400-401. "There's a family . . .

1370.   "Requiem." [anon.] *Farm Journal*, Sept. 1906, p. 282. Also in *Hol-
         land's Magazine*, Apr. 1913, p. 10a. See also item 1218. Scbk. 8.
         "Summer, the Summer is . . ."

1371.   "When Autumn Comes." *Zion's Herald*, 19 Sept. 1906, p. 1198.
         Scbk. 8. "The city is around us . . ."

1372.   "Wind in the Poplars." *Sports Afield*, Oct. 1906, p. 318. Scbk. 8.
         "Sad and strange as some . . ."

1373.   "Since Mother Died." *Ram's Horn*, 20 Oct. 1906, p. 3. "Since Moth-
         er died how long each . . ."

1374.   "Nutting Song." *Farm Journal*, Nov. 1906, p. 374. Scbk. 8. "Light,
         light rings our . . ."

1375.   "I Asked of God." *Sunday School Times*, 10 Nov. 1906, p. 637. Also
         in *Young People*, 5 Jan. 1907, p. 3. Scbk. 8 (2). "Humbly I asked of
         God to give me . . ."

1376.   "Last Night in Dreams." By Ella Montgomery. *American Agricul-
         turist*, 10 Nov. 1906, p. 447. Also in *Holland's Magazine*, Aug.
         1915, p. 6. Scbk. 8. "Last night in dreams I went once more . . ."

1377.   "God's Gifts." *King's Own*, 17 Nov. 1906, p. 184. "God gave our
         lips to me and you . . ."

1378.   "An Autumn Evening." *Youth's Companion*, 29 Nov. 1906, p. 614.
         Rpt. *Watchman*. Scbk. 8. "Dark hills against . . ."

1379.   "The Garden in Winter." *New Idea Woman's Magazine*, Dec. 1906,
         p. 18. Rpt. *Watchman*. Scbk. 8. "Frosty, white and cold . . ."

1380.   "An Old Man's Grave." *Youth's Companion*, 6 Dec. 1906, p. 628.
         Rpt. *Watchman* and *Aln*, chap. 22. Scbk. 8. "Make it where the
         winds . . ."

1381.   "A Prayer." *American Messenger*, Jan. 1907, p. 6. See also item
         1469. Scbk. 8. "Dear Lord, this boon . . ."

1382.   "When Mother Tucked Us In." *Farm Journal*, Jan. 1907, p. 18.
         Scbk. 8. "The sweetest memory . . ."

1383.   "A Good Memory." *Children's Visitor*, 13 Jan. 1907, p. 1. Scbk. 8.
         "I would hold . . ."

1384.   "Echo." *Sports Afield*, Mar. 1907, p. 206. Scbk. 8. "Here in my bosky glen . . ."

1385.   "My Queen." *Farm Journal*, Mar. 1907, p. 166. "She rules a kingdom . . ."

1386.   "A Shore Twilight." *Canadian Magazine*, Mar. 1907, p. 463. Rpt. *Watchman*. Scbk. 8. "Lo, here we find . . ."

1387.   "When the Boats Come In." *Forward*, 6 Apr. 1907, p. 107. Also in *Young People*, 25 May 1907, p. 163; and in *East and West*, 20 July 1907, p. 228. Scbk. 8. "The dusk creeps over . . ."

1388.   "Bird Song." *American Messenger*, May 1907, p. 94. Also in *Advocate and Guardian*, 1 June 1907, p. 161. Scbk. 8 (2). "In a plum-tree snowy . . ."

1389.   "The Little Gable Window." *Designer*, May 1907, p. 58. Scbk. 8. "There's a little gable window in a . . ."

1390.   "Some Day." *Home Herald [Ram's Horn]*, 22 May 1907, p. 3. "Some day in near or far . . ."

1391.   "A Day in the Open." *Outlook*, 25 May 1907, p. 203. Rpt. *Watchman*. Scbk. 8. "Ho, a day . . ."

1392.   "The Treasures." *Christian Endeavor World*, 30 May 1907, p. 708. Scbk. 8. "These I may not take . . ."

1393.   "Morning Song." *American Messenger*, July 1907, p. 124. Scbk. 8. "How glad the world . . ."

1394.   "Homestead Fields." *Advocate and Guardian*, 25 July 1907, p. 221. Scbk. 8. "Lovely and dear are . . ."

1395.   "Morning along Shore." *St. Nicholas*, Aug. 1907, p. 867. Rpt. *Watchman*. Scbk. 8. "Hark, oh hark, the elfin . . ."

1396.   "Don't." *Children's Visitor*, 18 Aug. 1907, p. 5. "My lad, dont' be . . ."

1397.   "In an Old Garden." *Canadian Magazine*, Sept. 1907, p. 439. Scbk. 8. "To-day I walked . . ."

1398.   "When the Tide Goes Out." *Sports Afield*, Sept. 1907, p. 218. Scbk. 8. "The boats sail out . . ."

1399.   "The Forsaken Home." *Ladies' Journal*. Also in *Zion's Herald*, 4 Sept. 1907, p. 1136. Scbk. 6. "Beneath its guardian . . ."

1400.   "I Thank Thee." *American Messenger*, Nov. 1907, p. 215. Scbk. 8.
         "I thank thee, Father, for my . . ."

1401.   "When the Dark Comes Down." *Youth's Companion*, 7 Nov. 1907, p.
         564. Rpt. *Watchman*. Scbk. 8. "When the dark comes down, oh,
         the wind . . ."

1402.   "Evening Boat Song." *Canadian Magazine*, Dec. 1907, p. 118. Scbk.
         8. "When the wind comes . . ."

1403.   "If Mary Had Known." *Forward*, 21 Dec. 1907, p. 413. Rpt.
         Watchman. Scbk. 8. "If Mary had known / When she held her . . ."

1404.   "A Boy's Best Creed." *Boys' World*, 28 Dec. 1907, p. 5. Also in
         King's Own, 27 Nov. 1909, p. 192. Scbk. 8. "Be honest, lad . . ."

1405.   "Among the Pines." *Zion's Herald*, 8 Jan. 1908, p. 48. Rpt. *Watch-
         man*. Scbk. 8. "Here let us linger . . ."

1406.   "The Exile." *Youth's Companion*, 6 Feb. 1908, p. 68. Rpt. *Watch-
         man*. See also item 1477. Scbk. 8. "We told her that . . ."

1407.   "A Winter Day." *Christian Endeavor World*, 6 Feb. 1908, p. 383.
         Rpt. *Watchman*. Scbk. 8. "The air is silent . . ."

1408.   "Let Us Be Glad." *Boys' World*, 18 Apr. 1908, p. 6. Scbk. 8. "Let
         us be glad for the glory of . . ."

1409.   "Delight in Life." *American Agriculturist*, 9 May 1908, p. 558.
         Scbk. 8. "Dear to me the dappled . . ."

1410.   "What Children Know." *American Agriculturist*, 16 May 1908, p.
         577. Also in *New England Homestead*, 16 May 1908, p. 600. Scbk.
         8. "Many things the . . ."

1411.   "The Transformation." *Sunday School Times*, 23 May 1908, p. 249.
         Scbk. 8. "Upon the marsh mud . . ."

1412.   "The Book of the Year." *Craftsman*, June 1908, p. 300. Scbk. 8.
         "The page of spring . . ."

1413.   "Sweet Clover." *American Messenger*, June 1908, p. 105. Scbk. 8.
         "How dear the pale sweet . . ."

1414.   "Let Us Walk with Morning." *East and West*, 20 June 1908, p. 195.
         Scbk. 8. "Come, let us walk with morning, let us go to . . ."

1415.   "In Wheaten Meadows." *Farm Journal*, July 1908, p. 274. Scbk. 8.
         "There are winds that . . ."

1416.   "On the Bay." *Youth's Companion*, 23 July 1908, p. 350. Also in
        Young People, 26 Sept. 1908, p. 312. Rpt. *Watchman*. Scbk. 8.
        "When the salt wave laps . . ."

1417.   "Drought." *Farm Journal*, Aug. 1908, p. 298. Scbk. 8. "So long it
        is since . . ."

1418.   "The Seeker." *American Messenger*, Aug. 1908, p. 145. Rpt.
        Watchman. Scbk. 8. "I sought for my . . ."

1419.   "Lost -- A Smile." *Children's Visitor*, 2 Aug. 1908, p. 3. Also in
        Jewels. Scbk. 8. "Something dreadful's . . ."

1420.   " 'Mizpah'." [anon.] *Family Story Paper*, 8 Aug. 1908, p. 6. " 'Twixt
        thee and me . . ."

1421.   "Twilight in the Garden." *Congregationalist*, 22 Aug. 1908, p. 241.
        Rpt. *Watchman*. Scbk. 8. "The scent of the earth . . ."

1422.   "Wild Rose Song." *Sports Afield*, Sept. 1908, p. 223. Scbk. 8. "I
        am queen of the . . ."

1423.   "Island Hymn." 9 Sept. 1908 (see item 1746, below). In *Lucy Maud
        Montgomery: the Island's Lady of Stories*. Women's Institute,
        Springfield, P.E.I., 1963. "Fair island of the . . ."

1424.   "My Rose Jar." *Youth's Companion*, 10 Sept. 1908, p. 424. Scbk. 8.
        "Lo! here's the haunting . . ."

1425.   "For Him." *King's Own*, 26 Sept. 1908, p. 158. Scbk. 8. "The glory
        is not in . . ."

1426.   "After Drought." *Christian Advocate*, 1 Oct. 1908, p. 1634. Scbk.
        8. "Last night through all . . ."

1427.   "October Rain." *Zion's Herald*, 21 Oct. 1908, p. 1360. Scbk. 8.
        "Over hills and meadows . . ."

1428.   "A Perfect Day." *Canadian Magazine*, Dec. 1908, p. 144. Scbk. 8.
        "A day came up this . . ."

1429.   "We Have Seen His Star." *Zion's Herald*, 16 Dec. 1908, p. 1615.
        Scbk. 8. "Across the yellow . . ."

1430.   "One of the Shepherds." *Christian Endeavor World*, 24 Dec. 1908,
        p. 280. Rpt. *Watchman*. Scbk. 8. "We were out on the hills . . ."

1431.   "A New Year Wish." *American Agriculturist*, 9 Jan. 1909, p. 50.
        Also in *New England Homestead*, 9 Jan. 1909, p. 54. Scbk. 8.
        "What, oh friend, shall . . ."

1432. "Tomorrow." *Zion's Herald*, 13 Jan. 1909, p. 46. Scbk. 8. "What holds within its . . ."

1433. "For Little Things." *Christian Endeavor World*, 21 Jan. 1909, p. 359. Rpt. *Watchman*. Scbk. 8. "Last night I looked . . ."

1434. "Our Temples." *Sunday School Visitor*. Also in *King's Own*, 20 Mar. 1909, p. 47. Scbk. 6. "Builded by toil . . ."

1435. "The Poet's Thought." *Canadian Magazine*, Apr. 1909, p. 511. Rpt. *Watchman*. Scbk. 8. "It came to him . . ."

1436. "The Old Home Calls." *Youth's Companion*, 1 Apr. 1909, p. 160. Also in *Woman's Century*, 7 June 1921, p. 2. Rpt. *Watchman*. Scbk. 5 (2). "Come back to me . . ."

1437. "Waken." *American Agriculturist*, 24 Apr. 1909, p. 551. Also in *New England Homestead*, 24 Apr. 1909, p. 543. Scbk. 8. "Here's an April day . . ."

1438. "The Morning Land." *Boys' World*, 8 May 1909, p. 3. Scbk. 8. "I saw a land adown . . ."

1439. "June Sunrise." *Forward*, 5 June 1909, p. 181. Scbk. 8. "Over a world that is . . ."

1440. "In the Morning." *American Messenger*, July 1909, p. 125. Scbk. 8. "All the light is gone . . ."

1441. "The Rovers." *Christian Endeavor World*, 8 July 1909, p. 839. Rpt. *Watchman*. Scbk. 8. "Over the fields we go . . ."

1442. "Old Aunt Sally." *Boys' World*, 10 July 1909, p. 6. Scbk. 8. "Old Aunt Sally says, says she, . . ."

1443. "Mother's Mending Basket." *Ram's Horn*, 15 Sept. 1909, p. 11. "Mother's mending basket . . ."

1444. "Down Home." *Youth's Companion*, 16 Sept. 1909, p. 452. Rpt. *Watchman*. Scbk. 8. "Down home to-night the . . ."

1445. "On the Hills." *Zion's Herald*, 6 Oct. 1909, p. 1265. Rpt. *Watchman*. Scbk. 8. "Through the pungent . . ."

1446. "The Last Bluebird." *East and West*, 30 Oct. 1909, p. 352. Scbk. 8. "The grasses are sere . . ."

1447. "Before Storm." *Canadian Magazine*, Nov. 1909, p. 44. Rpt. *Watchman*. Scbk. 8. "There's a grayness over . . ."

1448.   "The Rain on the Hill." *Christian Endeavor World*, 4 Nov. 1909, p. 81. Rpt. *Watchman*. Scbk. 8. "Now on the hill . . ."

1449.   "November Evening." *Youth's Companion*, 18 Nov. 1909, p. 604. Rpt. *Watchman*. Scbk. 8. "Come, for the dusk is . . ."

1450.   "In the River Meadows." *Smith's Magazine*, Dec. 1909, p. 464. Scbk. 8. "The breeze blows over . . ."

1451.   "Unrecorded." *Forward*, 18 Dec. 1909, p. 419. Rpt. *Watchman*. Scbk. 8. "I like to think . . ."

1452.   "Genius." *Youth's Companion*, 27 Jan. 1910, p. 48. Rpt. *Watchman*. Scbk. 8. "A hundred generations . . ."

1453.   "Now." *Young People's Paper*. Also in *American Messenger*, Feb. 1910, p. 26. Scbk. 2. "If you have a word of . . ."

1454.   "Music of the Morning." *East and West*, 19 Feb. 1910, p. 60. Scbk. 8. "When I waken in the . . ."

1455.   "A Shore Picture." *Canadian Magazine*, Apr. 1910, p. 514. Scbk. 8. "A windy, hollow sky . . ."

1456.   "The Revelation." *Zion's Herald*, 6 Apr. 1910, p. 429. Scbk. 8. "Once to my side . . ."

1457.   "In Lilac Time." *Mayflower*. Also in *American Agriculturist*, 21 May 1910, p. 730; and in *New England Homestead*, 21 May 1910, p. 747. Scbk. 6. "When the hills in the . . ."

1458.   "Companioned." *Canadian Magazine*, Aug. 1910, p. 345. Rpt. *Watchman*. See also item 1461. Scbk. 8. "I walked to-day, but . . ."

1459.   "Gratitude." *Christian Endeavor World*, 25 Aug. 1910, p. 927. See also item 1541. "Dear God, I thank Thee . . ."

1460.   "Bob's Stories." *Ladies' Journal*. Also in *Farm Journal*, Oct. 1910, p. 466. Scbk. 1. "The sky was a windy . . ."

1461.   "Companioned." *American Messenger*, Oct. 1910, p. 178. See also item 1458. Scbk. 8. "Even when most alone . . ."

1462.   "Harbor Night." *East and West*, 26 Nov. 1910, p. 380. Scbk. 8. "In the lucent dome . . ."

1463.   "The Watchman." *Everybody's*, Dec. 1910, pp. 778-83. Rpt. *Watchman*. "Claudia, . . ."

1464.   "Do You Remember?" *Canadian Magazine*, Jan. 1911, p. 301.
        Scbk. 8. "Do you remember that lone, ancient . . ."

1465.   "The Answers." *Smith's Magazine*, Apr. 1911, p. 68. Scbk. 8. "I
        asked of the stars . . ."

1466.   "An April Night." *Canadian Magazine*, Apr. 1911, p. 538. Rpt.
        Watchman. Scbk. 8. "The moon comes up . . ."

1467.   "Dawn." *Farm Journal*, Apr. 1911, p. 244. Also in *Zion's Herald*, 15
        July 1914, p. 882. Scbk. 8. "There's a silken fringe . . ."

1468.   "Fields o' May." *Zion's Herald*, 10 May 1911, p. 589. Scbk. 8. "Oh,
        the time of blossom . . ."

1469.   "A Prayer." *American Messenger*, June 1911, p. 105. See also item
        1381. "Lord, take my life . . ."

1470.   "The Pathway That Runs Through the Pines." *Messenger of the
        Sacred Heart*. Also in *Zion's Herald*, 5 July 1911, p. 846. Scbk. 6.
        "In the ripe, purple dusk . . ."

1471.   "Where the Iris Grows." *Zion's Herald*, 8 May 1912, p. 594. Scbk.
        8. "A breeze among the . . ."

1472.   "Harbour Moonrise." *Canadian Magazine*, June 1912, p. 157. Rpt.
        Watchman. Scbk. 8. "There is never a wind . . ."

1473.   "In Twilight Fields." *Illustrated Youth and Age*. Also in *Zion's
        Herald*, 17 July 1912, p. 1. Scbk. 2. "O'er dewy meadows . . ."

1474.   "Memory Pictures." *Canadian Magazine*, Sept. 1912, p. 403. Rpt.
        Watchman. Scbk. 8. "A wide spring meadow . . ."

1475.   "The Old Garden." *Holland's Magazine*, Oct. 1912, p. 7. See also
        item 1293. Scbk. 8. "Here white and red . . ."

1476.   "What I Would Ask of Life." *American Messenger*, Dec. 1912, p.
        219. Scbk. 8. "Life, as thy gift I ask . . ."

1477.   "The Exile." *Zion's Herald*, 22 Jan. 1913, p. 110. See also item
        1406. Scbk. 8. "The roses are very . . ."

1478.   "You." *Canadian Magazine*, Mar. 1913, p. 444. Also *ibid.*, July
        1918, p. 272. Rpt. *Watchman*. Scbk. 8 (2). "Only a long, low-lying
        . . ."

1479.   "Along Shore." *Christian Endeavor World*, 17 Apr. 1913, p. 567.
        Scbk. 8. "The chill and freakish . . ."

1480.   "Love's Gifts." *American Messenger*, May 1913, p. 87. Scbk. 8.
        "Love gave with Love's . . ."

1481.   "A White Fog." *Zion's Herald*, 13 Aug. 1913, p. 1041. Scbk. 8.
        "Softly we float out . . ."

1482.   "Echo Dell." *Canadian Magazine*, Sept. 1913, p. 476. Rpt. *Watch-
        man*. Scbk. 8. "In a lone valley . . ."

1483.   "The Wood Pool." *Christian Endeavor World*, 11 Sept. 1913, p. 987.
        Rpt. *Watchman*. Scbk. 8. "Here is a voice . . ."

1484.   "The Pathways." *Christian Endeavor World*, 23 Oct. 1913, p. 63.
        Scbk. 8. "Joy's roses bloom along . . ."

1485.   "Until We Meet." *Zion's Herald*, 3 Dec. 1913, p. 1549. Scbk. 8.
        "Until we meet / May He between us . . ."

1486.   "Love's Prayer." *Canadian Magazine*, Feb. 1914, p. 442. Rpt.
        Watchman. Scbk. 8. "Beloved, this the heart . . ."

1487.   "Down at Aunty's." *Holland's Magazine*, Apr. 1914, p. 64. Scbk. 8.
        "It's a jolly place to . . ."

1488.   "Evening Star." *Portland Transcript* [1901]. Also in *Zion's Herald*,
        1 July 1914, p. 814. Scbk. 2. "Calm-browed and white . . ."

1489.   "We Who Wait." *Zion's Herald*, 12 Aug. 1914, p. 1003. Scbk. 8.
        "Not ours to join in . . ."

1490.   "When I Go Home Again." *American Messenger*, Sept. 1914, p. 157.
        Scbk. 8. "Oh, I am hungering for . . ."

1491.   "With Tears They Buried You To-day." *Canadian Magazine*, Sept.
        1914, p. 470. Rpt. *Watchman*. Scbk. 5. "With tears they buried
        you to-day / But well I knew . . ."

1492.   "Twilight and I Went Hand in Hand." *Canadian Magazine*, Nov.
        1914, p. 54. Rpt. *Watchman*. Scbk. 8. "Twilight and I went hand
        in hand / As lovers walk . . ."

1493.   "A Pair of Slippers." *Good Housekeeping*. Also in *Holland's Maga-
        zine*, Nov. 1914, p. 46. Scbks. 1 and 8. "A pair of slippers worn,
        you know, . . ."

1494.   "Realization." *Canadian Magazine*, Feb. 1915, p. 372. Rpt.
        Watchman. Scbk. 8. "I smiled with skeptic . . ."

1495.   "A Request." *Canadian Magazine*, Aug. 1915, p. 324. Rpt. *Watch-
        man*. Scbk. 8. "When I am dead . . ."

1496.   "The Lost Friend." *Zion's Herald*, 25 Aug. 1915, p. 1068. Scbk. 8.
        "A friend of mine went . . ."

1497.   "Longing." *Zion's Herald*, 8 Sept. 1915, p. 1140. Scbk. 8. "If I
        could see you . . ."

1498.   "Great-Grandmamma's Portrait." 1st publ. not found. Also in
        Maclean's, Nov. 1915, p. 20. Scbks. 5 and 8. "On the pictured walls
        . . ."

1499.   "The Way to Slumbertown." *Holland's Magazine*, Apr. 1916, p. 56.
        Scbk. 5. "If we could go to . . ."

1500.   "Day Lilies." *Messenger of the Sacred Heart*. Also as "June Lil-
        ies," *Zion's Herald*, 21 June 1916, p. 786. Scbk. 8. "God took the
        whiteness . . ."

1501.   "The Sunset Bells." *Sports Afield*. Also in *Zion's Herald*, 27 July
        1916, p. 5. Scbk. 8. "Dreamily sweet across . . ."

1502.   "Forever." *Canadian Magazine*, Aug. 1916, p. 315. Rpt. *Watch-
        man*. See also item 1191. "With you I shall . . ."

1503.   "By an Autumn Fire." *Maclean's*, Nov. 1916, p. 14. Rpt. *Watch-
        man*. Scbk. 5. "Now at our casement . . ."

1504.   "If I Were King." *Everywoman's World*, Jan. 1917, p. 15. Scbk. 5.
        "If I were king in some fair . . ."

1505.   "The Wound." *Zion's Herald*, 17 Jan. 1917, p. 84. Scbk. 8. "A
        stranger sneered -- . . ."

1506.   "Summer Afternoon." *Canadian Magazine*, Aug. 1917, p. 306.
        "Hush! Hath the world . . ."

1507.   "My Love Has Passed This Way." *Canadian Magazine*, Dec. 1917, p.
        138. Scbk. 5. "I know my love has passed this way / To walk . . ."

1508.   "Our Women." In *Canadian Poems of the Great War*. Ed. John W.
        Garvin. Toronto: McClelland and Stewart, 1918, p. 158. "Bride of
        a day . . ."

1509.   "Midsummer." *Canadian Magazine*, July 1918, p. 226. See also
        item 1365. Scbk. 5. "The year dreams idly . . ."

1510.   "Dusk." *Canadian Magazine*, May 1919, p. 44. Scbk. 8. "Pale saf-
        fron clouds . . ."

1511.   "The Gate of Dream." *Canadian Magazine*, Dec. 1919, p. 158.
        Scbk. 5; BQ, pp. 193-94. "I seek a little hidden . . ."

1512.   "Premonitions." *Canadian Magazine*, Nov. 1921, p. 72. Scbk. 5. "To-day the west wind . . ."

1513.   "Spring Song." *Verse and Reverse 1922*. Toronto Women's Press Club. Toronto: Goodchild, 1922, p. 8. See also item 1550. Scbk. 5; BQ, pp. 425-26. "O gypsy winds that pipe and sing . . ."

1514.   "Grief." *Canadian Magazine*, Mar. 1922, p. 453. Scbk. 5. "To my door came grief . . ."

1515.   "By the Sea." *Canadian Magazine*, Dec. 1922, p. 105. Scbk. 5. "Lass, this hour is all . . ."

1516.   "Farewell to an Old Room." *Ladies' Home Journal*, Oct. 1924, p. 136. Scbk. 5; BQ, pp. 146-47. "In the gold of sunset . . ."

1517.   "To a Desired Friend." *Commonweal*, 5 Jan. 1927, p. 236. Scbk. 5; BQ, pp. 80-81. "I have a right to you -- . . ."

1518.   "An Old Face." *Commonweal*; 28 Sept. 1927, p. 502. Also in *Literary Digest*, 22 Oct. 1927, p. 34: "from *Commonweal*" and in *American Federationist*, Nov. 1928, p. 1325, with additional first stanza: "Calm as a reaped harvest . . ." Scbks. 1 and 5 (3); BQ (in full), pp. 195-96. "Many a wild, adventurous . . ."

1519.   "The Parting Soul." *Commonweal*, 25 Jan. 1928, p. 985. Scbk. 5. "Open the casement . . ."

1520.   "The Haunted Room." *Canadian Magazine*, Jan 1929, p. 25. Also as "The Room" in BQ, pp. 402-3. See also item 1579. "This is a haunted room . . ."

1521.   "Canadian Twilight." In *Canadian Verse for Boys and Girls*. Ed. John W. Garvin. Toronto: Nelson, 1930, p. 139. Rpt. as "Twilight in Abegweit," in *Lucy Maud Montgomery: the Island's Lady of Stories*, Women's Institute, Springfield, P.E.I., 1963, and in *RY*. Scbk. 5. "A filmy western sky . . ."

1522.   "Oh, We Will Walk with Spring To-day!" In *Canadian Verse for Boys and Girls*. Ed. John W. Garvin. Toronto: Nelson, 1930, p. 140. Scbk. 5; BQ, pp. 398-99. "Oh, we will walk with spring today . . ."

1523.   "Interlude." *Saturday Night*, 13 Dec. 1930, p. 15. Scbk. 5; BQ, p. 338. "To-day a wind of dream . . ."

1524.   "Success." *Saturday Night*, 9 May 1931, p. 9. Scbk. 5; BQ, p. 191. "Come, drain the cup . . ."

1525.   "Secret Knowledge." *Maclean's*, 15 Oct. 1931, p. 42. "I know not the high . . ."

1526.   "The New House." *Chatelaine*, Jan. 1932, p. 3. Scbk. 5; BQ, pp. 21-22. "Milk-white against . . ."

1527.   "The Wild Places." *Saturday Night*, 20 Aug. 1932, p. 3. Scbk. 5; BQ, pp. 344-45. "Oh, here is joy . . ."

1528.   "Night." *Canadian Magazine*, Jan. 1935, p. 21. Scbk. 5; BQ, p. 24. "A pale, enchanted room . . ."

1529.   "I Wish You." *Good Housekeeping*, Jan. 1936, p. 17. Scbk. 5; BQ, pp. 1-2. "Friend o' mine, in the . . ."

1530.   "The Difference." *Saturday Night*, 20 Jan. 1940, p. 2. See also 1537. Scbk. 5; BQ, p. 346. "There is no difference . . ."

1531.   "The Piper." *Saturday Night*, 2 May 1942, p. 25. Published posthumously. BQ, p. 429. "One day the Piper came . . ."

Poems reprinted in The Watchman, and Other Poems

Listed here are poems found either in the scrapbooks or mentioned in the ledger list.

1532.   "As the Heart Hopes." Scbk. 8. "It is a year, dear one . . ."

1533.   "At Nightfall." "The dark is coming . . ."

1534.   "At the Long Sault." *The Standard*. Scbk. 8. "A prisoner under the . . ."

1535.   "The Call." Scbk. 8. "Mother of her who is . . ."

1536.   "A Day Off." Scbk. 5. "Let us put awhile away . . ."

1537.   "The Difference." See also item 1530. "When we were together . . ."

1538.   "Fancies." Scbk. 8. "Surely the flowers . . ."

1539.   "The Farewell." "He rides away with . . ."

1540.   "Forest Path." "Oh, the charm of idle . . ."

1541.   "Gratitude." See also item 1459. Scbk. 8. "I thank thee, friend . . ."

1542.   "In Memory of Maggie." "Naught but a little cat . . ."

1543.   "The Mother." "Here I lean over you . . ."

1544. "Out o' Doors." Scbk. 8. "There's a gypsy wind . . ."

1545. "The Poet." "There was strength . . ."

1546. "Sea Sunset." Scbk. 8. "A gallant city has been . . ."

1547. "The Sea to the Shore." "Lo, I have loved thee . . ."

1548. "September." Scbk. 8. "Lo! a ripe sheaf of . . ."

1549. "Song of the Sea Wind." Scbk. 5. "When the sun sets over . . ."

1550. "Spring Song." See also item 1513. Scbk. 8. "Hark, I hear a robin
       . . ."

1551. "The Three Songs." Scbk. 8. "The poet sang of a . . ."

1552. "To One Hated." "Had it been when I came . . ."

1553. "The Truce o' Night." "Lo, it is dark . . ."

1554. "The Voyagers." "We shall launch our . . ."

1555. "While the Fates Sleep." "Come, let us to the . . ."

Poems Found Only in Scrapbooks and Manuscripts

Listed here are poems found either in the scrapbooks or in the manuscript
"The Blythes Are Quoted," including those poems where the periodical
source has been given in the scrapbooks, but which we have been unable to
verify.

1556. "The Aftermath." BQ, pp. 426-27, "Yesterday we were young who
       now are old . . ."

1557. "Aim and Endeavor." Scbk. 8. "Mean to be something . . ."

1558. "April Rain Song." *Forward*. Scbk. 1. "Oh, I'm the herald . . ."

1559. "As It Was in the Beginning." Scbk. 5, typescript. "I looked in your
       eyes . . ."

1560. "At New-Moon Time." *Illustrated Youth and Age*, p. 367. Scbk. 2.
       "Above the gold-rimmed . . ."

1561. "At Rising Tide." Scbk. 8. "The boats at anchor . . ."

1562. "Attainment." *Waverley Magazine*. Scbk. 6. "A glorious bubble
       . . ."

1563.   "The Benediction." *Wellspring*. Scbk. 6. "Speaks the Old Year . . ."

1564.   "The Book." *Designer* [1906]. Scbk. 8. "I wrote therein the . . ."

1565.   "The Bride Dreams." Scbk. 5. "Love, is it dawn . . ."

1566.   "Buttercup Hill." *Wellspring*. Scbk. 8. "The west wind is out . . ."

1567.   "Christmas Eve." *Farm and Home*. Scbk. 1. "Queerest sounds are . . ."

1568.   "Coiling up the Hay." Scbk. 8. "There's many a thing . . ."

1569.   "Come, Let Us Go." BQ, pp. 339-40. "Friendly meadows touched with spring . . ."

1570.   "The Coming of Spring." Scbk. 8. "Away down in the . . ."

1571.   "A Country Boy." *Farm and Home*. Scbk. 1. See also item 1177. "There are lots of things . . ."

1572.   "Daisy's Story." *Bluenose*. Scbk. 2. "It was Aunty told me . . ."

1573.   "Dandelion Song." Scbk. 8. "When the leaves peep . . ."

1574.   "A Dream Fancy." Scbk. 8. "When you see a little . . ."

1575.   "Earth's Vigils." *Forum*. Scbk. 6. "Through the winter I . . ."

1576.   "For Its Own Sake." BQ, p. 345. "I cherish love but for its own sweet sake . . ."

1577.   "Good Night." Scbk. 5. "Good night--'tis hard to say . . ."

1578.   "Guest Room in the Country." BQ, p. 5. "Old friend, who art my guest tonight . . ."

1579.   "The Haunted Room." BQ, pp. 149-50. See also item 1520. "The old clock ticks behind the door . . ."

1580.   "He Knows." Scbk. 8. "He knows the pain we hid . . ."

1581.   "I Know--." Scbk. 5; BQ, pp. 347-48. "I know a dell of violets . . ."

1582.   "I Want." Scbk. 5; BQ, pp. 422-23. "I'm weary of the city's . . ."

1583.   "I Would be Well." Scbk. 2. "I would be well if once again . . ."

1584.   "In an Autumn Road." Scbk. 8. "Babble of brook . . ."

1585.   "In Blossom Time." *Home and Flowers.* Scbk. 8. "The earth has awakened . . ."

1586.   "In Childland." Scbk. 8. "Oh, there it is always . . ."

1587.   "In Primrose Lane." Scbk. 8. "Down here in primrose lane / The dusk . . ."

1588.   "The Interpreter." Scbk. 8. "He drew his bow . . ."

1589.   "It Is Well." *Forward.* Scbk. 1. "It is well, O my heart, in a . . ."

1590.   "It Is Well." *Wellspring.* Scbk. 3. "Sing, oh my heart, what . . ."

1591.   "A June Day." Scbk. 5. BQ, pp. 341-42. "Come, 'tis a day that . . ."

1592.   "A June Evening." Scbk. 5. "The winds are out . . ."

1593.   "A June Memory." Scbk. 8. "There was a young moon . . ."

1594.   "Just Suppose." Scbk. 8. "When things wear a frown . . ."

1595.   "Laughing Lass and Grumble Girl." *Sunday School Visitor.* Scbk. 6. "There's a little maid . . ."

1596.   "Little Cheery Heart." *Morning Star.* Scbk. 3. "On her face the sun . . ."

1597.   "Love's Guerdon." Scbk. 8. "Said a human heart . . ."

1598.   "Man and Woman." BQ, pp. 25-26. "Sweet, I must be for you . . ."

1599.   "Many the Mother." *New Idea Woman's Magazine.* Scbk. 8. "Here with my Baby I . . ."

1600.   "May Song." Scbk. 5. "Across the sunlit sea . . ."

1601.   "Memories." Scbk. 5. "A window looking out . . ."

1602.   "A Midsummer Day." Scbk. 5; BQ, pp. 106-7. "When the pale east . . ."

1603.   "The Morning." Scbk. 5. "I stand on the orient . . ."

1604.   "Not to Be Taken Away." *Forward.* Scbk. 3. "It may not be ours to . . ."

1605.   "November Plowing." Nov. 1898. Scbk. 2. "When all the golden . . ."

1606.   "The Old Path Round the Shore." Scbk. 5; BQ, pp. 3-4. "It winds beneath the . . ."

1607.   "On Guard." *Sunday School Visitor.* Scbk. 6. "Guard well your lips . . ."

1608.   "The Only Way." See also item 1217. Scbk. 8. "To chisel a statue . . ."

1609.   "Pansy Faces." Scbk. 8. "Right down in the heart . . ."

1610.   "The Pilgrim." Scbk. 5; BQ, pp. 423-24. "The wind is on the hill . . ."

1611.   "The Quest." Scbk. 5, typescript. "I sit beside my harp . . ."

1612.   "Rain in the County." *Farm Journal.* Scbk. 1. "Here in the country . . ."

1613.   "Remembered." Scbk. 5; BQ, pp. 110-11. "Through the shriek of . . ."

1614.   "Robin Vespers." Scbk. 5; BQ, pp. 22-23. "When winds blow soft . . ."

1615.   "A Row in the Morning." Scbk. 8. "Pull blithely out . . ."

1616.   "Sandshore in September." Scbk. 8. "Dim dusk on the sea . . ."

1617.   "The Sea-Shell." Scbk. 8. "Where the old shores . . ."

1618.   "Sea Song." Scbk. 5; BQ, pp. 48-49. "Sing to me / Of the . . ."

1619.   "Sleep." Scbk. 8. "Slowly across the fields . . ."

1620.   "A Song of Summer." Scbk. 5. "Come, 'tis a time . . ."

1621.   "Song of Winter." Scbk. 5; BQ, p. 151. "Fast to-night the frost . . ."

1622.   "The Summons." Scbk. 8. "Today in the turbid city . . ."

1623.   "A Sunshiny Morning." Scbk. 8. "All night there was . . ."

1624.   "The Test." Scbk. 8. "All the great house sat . . ."

1625.   "There Is a House I Love." Scbk. 5. "There is a house I love / Beside a calling sea . . ."

1626.   "There is Always Time." Scbk. 8; BQ, p. 47. "There is always time to sing a song . . ."

1627.   "Two Foes." Scbk. 8. "Today I won a victory . . ."

1628.   "Unnatural." *Ladies' Journal.* Scbk. 1. "The proofs came up . . ."

1629.   "Vacant." Scbk. 8. "This is her room . . ."

1630.   "What They Can Do." *Sunday School Visitor.* Scbk. 6. "What can little hands . . ."

1631.   "When the Old House Dreams." Scbk. 5. "In the soft blue dusk . . ."

1632.   "When the Wild Plum Blossoms." Scbk. 5. "When the wild plum blossoms in the lane . . ."

1633.   "The Wind." See also item 1272. Scbk. 5. "Out in the ways of . . ."

1634.   "Wind Music." Scbk. 8. "The wind has stolen . . ."

1635.   "The Wind of a Day." *New Idea Woman's Magazine.* Scbk. 8. "In the fresh, sweet . . ."

1636.   "Wind of Autumn." Scbk. 5; BQ, pp. 342-43. "I walked with . . ."

1637.   "A Wood Road." Scbk. 8. "There's a wild, dear . . ."

Unverified Ledger Titles

Listed here are the poems entered in the ledger list, but which have not been found in print.

1638.   "The Deserted Home."

1639.   "Different Opinions."

1640.   "Going for Cows."

1641.   "Her Gifts."

1642.   "If We Knew."

1643.   "Needed."

1644.   "On the Sandshore."

1645.   "The Rain."

1646.   "Say It Now."

1647.   "The Secret."

1648.   "Six Pass Words."

1649.   "The Stile." *Farm Journal.*

1650.   "Ted's Pocket."

1651.   "To Our Boys."

1652.   "Two Opinions."

1653.   "Two Students."

1654.   "Wood Music."

MISCELLANEOUS PIECES

1655.   "The Wreck of the 'Marco Polo.' " *Montreal Witness,* Feb. 1891. Also in *Daily Patriot* (Charlottetown), 11 Mar. 1891, p. 1. Scbk. 7. (Third prize in an essay contest.)

1656.   "A Western Eden." *The Prince Albert Times and Saskatchewan Review,* 17 June 1891, p. 4. Scbk. 7.

1657.   "From Prince Albert to P.E. Island." *Daily Patriot* (Charlottetown), 31 Oct. 1891, p. 1. Scbk. 7.

1658.   "The Usual Way." *College Record* (Prince of Wales College, Charlottetown), Mar. 1894. Scbk. 7. A playlet.

1659.   "Extracts from the Diary of a Second-Class Mouse." *College Record* (Prince of Wales College, Charlottetown), Apr. 1894. Scbk. 7.

1660.   "High School Life in Saskatchewan." *College Record* (Prince of Wales College, Charlottetown), May 1894. Scbk. 7.

1661.   " 'Portia'--A Study: Miss Montgomery's Essay at the P. of W. Convocation." *Daily Guardian* (Charlottetown), June 1894. Also in *Daily Patriot* (Charlottetown), 11 June 1894; and in *Examiner* (Charlottetown), 11 June 1894, p. 2. Scbk. 7.

1662.   "Valedictory." *Examiner* (Charlottetown), June 1894. Scbk. 7. (The valedictorian of 1894 was James H. Stevenson, but the speech was ghost written by LMM.)

1663.   "Patience." By Belinda Bluegrass. *Evening Mail* (Halifax), Feb.
        1896. Scbk. 7. A poem submitted to a letter-writing contest.

1664.   "The Bad Boy of Blanktown School." By L.M.M. *Dalhousie
        Gazette*, Mar. 1896, pp. 220-23. Scbk. 7.

1665.   "Crooked Answers." By L.M.M. *College Observer* (Dalhousie Col-
        lege, Halifax), Mar. 1896. Scbk. 7.

1666.   "A Girl's Place at Dalhousie College." *Halifax Herald*, Apr. 1896.
        Scbk. 7.

1667.   "James Henry, Truant." By L. *College Observer* (Dalhousie Col-
        lege, Halifax), Apr. 1896. Scbk. 7.

1668.   "Ladies' College Recital." [1896.] Scbk. 7.

1669.   "Around the Table." By Cynthia. *Daily Echo* (Halifax), Oct.
        1901-June 1902. Scbk. 3. A weekly column.

1670.   "A Half-hour in an Old Cemetery." By M.M. [1901/02.] Scbk. 3.

1671.   "Dalhousie College Convocation." By Cynthia. *[Daily Echo* (Hali-
        fax), 1902]. Scbk. 3.

1672.   "The Woods." 4 parts: "Spring in the Woods," "The Woods in Sum-
        mer," "The Woods in Autumn," "The Woods in Winter." *Canadian
        Magazine*, May, Sept., Oct., Dec. 1911, pp. 59-62; 399-402; 574-77;
        62-64.

1673.   "What Twelve Canadian Women Hope to See as the Outcome of the
        War." *Everywoman's World*, Apr. 1915, p. 7.

1674.   "The Alpine Path." *Everywoman's World*, June-Nov. 1917. In six
        instalments, later republished as a book; see 622, above.

1675.   "How I Became a Writer." *Winnipeg Free Press*, 6 Dec. 1921.

1676.   Hoffman, Arthur Sullivant, ed. *Fiction Writers on Fiction Writing*.
        Indianapolis: Bobbs-Merrill, 1923. Short essay by LMM in response
        to questionnaire on writing, pp. 160-61.

1677.   "The 'Teen-age Girl." *Chatelaine*, Mar. 1931, pp. 9, 32, 37.

1678.   "An Open Letter from a Minister's Wife." *Chatelaine*, Oct. 1931,
        pp. 8, 53.

1679.   "Is This My Anne?" *Chatelaine*, Jan. 1935, pp. 18, 22.

1680.   Foreword, in Jessie Findlay Brown, *Up Came The Moon.* Oshawa, Toronto, Whitby: Mundy-Goodfellow Printing Co., 1936. vi, 79 pp.

ANTHOLOGIZED WORKS: A SELECTED LISTING

1681.   Garvin, J.W., ed. *Canadian Poets.* Toronto: McClelland, Goodchild and Stewart, 1916. 471 pp. Contains "The Old Home Calls," p.358; "The Old Man's Grave," pp. 357-58; "Off to the Fishing Ground," pp. 356-57; "Sunrise Along Shore," pp. 355-56; "When the Dark Comes Down," p. 355. New edition: Toronto: McClelland and Stewart, 1926. 536 pp.; contains the same poems in the same order, pp. 229-34.

1682.   Caswell, Edward S. *Canadian Singers and Their Songs: A Collection of Portraits and Autograph Poems.* Toronto: McClelland and Stewart, 1919. 157 pp. Photograph of LMM, with facing page poem "Love's Prayer," pp. 88-89.

1683.   Members of the Toronto Women's Press Club. *Verse and Reverse.* Toronto: Toronto Women's Press Club, 1921. 47 pp. Contains "Winter Song," p. 16, "The Gate of Dream," p. 29.

1684.   Garvin, John W., ed. *Canadian Verse for Boys and Girls.* Toronto: Nelson, 1930. 215 pp. Contains "The Way to Slumber Town," pp. 137-39; "Canadian Twilight," p. 139; "Oh, We Will Walk with Spring To-day!", p. 140.

1685.   Ritchie, Eliza, ed. *Songs of the Maritimes: An Anthology of Poetry of the Maritime Provinces of Canada.* Toronto: McClelland and Stewart, 1931. 213 pp. Contains "The Old Man's Grave," p. 150; "Our Women (Written in War-time)," p. 113; "When the Dark Comes Down," p. 48.

1686.   Bird, W. R., ed. *Atlantic Anthology.* Toronto: McClelland and Stewart, 1959. 510 pp. Contains "Anne's Company Gets Drunk," pp. 204-11, from *Anne of Green Gables.*

1687.   Toye, William, ed. *A Book of Canada.* London: Collins, 1962. 416 pp. Contains "Calling a Minister," pp. 359-66, from *Rainbow Valley.*

1688.   Graham, Allan, ed. *Island Prose and Poetry: An Anthology.* Collected by the P.E.I. 1973 Centennial Commission Literary Committee. Charlottetown: P.E.I. 1973 Centennial Commission, 1972. 225 pp. Contains chapter 6 of *Emily of New Moon,* pp. 102-111.

1689.   Edwards, Mary Jane, Paul Denham and George Parker, eds. *The Evolution of Canadian Literature in English: 1867-1914.* Toronto:

Holt, Rinehart and Winston, 1973. 335 pp. Critical introduction, pp. 313-15; "Aunt Olivia's Beau" (from *Chronicles of Avonlea*), pp. 315-25.

1690. Rubio, Mary, and Glenys Stow, eds. *Kanata: An Anthology of Canadian Children's Literature.* London: Evans, 1976. 244 pp. Contains "Vanity and Vexation of Spirit," pp. 152-62, from *Anne of Green Gables.*

1691. Bell, John, and Leslie Choyce, eds. *Visions from the Edge: An Anthology of Atlantic Canada Science Fiction and Fantasy.* Porters Lake, N.S.: Pottersfield Press, 1981. Contains "House Party at Smoky Island," pp. 130-37, first published in *Weird Tales*, August 1935, reprinted in *Startling Mystery Stories*, Fall 1968.

1692. Bolger, Francis W. P., ed. Photographs by Wayne Barrett and Anne MacKay. *Spirit of Place: Lucy Maud Montgomery and Prince Edward Island.* Toronto: Oxford University Press, 1982. 86 pp. Colour photographs of P.E.I., with facing page extracts from LMM's works.

1693. Bolger, Francis W. P., ed. *L.M. Montgomery no shima.* (Japanese translation of *Spirit of Place*, no. 1692, above.) Tr. Junzo Miyatake and Noriko Miyatake. Tokyo: Shinozaki Shorin, 1983. 104 pp. Photographs as in the original, *Spirit of Place*, ed. Francis W. P. Bolger, Toronto, 1982.

Part 5

ARCHIVAL HOLDINGS

The entries are arranged alphabetically, first by province, then by the name of the repository.

ONTARIO

Guelph, University of

McLaughlin Library.

Diaries and Journals:

1694.   Diaries. XZ5 MS A001. 10 vols. 20 x 36 cm. 1889-1942. Each volume has 500-600 pages, with numerous photographs and other memorabilia. These diaries, reported to be highly personal in nature, are without doubt the single most important archival collection relating to the personal and public life of LMM. However, they will not be open to researchers (including the present bibliographers) until after 1992, except for selected people at the University of Guelph. As we go to press, the first volume of edited selections of the journals has appeared in print; see item 629, above.

Manuscripts:

1695.   "House Party at Smoky Island." XZ1 MS A082. Original typescript of story, 11 pp., published in *Weird Tales Magazine*, [Aug. 1935, pp. 152-55].

1696.   "The Blythes Are Quoted." XZ1 MS A098001. A draft version, typed with numerous corrections; 429 pp. plus a section of unnumbered pages; 21.7 x 18 cm., pages of standard bond and onion-skin paper. A copy of the complete manuscript (624 pp.) is held at McMaster University (see below).

1697.   "The Blythes Are Quoted." XZ1 MS A098002. Carbon copy, 429 pp., 21.7 x 28 cm.

1698.   "The Blythes Are Quoted." XZ1 MS A098003. Typescript, 429 pp., 21.7 x 28 cm., editor's copy used to produce *The Road to Yesterday*. See the entry for "The Blythes Are Quoted" held at McMaster University, below.

1699.   Typed manuscript for *The Doctor's Sweetheart*. XZ1 MS A098006.

Miscellanea:

1700.   Part of LMM's personal library was sold to the University of Guelph in 1983. This part of the Guelph collection consists of 48 published titles, some of them duplicates, most of them with LMM's own signature on the flyleaf or inscribed there by her to one of her sons. The collection includes a number of translations (mostly Polish, but a few Dutch, French, Swedish, Finnish, Italian, and Japanese, many of which were published after LMM's death). The copy of *Rilla of Ingleside* contains a clipping of the poem entitled "The Piper," author anonymous, which figures as an important detail in the plot of *Rilla of Ingleside*. This is not the same poem, though it has the same title, as that in the Introduction to "The Blythes are Quoted" (McMaster University Library collection). Another version of "The Piper" exists in the Guelph collection of books from LMM's personal library; this is a handwritten copy of a poem in three stanzas, author anonymous, pasted in the back of a copy of *Rainbow Valley*. Another annotation of interest is the description of the legal proceedings brought by LMM against Page over the publication of *Further Chronicles of Avonlea*, without her permission. The note, dating from after 1928, is found in a presentation copy of *Further Chronicles of Avonlea* sent by the publisher to LMM, and is addressed to her son, Stuart. It outlines the publishing history of the book and the subsequent lawsuit with Page, eventually won by LMM. (See item 372, above).

1701.   Book Price Record Book, 1908-1942. XZ1 MS A098043. This is the item called the Ledger List by Rea Wilmshurst in her 1983 article (see above, Introduction to Part 4).

Personal Scrapbooks:

These scrapbooks, like the diaries, are closed to researchers until sometime after 1992. We gather that the first four scrapbooks listed here are of the same type available to the public in the Confederation Centre collection in Charlottetown, and contain clippings and memorabilia. The last one, less personal in nature, contains the only known compilation of reviews of LMM's works, sent by her clipping service and derived from publications in many countries.

1702.   Scrapbook, 1910-1914, 114 pp.

1703.   Scrapbook, 1913-1926, 122 pp.

1704.   Scrapbook, 1923-1933, 104 pp.

1705.   Scrapbook, 1931-1937, 79 pp.

1706.   Scrapbook, 1911-1936, 473 pp.

McMaster University, Hamilton

Mills Memorial Library Archives.

Manuscripts:

1707.   "The Blythes Are Quoted." McClelland and Stewart Papers. M12
        26. Typewritten manuscript, carbon copy. 624 pp., 21.7 x 18 cm.
        This seems to be a duplicate of the manuscript which was found
        among his mother's papers by the author's son, Stuart Macdonald,
        and edited and published by McGraw-Hill Ryerson as *The Road to
        Yesterday* in 1974. Among the sections of this ms. deleted for the
        McGraw-Hill Ryerson edition was LMM's Introduction. In the
        Introduction LMM includes the text of the poem "The Piper" which
        figured as an important symbol in *Rilla of Ingleside*. She says,
        "Although the poem had no real existence many people have writ-
        ten me asking where they could get it. It has been written recent-
        ly, but seems even more appropriate now than then." The poem
        was published in *Saturday Night*, 2 May 1942, p. 25. See the entry
        under Miscellanea, Guelph, above.

Miscellanea:

1708.   Printer's proofs. McClelland and Stewart Papers. M11 26. *Anne
        of Windy Poplars* (Canadian Favourites edition, 1973).

1709.   Printer's proofs. McClelland and Stewart Papers. M11 26, M11 35.
        Rainbow Valley.

Public Archives of Canada, Ottawa

The Public Archives' holdings of copies of letters (of which the originals are
in the University of P.E.I. collection) are not listed here.

Letters:

1710.   George MacMillan Papers. MG 30, D 185. Letters to George Mac-
        Millan from LMM. A selection of these letters was published as *My
        Dear Mr. M.*, eds. F. W. P. Bolger, E. R. Epperly, 1980.

1711.   Ephraim Weber Papers. MG 30, D 53. Letters to Ephraim Weber
        from LMM. Published as *The Green Gable Letters*, ed. W. Eggle-
        ston, 1960.

Queen's University, Kingston

Queen's University Archives, Kathleen Ryan Hall.

Manuscripts:

1712.   Accession No. 75 - 147. Manuscript for "Dog Monday's Vigil." Typescript, 7 pp., no date. Adapted from *Rilla of Ingleside*.

PRINCE EDWARD ISLAND

Confederation Centre of the Arts, Charlottetown

Confederation Museum Permanent Collection.

Manuscripts: (listed alphabetically by title)

1713.   Manuscript for *Anne of Green Gables*. CM. 67.5.1. Holograph, unbound manuscript, pen and ink on paper; 21.8 x 16.6 x 6.8 cm. 38 chapters, 716 pp., plus 137 pp. of notes; written on both sides of the paper, occasionally on the back of scrap paper.

1714.   Manuscript for *Anne of Ingleside*. CM. 67.5.4. Holograph, unbound manuscript, pen and ink on paper; 20.5 x 16.7 x 4.0 cm. 389 pp.

1715.   Manuscript for "Anne of Redmond" (published as *Anne of the Island*). CM. 78.5.5a. Holograph, unbound manuscript, pencil on paper; incomplete, ending in mid-sentence on p. 249 of 256 pp.; typewritten manuscript of *The Golden Road* on the reverse side (see item 1722); 28.4 x 21.6 x 3.0 cm. 256 pp.

1716.   Manuscript for *Anne of Windy Poplars*. CM. 67.5.7. Holograph, unbound manuscript, pen and ink on paper of varying sizes; 26.0(longest) x 19.5 x 5.0 cm. 234 pp.

1717.   Manuscript for *Anne's House of Dreams*. CM. 67.5.2. Holograph, unbound manuscript, pen and ink on paper; 21.8 x 16.8 x 5.5 cm. 40 chapters, 569 pp., plus 6-page Introduction.

1718.   Manuscript for *The Blue Castle*. CM. 67.5.9. Holograph, unbound manuscript, pen and ink on paper of several sizes; 21.5(largest) x 17.0 x 3.7 cm. 378 pp. Stored in Book Box with title: Canadian Cities of Romance by Katherine Hale.

1719.   Manuscript for *Emily Climbs*. CM. 67.5.6. Holograph, bound with paper tacks, pen and ink on paper; 22.0 x 18.0 x 5-10 cm. 25 chapters, 960 pp.

1720.   Manuscript for *Emily of New Moon*. CM. 67.5.8. Holograph, bound with paper tacks by chapter, pen and ink on paper; several sizes: 33.5(largest) x 22.5 x 2.5-6.5 cm. 31 chapters, 447 pp.

1721.   Manuscript for *Emily's Quest*. CM. 78.5.1. Holograph, unbound manuscript, pencil and pen and ink on paper; 20.5 x 16.7 x 3.8 cm. 582 pp. Title page: Emily's Quest by L.M. Montgomery, author of Anne of Green Gables, Rainbow Valley, The Story Girl.

1722.   Manuscript for *The Golden Road*. CM. 78.5.5b. Typewritten, unbound, on the reverse side of the manuscript for *Anne of the Island* (originally "Anne of Redmond"); 28.4 x 21.6 x 3.0 cm. 256 pp.; pages are out of order for *The Golden Road* but in correct order for "Anne of Redmond."

1723.   Manuscript for *Jane of Lantern Hill*. CM. 67.5.3. Holograph, unbound manuscript, pen and ink on paper; 22.6 x 15.5 x 6.8 cm. 683 pp.; wrapped in brown paper, tied in string.

1724.   Manuscript for *Magic for Marigold*. CM. 78.5.3. Holograph, unbound manuscript, pen and ink on paper of several sizes; 30.0(largest) x 23.0 x 4.5 cm. 21 chapters and notes, 462 pp., with 53 pp. wrapped separately.

1725.   Manuscript notes for *Mistress Pat*. CM. 78.5.6. Holograph, unbound manuscript, typed and handwritten on paper; 28.5 x 21.0 x 4.0 cm. 545 pp.; includes notes for *Mistress Pat*, part of an unidentified manuscript (possibly *Anne of the Island*) and several short stories.

1726.   Manuscript for *Pat of Silver Bush*. CM. 78.5.4. Holograph, unbound manuscript, pen and ink and typewritten on paper; 21.5 x 17.8 x 5.5 cm. 39 chapters, 759 pp., plus 235 pp. of notes.

1727.   Manuscript for *Rainbow Valley*. CM. 78.5.2. Holograph, unbound manuscript, pen and ink and typewritten on paper; 28.0 x 20.6 x 4.6 cm. 35 chapters, 408 pp., plus 31 pp. of notes; several pages have been laminated.

1728.   Manuscript for *A Tangled Web*. CM. 67.5.5. Holograph, unbound manuscript, pen and ink on paper of two sizes; 24.5 x 18.5 x 3.6 cm. 702 pp.

Personal Scrapbooks: (listed numerically, by acquisition number)

1729.   CM. 67.5.11. 1930s. Contains clippings of published poems, short stories, typewritten poems. Bound with black lacing, black cover. Two poems, "The Old Mirror" and "Grief," have been corrected in ink. 39.9 x 26.5 cm. 29 pp. (Our Scrapbook 5.)

1730.   CM. 67.5.12. Late 1890s, early 1900s. Contains mixed memorabi-
         lia, photos, articles, flowers, intermittent notes in ink. Cloth cov-
         er, red, black and silver, with floral design, with oval picture in
         centre, entitled "Album"; 38.5 x 27.0 cm.

1731.   CM. 67.5.13. 1893-1896. Contains poems, articles, diagrams.
         Cloth binding, crimson and gold floral and animal design.
         Inscribed, inside front cover: "Lucy M. Montgomery (M.L. Cavend-
         ish) 'Tis pleasant sure to see one's name in print. A book's a book
         although there's nothing in it.' Byron." 45 pp. (Our Scrapbook 7.)

1732.   CM. 67.5.14. 1890s. Contains newspaper clippings of stories pub-
         lished in the 1890s; intermittent notes written in ink. Bound in
         black and green leather. Cover: 27.5 x 22.0 cm.; pages: 26.5 x 20.5
         cm. 44 pp. (Our Scrapbook 1.)

1733.   CM. 67.5.15. Contains pictures, poems, mixed memorabilia.
         Bound, blue cloth with black floral design. 35.8 x 30.4 x 4.0 cm.

1734.   CM. 67.5.16. Contains unidentified newspaper clippings of stories
         and poems published in the 1890s. Titles added in ink. Maroon
         cover, embossed with gold border. 35.4 x 28.1 cm. 56 pp. (Our
         Scrapbook 8.)

1735.   CM. 67.5.17. "Stories and Poems late 1890s early 1900s." Contains
         clippings of stories and poems published in the late 1890s and early
         1900s. Bound scrapbook album, green cover embossed in silver and
         black, picture of boy and girl skating on cover. Periodical names
         and corrections added in ink. 38.6 x 27.5 cm. 61 pp. (Our Scrap-
         book 6.)

1736.   CM. 67.5.18. "Scrapbook 1898--Stories and Poems." Contains clip-
         pings of stories and poems, with intermittent notes written in ink.
         Bound, green and gold cloth cover, "Scrapbook" in gold on cover.
         Inscribed: "L.M. Montgomery Cavendish P.E. Island May 17th 1898,
         'Authors are partial--'tis true. But are not critics within judgement
         too?' Pope." Cover: 31.0 x 25.0 cm.; pages: 30.0 x 23.5 cm. 48 pp.
         (Our Scrapbook 2.)

1737.   CM. 67.5.19. Contains clippings of articles written by L.M. Mont-
         gomery for *The Halifax Echo*, Fall 1901 to June 1902. Bound, bur-
         gundy and red leather, with gold lines. 27.9 x 23.5 cm. 56 pp. (Our
         Scrapbook 3.)

1738.   CM. 67.5.20. Early 1900s, after *Anne of Green Gables*. Contains
         clippings from various newspapers and magazines, with handwritten
         notes. Brown paper parchment cover, loose pages. Cover: 28.3 x
         20.4 cm.; pages: 25.0 x 17.4 cm. 208 pp. (Our Scrapbook 4.)

1739. CM. 67.5.24. A collection of clippings from various publications: *Pure Words, Macleans, Zion's Herald, The Congregationalist and Christian World, Days of Youth, Western Christian Advocate, The Junior Herald, Western Christian Herald.* 198 pp. (Our Scrapbook 11.)

> Note: The following three scrapbooks, like the eleven listed above, were examined by Rea Wilmshurst. These three were found at the New London Birthplace Museum but, unlike the others, they are not listed as part of the official Confederation Centre collection.

1740. 1903-1907. A collection of clippings of stories from various publications: *American Home, Sunday Magazine, Boys' World.* Sewn gathering, 26.7 x 36.8 cm. 29 pp. (Our Scrapbook 9.)

1741. 1904-1907. A collection of clippings of stories from various publications: *Evenings at Home, Boys' World, Holland's Magazine.* Sewn gathering, 26.7 x 38.0 cm. 39 pp. (Our Scrapbook 10.)

1742. 1905-1916. A collection of clippings of stories from various publications: *East and West, Forward, Housewife.* Sewn gathering, 26.6 x 40.6 cm. 34 pp. (Our Scrapbook 12.)

Park Corner, Prince Edward Island

Private museum, called Silver Bush, run by Mrs. Ruth Campbell.

Miscellanea:

1743. In the house at Park Corner, now called Silver Bush, which belonged to LMM's uncle, there is a privately-owned museum of various memorabilia connected with LMM's life. Among its unofficially-catalogued holdings are a number of letters written by LMM, in general near the end of her life, to members of her family in P.E.I.

Prince Edward Island Public Archives, Charlottetown

The archival holdings include a number of items which we do not list here: copies of books, pamphlets, newspaper clippings (of items by and about LMM), and printed versions of "The Island Hymn."

Letters:

1744. Accession No. 2541/133. Letters to Muriel Smith from LMM, a) 2 pp., 20 July 1917; b) 2 pp., 12 June 1918.

1745.   Accession No. 2668/1. Letter to Mrs. Fred Uncles from LMM, 1
         page, April 24, 1940.

Manuscripts:

1746.   Accession No. 2305/22. "The Island Hymn." 2 pp., holograph man-
         uscript, dated Sept. 9, 1908.

Miscellanea:

1747.   Accession No. 2818/1. 8 photographs, with inscriptions, by LMM.

University of Prince Edward Island, Charlottetown.

Prince Edward Island Collection.

Letters:

1748.   Letters to Penzie Macneill from LMM. Includes 3 short notes,
         written at Cavendish; 4 letters dated 1886, written at Cavendish;
         16 letters written in Prince Albert, Saskatchewan, dated from
         August 1890 through June 1891; 1 letter written at Bideford, P.E.I.,
         1894. Selections from these letters were published in F.P. Bolger,
         The Years Before "Anne," 1974.

Part 6

WORKS ON LUCY MAUD MONTGOMERY

Books and Theses

1749.   Ridley, Hilda. *The Story of L. M. Montgomery.* Toronto: Ryerson, 1956. xiii, 137 pp. Illustrated with 6 photographs.

1750.   Ridley, Hilda. *The Story of L. M. Montgomery.* London: Harrap, 1956. 143 pp. Illustrated with 7 photographs, 6 of which are also in the Ryerson edition.

1751.   Joanne of the Christ, Sister (Gertrude McLaughlin). "The Literary Art of L. M. Montgomery." Master's thesis, University of Montreal, 1961.

1752.   The Women's Institute, Springfield, P.E.I. *Lucy Maud Montgomery: The Island's Lady of Stories.* Springfield, P.E.I.: The Women's Institute, 1963. 20 pp.

1753.   St. Paul's Presbyterian Women's Association, Leaskdale, Ont. *L. M. Montgomery as Mrs. Ewan Macdonald of the Leaskdale Manse, 1911-1926.* Leaskdale, Ont.: St. Paul's Presbyterian Women's Association, 1965. 20 pp.

1754.   Bolger, Francis W. P. *The Years Before "Anne."* Charlottetown, P.E.I.: The Prince Edward Island Heritage Foundation, 1974. viii, 229 pp.

1755.   Gillen, Mollie. *The Wheel of Things: A Biography of L. M. Montgomery, Author of "Anne of Green Gables."* Toronto: Fitzhenry and Whiteside, 1975. 200 pp. Includes 32 pp. of photographs.

1756.   Gillen, Mollie. *The Wheel of Things: A Biography of L. M. Montgomery, Author of "Anne of Green Gables."* Goodread Biographies, Canadian Lives series, no. 9. Toronto: James Lorimer and Formac Publishing, 1983. 201 pp. Paperback. ISBN 088781099.

1757.   Gillen, Mollie. *Ummei no tsumugi-guruma* (Japanese translation of *The Wheel of Things*, item 1755, above.) Tr. Junzo Miyatake and Noriko Miyatake. Tokyo: Shinozaki Shorin, 1979. 268 pp. Illustrated with same photographs as the Fitzhenry and Whiteside edition of *The Wheel of Things.*

1758.   Jones, Susan Elizabeth. "Recurring Patterns in the Novels of L. M. Montgomery." Master's thesis, University of Windsor, 1977. 112 pp.

1759. Gillen, Mollie. *Lucy Maud Montgomery*. The Canadians series. Toronto: Fitzhenry and Whiteside, 1978. 62 pp. ISBN 0889022445. Illustrated with numerous photographs.

1760. Scanlon, L.D. "Lucy Maud Montgomery." Although listed in several sources as published in Ottawa by Borealis in 1980, this book was never in fact published.

Articles, Chapters in Books and Theses

1761. Mahon, A.W. "The Old Minister in *The Story Girl*." *Canadian Magazine*, Mar. 1912, pp. 452-54.

1762. Rhodenizer, V.B. "Who's Who in Canadian Literature: L. M. Montgomery." *Canadian Bookman* 9 (1927): 227-28.

1763. Hill, Maude Petitt. "Best Known Woman in Prince Edward Island: L. M. Montgomery." *Chatelaine*, May 1928, pp. 8-9, 65; June 1928, pp. 23, 41-42.

1764. McAnn, Aida B. "Life and Works of L.M. Montgomery." *The Maritime Advocate and Busy East* 32, nos. 10-11 (June-July 1942), pp. 19-22.

1765. Weber, Ephraim. "L. M. Montgomery as a Letter Writer." *Dalhousie Review* 22 (1942): 300-310.

1766. Weber, Ephraim. "L. M. Montgomery's 'Anne.' " *Dalhousie Review* 24 (1944): 64-73.

1767. Sclanders, Ian. "Lucy of Green Gables." *Maclean's Magazine*, 15 Dec. 1951, pp. 12-13, 33-36.

1768. Millen, Muriel. "Who Was Ephraim Weber?" *Queen's Quarterly* 68 (1961): 333-36.

1769. Rogers, Amos Robert. "American Recognition of Canadian Authors Writing in English: 1890-1960." Ph.D. dissertation, University of Michigan, 1964. 818 pp. Statistical study of 278 Canadian authors; references to LMM's work in several chapters, and in appendices 3, 6, 8, 9.

1770. Waterston, Elizabeth. "L. M. Montgomery." In *The Clear Spirit: Twenty Canadian Women and Their Times*, ed. Mary Q. Innis, pp. 198-220. Toronto: University of Toronto Press, 1966.

1771. Stevenson, Laura Alice. "The Image of Canada in Canadian Children's Literature." Master's thesis, University of Western Ontario, 1967. Deals with LMM in chapter 3, pp. 59-65.

1772. Fitzpatrick, H. "Anne's First Sixty Years." *Canadian Author and Bookman* 44 (1969): 5-7.

1773. Gillen, Mollie. "Maud Montgomery: The Girl Who Wrote *Green Gables.*" *Chatelaine*, July 1973, pp. 40-41, 52-55.

1774. Porter, Helen. "The Fair World of L. M. Montgomery." *Journal of Canadian Fiction* 2, no. 4 (Fall 1973), pp. 102-04.

1775. McKenna, I. "Women in Canadian Literature." *Canadian Literature*, no. 62 (Autumn 1974), pp. 69-78.

1776. *Canadian Children's Literature* 1, no. 3 (Autumn 1975). Special issue on LMM, articles listed separately, below.

1777. Cowan, Ann S. "Canadian Writers: Lucy Maud and Emily Byrd." *Canadian Children's Literature* 1, no. 3 (Autumn 1975), pp. 42-49.

1778. Fredeman, Jane Cowan. "The Land of Lost Content: The Use of Fantasy in L. M. Montgomery's Novels." *Canadian Children's Literature* 1, no. 3 (Autumn 1975), pp. 60-70.

1779. Little, Jean. "But What About Jane?" *Canadian Children's Literature* 1, no. 3 (Autumn 1975), pp. 70-81.

1780. Rubio, Mary. "Satire, Realism and Imagination in *Anne of Green Gables.*" *Canadian Children's Literature* 1, no. 3 (Autumn 1975), pp. 27-36.

1781. Sorfleet, John Robert. "L. M. Montgomery: Canadian Authoress." *Canadian Children's Literature* 1, no.3 (Autumn 1975), pp. 4-7.

1782. Thomas, Gillian. "The Decline of Anne: Matron vs. Child." *Canadian Children's Literature* 1, no. 3 (Autumn 1975), pp. 37-41.

1783. Whitaker, Muriel A. " 'Queer Children': L. M. Montgomery's Heroines." *Canadian Children's Literature* 1, no. 3 (Autumn 1975), pp. 50-59.

1784. Waller, Adrian. "Lucy Maud of Green Gables." *Reader's Digest*, December 1975, pp. 38-43.

1785. Frazer, F. M. "Scarcely an End." *Canadian Literature*, no. 63 (Winter 1975), pp. 89-92.

1786. Frazer, F. M. "Island Writers." *Canadian Literature*, no. 68-69 (Spring-Summer 1976), pp. 76-87.

1787. Sorfleet, John Robert, ed. *L. M. Montgomery: An Assessment.* Guelph, Ont.: Canadian Children's Press, 1976. 81 pp. Re-issue in book form of the special number of *Canadian Children's Literature* devoted to LMM.

1788. Willis, L. "Bogus Ugly Duckling: Anne Shirley Unmasked." *Dalhousie Review* 56 (1976): 247-51.

1789. Kiyokawa, Tae. ["Canada--Tour of P.E.I.--Visiting the Home Country of Red-Haired Anne"; translation of Japanese title]. *Saison de Non-no*, no. 12 (1976), pp. 37-49. Article in Japanese; illustrated with many colour photos.

1790. Bolger, F.W.P. "Lucy Maud's Island." *The Island Magazine*, no. 2 (Spring-Summer 1977), pp. 4-10. Transcription of address by F.W.P. Bolger to Belfast (P.E.I.) Historical Society, 26 Nov. 1976.

1791. Burns, Jane. "Anne and Emily: L.M. Montgomery's Children." *Room of One's Own* 3, no.3 (1977), pp. 37-48.

1792. Woodcock, George. *Faces from History: Canadian Profiles and Portraits.* Edmonton: Hurtig, 1978, pp. 200-201. Portrait with facing page of text.

1793. Vipond, Mary. "Best Sellers in English Canada, 1899-1918: An Overview." *Journal of Canadian Fiction*, no. 24 (1979), pp. 96-119.

1794. Norcross, E. Blanche. *Pioneers Every One: Canadian Women of Achievement.* Toronto: Burns and MacEachern, 1979, pp. 77-87.

1795. Ross, Catherine Sheldrick. "Calling Back the Ghost of the Old-Time Heroine: Duncan, Montgomery, Atwood, Laurence and Munro." *Studies in Canadian Literature*, no. 4 (1979), pp. 43-58.

1796. Berke, J. "Mother-I-Can-Do-It-Myself: [The] Self-Sufficient Heroine in Popular Girls' Fiction." *Women's Studies* 6 (1979): 187-203.

1797. Coldwell, Joyce-Ione Harrington. "Folklore as Fiction: The Writings of L. M. Montgomery." In *Folklore Studies in Honour of Herbert Halpert: A Festschrift*, pp. 125-36. St. John's, Nfld.: Memorial University of Newfoundland, 1980.

1798. Nodelman, Perry. "Progressive Utopia: Or, How to Grow Up Without Growing Up." In *Proceedings of the Sixth Annual Conference of Children's Literature Association, University of Toronto, March 1979*, pp. 146-54. Villanova, Penn.: Villanova University Press, 1980.

1799. Bliss, Michael. "Canada in 1907." *Financial Post*, 16 Jan. 1982, p. 5.

1800. Bumstead, J.M. "The Only Island There Is." In *The Garden Trans-formed: Prince Edward Island, 1945-1980*, eds. Verner Smitheram, David Milne and Satadal Dasgupta, pp. 32-33. Charlottetown: Rag-weed Press, 1982.

1801. Tausky, Thomas E. "L.M. Montgomery and 'The Alpine Path, so hard, so steep.' " *Canadian Children's Literature*, no. 33 (1983), pp. 5-20.

1802. Wilmshurst, Rea. "L.M. Montgomery's Short Stories: A Preliminary Bibliography." *Canadian Children's Literature*, no. 29 (1983), pp. 25-34.

1803. Wright, Shirley. "Images of Canada in English Canadian Literature for Children, or, After *Anne of Green Gables.*" In *Sharing: A Chal-lenge for All. Proceedings of the Eleventh Annual Conference, International Association of School Librarianship*, pp. 179-81. Kalamazoo, Mich.: Western Michigan State University, 1983.

1804. Katsura, Yuko. "Red-Haired Anne in Japan." *Canadian Children's Literature*, no. 34 (1984), pp. 57-60.

Audio-Visual Studies

Films:

1805. *The Road to Green Gables.*   Dir. Terence Macartney-Filgate. Ottawa and Toronto: National Film Board and Canadian Broad-casting Corporation, 1975. 16 mm. 86 minutes. Colour. Cast: Lin-da Goranson, Jill Cody. Narrators: Gordon Pinsent, Jackie Bur-roughs. Music: Eldon Rathburn. A study of LMM, based on her unpublished diaries.

Filmstrips:

1806. *Lucy Maud Montgomery; Anne of Green Gables.* Famous Canadians series, nos. 1526, 1527. Toronto: Robert B. Mansour Ltd., 1976. Filmstrips and cassette sound recordings, using illustrations and commentary; aimed at the elementary school audience. No. 1526 has 40 frames, 7 pp. script of recorded text; no. 1527 has 39 frames, 5 pp. script of recorded text.

1807. *L.M. Montgomery: Those Cavendish Years.* Directed by David Newman. Produced by Doug MacDonald. Ottawa: National Film Board, 1977. Filmstrip. Catalogue No. 20SC0177016. 61 frames; 16 minutes, 50 seconds narration on sound cassette.

Selected Articles from Reference Works

1808. *The Canadian Men and Women of the Time.* 2nd ed. Ed. James Henry Morgan. Toronto: William Briggs, 1912, p. 760.

1809. *Canada and its Provinces.* Vol. XII. Eds. Adam Shortt and Arthur G. Doughty. Toronto: Publisher's Association of Canada, 1913, pp. 564-65.

1810. MacMechan, Archibald. *Head-Waters of Canadian Literature.* Toronto: McClelland and Stewart, 1924, pp. 209-13.

1811. Stevenson, Lionel. *Appraisals of Canadian Literature.* Toronto: Macmillan, 1926, pp. 32, 128, 131, 134, 157.

1812. *The Canadian Who's Who.* Toronto: The Times Publishing Company, 1936, 2 (1936-37): 660.

1813. *Who's Who in Canada, 1936-37.* Toronto: International Press, 1937, p. 334.

1814. Kunitz, Stanley, and Howard Haycraft. *Twentieth Century Authors: A Biographical Dictionary of Modern Literature.* New York: H.W. Wilson, 1942, pp. 974-75.

1815. Thomas, Clara. *Canadian Novelists, 1920-45.* Toronto: Longmans, Green, 1946, pp. 83-84.

1816. Palk, Helen. *The Book of Canadian Achievement.* Toronto: Dent, 1951, pp. 146-49.

1817. Phelps, Arthur L. *Canadian Writers.* Toronto: McClelland and Stewart, 1951, pp. 85-93.

1818. Hackett, Alice Payne. *70 Years of Best Sellers 1895-1965.* New York: R. R. Bowker, 1967, pp. 70-74.

1819. Pacey, Desmond. *Creative Writing in Canada: A Short History of English-Canadian Literature.* Rev. ed. Toronto: McGraw-Hill Ryerson, 1967, pp. 89-92, 102-06.

1820. Rhodenizer, Vernon B. *Canadian Literature in English.* Montreal: Quality Press, 1965, p. 742, and frequent other mentions; see also Lois Mary Thierman, *Index to Vernon Blair Rhodenizer's Canadian Literature in English,* Edmonton: La Survivance Printing, [1968].

1821. Egoff, Sheila. *The Republic of Childhood: A Critical Guide to Canadian Children's Literature in English.* Toronto: Oxford University Press, 1967, pp. 252-53.

1822. *The Oxford Companion to Canadian History and Literature.* Ed. Norah Story. Toronto: Oxford University Press, 1967, pp. 586-87.

1823. Pacey, Desmond. *Essays in Canadian Criticism 1938-1968.* Toronto: Ryerson, 1969, pp. 24, 67, 126, 239, 274.

1824. Thomas, Clara. *Our Nature—Our Voices: a Guidebook to English-Canadian Literature.* Vol. 1. Toronto: New Press, 1973, pp. 76-78.

1825. Waterston, Elizabeth. *Survey: A Short History of Canadian Literature.* Toronto: Methuen, 1973, pp. 70, 102, 147.

1826. Fee, Margery, and Ruth Cawker. *Canadian Fiction: An Annotated Bibliography.* Toronto: Peter Martin Associates, 1976, pp. 79-81.

1827. *Literary History of Canada: Canadian Literature in English.* Ed. Carl F. Klinck. 3 vols. 2nd ed. Toronto: University of Toronto Press, 1976, 1: 345, 2: 137-38.

1828. *Encyclopedia Canadiana.* Toronto: Grolier, 1977, 7: 133-34.

1829. *Facts and Pictures about Authors and Illustrators of Books for Young People, from Early Times to 1960.* Vol. 1. Ed. Anne Commire. Detroit: Gale Research, 1977, pp. 182-92.

1830. *Twentieth-Century Children's Writers.* Ed. D.L. Kirkpatrick. New York: St. Martin's Press, 1978, pp. 905-08.

1831. *Macmillan Dictionary of Canadian Biography.* Ed. W. Stewart Wallace. 4th edition, rev. W. A. McKay. Toronto: Macmillan, 1978, pp. 586-87.

1832. Laugher, Charles T. *Atlantic Province Authors of the Twentieth Century: A Bio-Bibliographical Checklist.* Halifax: Dalhousie University School of Library Science, 1982, pp. 392-95.

1833. *Oxford Companion to Canadian Literature.* Ed. William Toye. Toronto: Oxford University Press, 1983, pp. 118-19, 528-29.

Selected Newspaper Articles

1834. *Star Weekly,* 18 Apr. 1914.

1835. Muir, Norman Phillips. "Famous Author and Simple Mother." *Star Weekly,* 28 Nov. 1926.

1836. Osborne, Eleanor. "Fair Avonlea." *Canadian Home Journal,* Jan. 1927.

1837.   Cowan, C.L. "Minister's Wife and Authoress." *Star Weekly*, 29 Dec. 1928.

1838.   "Poetry Her First Love Says LMM." *Mail*, 19 Mar. 1929.

1839.   "Author To Get No Profit as 'Green Gables' Filmed." *Toronto Star*, Sept. 1934.

1840.   "P.E.I.'s Famous Writer." *The Challenge*, 12 Jan. 1941. Reprinted from *The Adventure*, Kentville, Nova Scotia.

1841.   *Globe and Mail*, 3 Oct. 1974.

1842.   "Lucy Maud's Album." *The Canadian Magazine*, 6 Sept. 1975. [6 pp.]

1843.   "Anne et son île." *Le Devoir*, 27 May 1976.

Selected Reviews: Novels

The following small sample of reviews is drawn from existing printed indices of book reviews; as such it is not representative of the number of reviews of LMM's works. Since the scrapbooks of LMM contain clippings of reviews of her work, further details of these will be available sometime after 1992 when that part of the archival holdings becomes accessible to researchers.

Anne of Green Gables:

1844.   *New York Times Saturday Review of Books*, 18 July 1908, p. 404.

1845.   *Outlook*, 22 Aug. 1908, p. 956.

1846.   *Canadian Magazine*, Nov. 1908, p. 88.

1847.   *Tijidspiegel*, Mar. 1911. Review of *In veilige haven* (Dutch translation).

1848.   *Atlantic Advocate*, Aug. 1964, p. 94

Anne of Avonlea:

1849.   *Independent* 67 (1909): 1355.

1850.   *The Nation*, 2 Sept. 1909, p. 212.

1851.   *Outlook*, 2 Oct. 1909, p. 276.

1852.   *A.L.A. Booklist*, Dec. 1909, p. 134.

1853. *Tijidspiegel*, Feb. 1913. Review of *Anne van Avonlea* (Dutch translation).

1854. *Gulden Winckel*, Apr. 1913. Review of *Anne van Avonlea* (Dutch translation).

Kilmeny of the Orchard:

1855. *Athenaeum*, 30 July 1910, p. 122.

1856. *Independent*, 8 Aug. 1910, p. 362.

1857. *Spectator* (London), 24 Sept. 1910, p. 470.

1858. Sherwood, Margaret. "Lying Like Truth." *Atlantic Monthly*, Dec. 1910, p. 808.

1859. *The Nation*, 9 June 1910, p. 587.

The Story Girl:

1860. *A.L.A. Booklist*, Sept. 1911, p. 38.

1861. *Outlook*, 2 Sept. 1911, p. 46.

1862. *Catholic World*, Oct. 1911, p. 116.

1863. *The Nation*, 10 Aug. 1911, p. 122.

Chronicles of Avonlea:

1864. *Globe*, 6 Apr. 1912.

1865. *Outlook*, 29 June 1912, p. 500.

1866. *The Nation*, 22 Aug. 1912, p. 171.

1867. *Catholic World*, Oct. 1912, p. 103.

1868. *A.L.A. Booklist*, Nov. 1912, p. 127.

1869. *Globe and Mail*, 2 Nov. 1953.

The Golden Road:

1870. *Boston Transcript*, 20 Sept. 1913, p. 8.

1871. *Outlook*, 4 Oct. 1913, p. 280.

1872. *Literary Digest*, 18 Oct. 1913, p. 692.

1873. *Globe*, 25 Oct. 1913.

Anne of the Island:

1874. *Boston Transcript*, 7 Aug. 1915, p. 8.

1875. *Outlook*, 25 Aug. 1915, p. 1009.

1876. *The Nation*, 26 Aug. 1915, p. 263.

1877. *Publishers' Weekly*, 18 Sept. 1915, p. 790.

1878. *A.L.A. Booklist*, Oct. 1915, p. 35.

1879. *Wisconsin Library Bulletin*, Oct. 1915, p. 298.

1880. *Spectator* (London), 4 Dec. 1915, p. 796.

Anne's House of Dreams:

1881. *New York Times Review of Books*, 26 Aug. 1917, p. 318.

1882. *A.L.A. Booklist*, Nov. 1917, p. 61.

Rainbow Valley:

1883. *Publishers' Weekly*, 16 Aug. 1919, p. 484.

1884. *Outlook*, 17 Sept. 1919, p. 95.

1885. *New York Times Review of Books*, 21 Sept. 1919, p. 484.

1886. *Wisconsin Library Bulletin*, Oct. 1919, p. 215.

1887. *A.L.A. Booklist*, Nov. 1919, p. 59.

Rilla of Ingleside:

1888. *New York Times Book Review and Magazine*, 11 Sept. 1921.

1889. *Wisconsin Library Bulletin*, Oct. 1921, p. 157.

1890. *Globe*, 1 Oct. 1921.

1891. *Booklist*, Nov. 1921, p. 52.

Emily of New Moon:

1892. *New York Times Book Review and Magazine*, 26 Aug. 1923, p. 24.

1893. *Times Literary Supplement*, 13 Sept. 1923, p. 605.

1894.   *Wisconsin Library Bulletin*, Oct. 1923, p. 444.

1895.   *Montreal Star*, 22 Oct. 1923.

Emily's Quest:

1896.   *Canadian Bookman*, Sept. 1927, p. 273.

1897.   *Outlook*, 7 Sept. 1927, p. 28.

1898.   *Times Literary Supplement*, 6 Oct. 1927, p. 696.

1899.   *Globe*, 22 Oct. 1927.

1900.   *Wisconsin Library Bulletin*, Nov. 1927, p. 261.

Emily Climbs:

1901.   *Montreal Star*, 26 Sept. 1925.

1902.   *Canadian Bookman*, Oct. 1925, p. 164.

1903.   *Bookman* (London) 65 (1926): 234-35.

The Blue Castle:

1904.   *Globe*, 18 Sept. 1926.

1905.   *Saturday Review of Literature*, 18 Sept. 1926, p. 122.

1906.   *New York World*, 19 Sept. 1926, p. 4m.

1907.   *New York Times Book Review*, 26 Sept. 1926, p. 33.

1908.   *Times Literary Supplement*, 30 Sept. 1926, p. 657.

1909.   *Canadian Bookman*, Oct. 1926, p. 307.

1910.   *Mail*, 2 Oct. 1926.

1911.   *Literary Review*, 16 Oct. 1926, p. 12.

1912.   *Boston Transcript*, 23 Oct. 1926, p. 5.

1913.   *New York Herald Tribune*, 31 Oct. 1926, p. 16.

1914.   *Wisconsin Library Bulletin*, Nov. 1926, p. 299.

1915.   *Booklist*, Jan. 1927, p. 177.

Magic for Marigold:

1916. *Boston Transcript*, 2 Oct. 1929, p. 2.

1917. *Globe and Mail*, 3 Oct. 1929.

1918. *Times Literary Supplement*, 24 Oct. 1929, p. 848.

1919. *Canadian Bookman*, Jan. 1930, p. 13.

1920. *Italia*, 23 Apr. 1939, p. 67. Review of *La Bimba dal cuore esultante* (Italian translation).

A Tangled Web:

1921. *Wisconsin Library Bulletin*, Oct. 1931, p. 223.

1922. *Books*, 1 Nov. 1931, p. 23.

1923. *New York Times Book Review*, 20 Dec. 1931, p. 9.

1924. *Springfield Republican*, 27 Dec. 1931, p. 7e.

1925. *Canadian Bookman*, Jan. 1932, p. 8.

Pat of Silver Bush:

1926. *Times Literary Supplement*, 24 Aug. 1933, p. 562.

1927. *Canadian Bookman*, Sept. 1933, p. 123.

1928. *Books*, 1 Oct. 1933, p. 9.

1929. *Boston Transcript*, 7 Oct. 1933, p. 2.

1930. *Springfield Republican*, 17 Dec. 1933, p. 7e.

Mistress Pat:

1931. *Books*, 8 Sept. 1935, p. 15.

1932. *Springfield Republican*, 22 Sept. 1935, p. 7e.

1933. *Winnipeg Free Press*, 16 Nov. 1935.

1934. *Booklist*, Dec. 1935, p. 112.

Anne of Windy Poplars:

1935.   *Books,* 9 Aug. 1936, p. 8.

1936.   *Booklist,* Oct. 1936, p. 54.

1937.   *Winnipeg Free Press,* 10 Oct. 1936.

1938.   *Univeristy of Toronto Quarterly* 6 (1936-37): 361.

Jane of Lantern Hill:

1939.   *Books,* 8 Aug. 1937, p. 8.

1940.   *New York Times Book Review,* 15 Aug. 1937, p. 22.

1941.   *Springfield Republican,* 12 Sept. 1937, p. 7e.

1942.   *Saturday Night,* 23 Oct. 1937.

1943.   *Montreal Star,* 20 Nov. 1937.

Anne of Ingleside:

1944.   *Books,* 30 July 1939, p. 9.

1945.   *New York Times Book Review,* 30 July 1939, p. 7.

1946.   *Times Literary Supplement,* 12 Aug. 1939, p. 477.

1947.   *Globe,* 26 Aug. 1939.

1948.   *Winnipeg Free Press,* 2 Sept. 1939.

1949.   *Springfield Republican,* 24 Sept. 1939, p. 7e.

1950.   *Saturday Night,* 11 Nov. 1939, p. 8.

1951.   *University of Toronto Quarterly* 9 (1939-40): 300.

Selected Reviews: Other Books

The Watchman, and Other Poems:

1952.   *Globe,* 22 Nov. 1916.

1953.   *Book Review Digest,* July 1917.

The Alpine Path:

1954.   *Vancouver Sun*, 27 Dec. 1974.

1955.   *Toronto Star*, 1 Feb. 1975.

1956.   *In Review* 9, no. 3 (Summer 1975): 36.

The Green Gables Letters:

1957.   *Globe and Mail*, 30 Apr. 1960.

1958.   *Atlantic Advocate*, June 1960, p. 97.

1959.   *Canadian Literature*, no. 5 (Summer 1960), pp. 87-88.

1960.   *Canadian Forum*, Sept. 1960, p. 142.

1961.   *Dalhousie Review* 41 (1961): 429-31.

1962.   *University of Toronto Quarterly* 30 (1961): 422.

My Dear Mr. M.:

1963.   *Vancouver Sun*, 14 Nov. 1980.

1964.   *Quill and Quire* 47, no.1 (1981), p. 27.

1965.   *Canadian Literature*, no. 90 (Autumn 1981), pp. 141-43.

1966.   *Canadian Author and Bookman* 56 (Winter 1981): 27.

Selected Journals of L.M. Montgomery:

1967.   Powell, Marilyn. "The Ideals of a Lonely Little Girl." *The Globe and Mail*, 2 Nov. 1985, p. D21.

The Road to Yesterday:

1968.   *In Review* 8, no. 2 (Spring 1974), p. 43.

1969.   *Globe and Mail*, 23 Mar. 1974.

1970.   *Maclean's*, June 1974, p. 94.

1971.   *Quill and Quire*, July 1974, p. 19.

1972.   *Canadian Author and Bookman* 49 (Summer 1974): 26.

1973.   *New Yorker*, 2 Dec. 1974, p. 191.

1974. *Dalhousie Review* 54 (Winter 1974-75): 783-84.

1975. *Canadian Literature,* no. 63 (Winter 1975), pp. 89-92.

The Doctor's Sweetheart and Other Stories:

1976. *Books in Canada,* May 1979, p. 22.

1977. *Montreal Gazette,* 5 May 1979, p. 37.

1978. *Quill and Quire* 45, no. 8 (1979), pp. 48-49.

Selected Reviews and Study Guides: Film and Stage Versions

1979. *New York Times,* 22 Dec. 1919, p. 18. Review of 1919 film of *Anne of Green Gables.*

1980. Blum, Daniel. *A Pictorial History of the Silent Screen.* London: Spring Books, 1953. 2nd impression 1966. Photo from the 1919 film on p. 173.

1981. *New York Times,* 22 Dec. 1934, n.p. Review of the 1934 film of *Anne of Green Gables.*

1982. Motion Picture Producers and Distributors of America. *Teacher's Manual for the Screen Version of Anne of Green Gables.* New York: Motion Picture Producers and Distributors, 1934. 15 pp. Foreword to the teacher by Kenneth Macgowan.

1983. *New York Times,* 23 Aug. 1940, in *The New York Times Film Reviews, 1939-1948,* p. 1727. Review of the 1940 film of *Anne of Windy Poplars.*

1984. *New York Times,* 18 Apr. 1969. A review of the London (England) production (New Theatre, produced by Irving Wardle) of the musical *Anne of Green Gables* by Norman Campbell and Donald Harron.

1985. Barnes, Clive. *New York Times,* 25 Aug. 1969. Review of the same production.

1986. Brown, J. Frederick. "The Charlottetown Festival in Review," *Canadian Drama* 9 (1983): 227-368. This factual report covers musicals produced at the Charlottetown Festival from its inception in 1965 to 1983. The 12-page report on the Campbell/Harron musical production of *Anne of Green Gables* includes quotations from selected reviews in Canadian, British, American and Japanese newspapers.

1987.   Conlogue, Ray. "Anne of the Silver Screen." *Globe and Mail*, 27
        July 1985, p. E1. Article on the filming of the 1985 Sullivan ver-
        sion of *Anne of Green Gables.*

1988.   Groen, Rick. "Anne's a Winner of Hearts." *Globe and Mail*, 30 Nov.
        1985, p. D1. Review of the 1985 Sullivan film of *Anne of Green
        Gables.*

1989.   Widerman, Jane. "One More Juicy Role for Colleen Dewhurst."
        Broadcast Week of Nov.30-Dec.6, Globe and Mail, 30 Nov. 1985, p.
        7. Review of the 1985 Sullivan film of *Anne of Green Gables.*

Part 7

INDEX

Numbers in this index refer to the number of the item in the bibliographical listing. For Parts 1-5, titles of works cited are listed, as well as names of authors, translators, editors and directors, and titles of periodicals. In Part 6, for "Books and Theses" both the author and title are indexed, for "Articles, Chapters in Books and Theses" only the author is indexed, for "Audio-Visual Studies" and "Selected Articles from Reference Works" only the title is indexed, and the reviews are indexed only under the title of the work reviewed.